The
BIBLE DOESN'T
SAY THAT

ALSO BY DR. JOEL M. HOFFMAN

In the Beginning: A Short History of the Hebrew Language

*And God Said: How Translations Conceal
the Bible's Original Meaning*

*The Bible's Cutting Room Floor:
The Holy Scriptures Missing from Your Bible*

The
BIBLE DOESN'T
SAY THAT

40 BIBLICAL

MISTRANSLATIONS,

MISCONCEPTIONS,

AND OTHER

MISUNDERSTANDINGS

Dr. Joel M. Hoffman

THOMAS DUNNE BOOKS
ST. MARTIN'S PRESS NEW YORK

THOMAS DUNNE BOOKS.
An imprint of St. Martin's Press.

THE BIBLE DOESN'T SAY THAT. Copyright © 2016 by Joel M. Hoffman. All rights reserved.
Printed in the United States of America. For information, address St. Martin's Press, 175
Fifth Avenue, New York, N.Y. 10010.

www.thomasdunnebooks.com
www.stmartins.com
www.thebibledoesntsaythat.com

Library of Congress Cataloging-in-Publication Data

Names: Hoffman, Joel M., 1968–
Title: The Bible doesn't say that : 40 biblical mistranslations, misconceptions, and
    other misunderstandings / Dr. Joel M. Hoffman.
Description: First [edition]. | New York : Dunne Books, 2016. | Includes index.
Identifiers: LCCN 2015039459| ISBN 9781250059482 (hardcover) | ISBN
    9781466864566 (e-book)
Subjects: LCSH: Bible—Criticism, interpretation, etc. | Common fallacies. | Errors.
Classification: LCC BS511.3 .H64 2016 | DDC 220.6—dc23
LC record available at http://lccn.loc.gov/2015039459

Our books may be purchased in bulk for promotional, educational, or business use. Please
contact your local bookseller or the Macmillan Corporate and Premium Sales Department
at (800) 221-7945, extension 5442, or by e-mail at MacmillanSpecialMarkets@macmillan
.com.

First Edition: February 2016

10   9   8   7   6   5   4   3   2   1

ACKNOWLEDGMENTS

In the way that one thing leads unpredictably to the next, Irene Goodman can take double credit for this book. For nearly a decade she has been my agent, trusted friend, and guide to the world of publishing. She found a publisher first for my book about Bible translation, then for my exploration of material left out of the Bible; this time, she even suggested a topic, hoping that I would write this book. I did. Thank you, Irene, for your help and for your kindness.

Irene also introduced me to the wonderful folks at Thomas Dunne Books.

Though writing a book is mostly a solitary endeavor, publishing one requires a team, and the nature of that team in large part determines the quality of the experience. In this regard I have been fortunate. My primary contact at Thomas Dunne Books, Peter Joseph, has offered support and guidance that have made me a better writer, and his pleasant demeanor has made the process of creating this book a thoroughly enjoyable one. Thank you, Peter.

Peter's team includes a variety of other talented people, and I'm grateful to them: Melanie Fried, his assistant; Terry McGarry, for her diligent and insightful copy editing; Rob Grom, for designing the cover; Laura Clark, team leader; David Stanford Burr, production editor; Joy Gannon, production manager; Karlyn Hixson, in charge of marketing; and Kathryn Hough, publicist.

It was Tom Dunne's vision to put these people together, so I'm in his debt both for publishing my work and for introducing me to these people. I'm similarly indebted to Sally Richardson, St. Martin's Press Publisher.

Bowen Road, West Fourth Street, West Sixty-eighth Street, and Hooker Avenue have something in common: They have all been home to remarkable communities of creativity, support, collegiality, and enthusiasm. It has been my great fortune to be part of all four, and I'm especially grateful to the people I met at each one.

Space obviously doesn't permit me to list every person who has helped me reach where I am today, but I must single out a few, starting with my father, Rabbi Lawrence A. Hoffman, Ph.D. In addition to everything else that he has done for me, he has been my lifelong study partner.

I'm also particularly grateful to: Rabbi Gary Bretton-Granatoor, who helped me thrive; Marc Brettler, for his compassion and knowledge; Rabbi Billy and Cantor Ellen Dreskin, for their support, honesty, and wisdom; David and Karen Frank, for their kindness and thoughtfulness, and for opening so many doors; Rabbi Stuart Geller, for his compassion, support, and humor; Rabbis Paul Golomb and Shoshana Hantman, for keeping me sane (or am I assuming facts not in evidence?); Jennifer Hammer at NYU Press, for publishing my first book in a way that made me want to continue; Danny Maseng, for expanding my horizons; Doug Mishkin, who lives his life with the same musicality, joy, purpose, and tenderness that he brings to his music; Lauren Rose, for her support and enthusiasm; Rabbi Allan "Smitty" Smith, for believing in me; Rabbi Jaimee Shalhevet, for her insight; Tal Varon, who by personal example reminds me to walk humbly; Janet Walton, for being clear on what matters; and Rabbi Danny Zemel, a modern-day prophet.

Finally and mostly, I remain endlessly grateful to my parents, Sally and Larry, for giving me a good life.

CONTENTS

INTRODUCTION

The Bible doesn't say that God performed miracles.

The Bible doesn't say "Thou shalt not covet" or "God so loved the world," doesn't say that homosexuality is a sin, and hardly says anything about modern baptism or kosher food, the rapture, monogamy, or evolution.

These misconceptions and many more like them stem from a fundamental misunderstanding about how to read the Bible, combined, frequently, with ignorance or ideology that leads people to misrepresent the Bible to others.

An old joke asks a reporter to boil down an economist's evaluation of the economy to one word. "Good," says the reporter, accurately quoting the economist. Then when asked to expand the economist's message to two words, the reporter quotes, just as accurately, "Not good."

The same thing happens with the Bible. People quote a word or a phrase out of context as "what the Bible says." In a strict literal sense, the Bible does say what they report, but only in the way that the economist who thought the economy was failing did say, ". . . good."

This is just one way out of many that modern readers misunderstand what the Bible says.

Technically, of course, the Bible doesn't "say" anything. Like all other written texts, it sits there waiting to be read. But even so, most people have a sense that the point of reading a text is to figure out what's there, and the "what's there" part is what the text says.

As it happens, a variety of intellectual movements arose last century to question even this basic premise. Researchers wondered if a text had any meaning without a reader. They asked whether the author or the reader gets to decide what a text means. They concluded that all reading is a matter of interpretation. But even so, most people have a sense of what kinds of interpretation are acceptable when it comes to figuring out what a text says.

For example, on April 16, 1912, *The New York Times* ran the headline "Titanic Sinks Four Hours After Hitting Iceberg." Even though it was a headline, most people agree that the newspaper "says" that the *Titanic* sank four hours after it hit an iceberg.

A devious reader might wonder if maybe the newspaper was vague about how long after hitting the iceberg the *Titanic* sank, because "four" sounds like "for," and maybe the newspaper only says that the *Titanic* was in the process of sinking "for hours." But most people know that that's not what the *Times* headline says, in spite of the coincidence of two words that happen to sound the same.

Another example comes from Shakespeare's Juliet, who laments, "O Romeo, Romeo! wherefore art thou Romeo?" In this case, many modern-English speakers need to learn a little bit about seventeenth-century English to understand the poetry. The word "wherefore" means "why," not "where." The words "art" and "thou" match our modern "are" and "you." Juliet is asking Romeo why he had to be Romeo, whom she couldn't marry, instead of someone she could marry. So most people agree that Shakespeare's Juliet asked "Why are you Romeo?" And even if there's a stage of interpretation that converts Shakespeare's English into our own, most people agree that it's reasonable.

By contrast, it would be entirely unreasonable to suggest a connection to the arts based on the word "art," and even more absurd to wonder if Juliet chose the nine-letter word "wherefore" because she wanted to show how she felt about Romeo, and another word that has nine letters is "affection." To claim that Shakespeare's Juliet was expressing affection for Romeo with her choice of the word "wherefore" is to misrepresent what the text says.

However, when it comes to reading the Bible, these sorts of interpretations have become standard. Words get swapped for other words that sound the same, or that have the same letters, or the same number of letters, or letters whose numerical values have some particular importance, and so on. Or passages that share a word are interpreted as reinforcing each other even if they are otherwise unrelated.

These kinds of interpretations—and many more like them—strike many modern readers as odd or even worthless. But though they do not tell us "what the Bible says," they are not without value. They are not more bizarre or less insightful than, say, Impressionism or Cubism in art.

The impressionist painter Monet painted his famous water lilies in hundreds of different ways, each one capturing a different aspect of his flower garden. It is hardly the point that none of the oil paintings is as accurate as a photograph would be. Likewise, some of Picasso's art barely resembles what that great twentieth-century artist was depicting. In 1932, for instance, he painted his then-mistress Marie-Thérèse Walter in a work called *Le Rêve* (*The Dream*). In the painting, Ms. Walter's left eye is detached from her head, but the critic who argues that eyes don't separate in this way has simply missed the point of art.

Similarly, the various religious methods of interpreting the Bible bring it to light in unique and meaningful religious ways. It makes little sense to condemn those religious approaches in terms of how they might work in secular settings, just as it is a mistake to use accuracy as the only metric of art.

On the other hand, a curious soul might wonder what Monet's flower garden or Picasso's Marie-Thérèse actually looked like. Equally, many modern readers wonder what the Bible said before it was interpreted and filtered through religious rhetoric.

Our goal here is to answer that question, to explore the original Bible.

Or to look at things differently, we might imagine a particularly cherished vacation destination: the Galápagos Islands for some, New York City for others, or Jerusalem, or the Vatican, or maybe our parents' birthplace. We've heard stories, but they are both incomplete, missing some aspects of what the place is like, and exaggerated, overstating other aspects. The storytellers have their biases, so they emphasize what is important to them, inadvertently or even purposely tailoring their descriptions. We may have photographs, too, but how can a photograph truly capture the original?

Guidebooks about this destination are plentiful as well, but they all distort the actual place. A color photo of one building focuses our attention on it, but it also necessarily diverts our attention from something else. And the descriptions reflect the prejudices of the authors: An architect might write a book stressing the building styles, where a cyclist might care more about car-free zones; one gourmand might care more about fine dining, while another might emphasize dessert spots. And the guidebooks might even contain mistakes.

So, too, people who read the Bible primarily in translation and guided by established religious trends get great insight into those religious trends and the role the Bible plays in them, but the focus on one particular view of the Bible necessarily presents a warped view of the original Bible.

In this sense, our journey here over the next couple of hundred pages will be like visiting the Bible itself, stripped of its later interpretations, the biases from agenda-laden theologians, the distortions of both accidental and purposeful mistranslations, and the various impacts of history.

We'll see that some of the most familiar biblical passages are the most severely misrepresented today: the theological creeds, the ethical guidelines, and the key stories. We should hardly be surprised. Those passages achieved their fame because of their centrality, and that very centrality came only as the passages were continuously reinterpreted.

As we work through the texts, we'll see five recurring themes.

The first is simple ignorance. That's a strong word—and it often conveys a sense of shame, as if to say, "What's wrong with you that you don't know that?" But that's not our point here. Rather, we simply mean the understandable lack of knowledge among people who can't reasonably be expected to be experts in ancient languages and culture. When we say that someone is ignorant about how the New Testament quotes the Old Testament, we mean it in the same way that even a frequent flier on an airline might be ignorant about how turbulence and velocity impact aerodynamic lift.

Still, those frequent fliers don't usually pass themselves off as engineering experts. But people who haven't read the Bible carefully sometimes nonetheless spout proclamations about it, either to bolster its value or to mock it. The Rapture (which, as we'll see in chapter 30, is when nonbelievers will be left on earth as believers are transported to be with the Lord) isn't in the Bible, so believing in the Rapture is no reason to value the Bible. And the Bible doesn't contradict evolution (chapter 2), so believing in evolution is no reason to dismiss it.

Related to ignorance is the second theme: historical accident. Some passages were inadvertently misinterpreted before the Bible spread around the world, so the mistaken interpretations became mainstream. This is where we get Adam and Eve's famous apple from the Garden of Eden (chapter 26), which wasn't an apple, and two very different understandings of the theologically important "Man does not live by bread alone" (chapter 21).

The third theme is a culture gap. Our modern, scientific, Western approach to life is all most of us know, just as the cultures of the Ancient Near East, which created the Bible, were all the ancient readers knew. So when we read biblical texts through a modern lens, we necessarily miss some of the ancient impact. Psalm 23 ("The Lord is my shepherd") compares God to a person most people have never met: a shepherd. But the ancient imagery was one of familiarity, and (as we'll see in chapter 16) the shepherding wasn't even the original point; it was simply the cultural backdrop against which the poetry was painted.

The fourth theme is mistranslation. The Bible has been translated into literally hundreds, perhaps even thousands of versions. Some of these became mainstream, like the Septuagint, the early translation of the Old Testament from Hebrew into Greek; the Vulgate, the mid-first-millennium-A.D. translation of the Old and New Testaments into Latin; and the King James Version, the seventeenth-century translation of the Old and New Testaments into English. Not surprisingly, these translations were imperfect, but because of their centrality, the errors in them often became just as mainstream as the original words themselves. This is where we get famous but inaccurate renditions like "In the beginning God created . . ." for the start of Genesis (our chapter 1) and the equally famous but just as inaccurate "God so loved the world" for John 3:16 (our chapter 10).

The fifth and final theme is misrepresentation. From time to time, people purposely misquote and otherwise misrepresent the Bible's text, in furtherance of a particular agenda. This is where we get the virgin birth of Isaiah 7:14 to which Jesus is compared in Matthew 1:18 (our chapter 24); in the original there was no virgin birth in Isaiah. And it's frequently where we get the texts that are cited in support of or opposition to today's most bitter cultural debates: homosexuality, abortion, marriage, pacifism, the death penalty, and so forth. The Bible doesn't say that homosexuality is a sin (as we discuss in chapter 39), in spite of prominent leaders who say it does; and it doesn't say that war is always evil, in spite of people who like to quote Isaiah: "Nation shall not lift up sword against nation" (our chapter 20).

These five ways of distorting the Bible's original message have various common elements. Two are worth pointing out here.

The first is mistaking tradition for the original. One early tradition about the Ten Commandments quotes them as saying "Do not covet," but, in fact, that is not what the original Hebrew means (our chapter 8). Similarly, modern Jewish dietary laws—"keeping kosher"—find their roots in the Bible. But most of the modern details come from tradition. For instance, even though cheeseburgers aren't kosher today, there's nothing in the Bible that even mentions them (our chapter 29).

A more subtle way of mixing up tradition with the original is to assume that a traditional interpretation of a biblical passage is the only way of reading that passage. In the context of homosexuality (our chapter 39), for instance, one common argument in support of same-sex couples is the observation that the same word, "cling," describes both Adam's relationship to Eve and the relationship of one woman, Ruth, toward another, Naomi. That kind of reasoning may make for an interesting discussion, but the similarity of language doesn't mean that the Bible says Ruth and Naomi were lesbians.

A second common element is ignoring the context of an original passage. The joke above about the reporter and the economist shows how misleading that can be.

We see that an accurate quotation out of context is just as bad as an inaccurate quotation. This lack of context is why many people think that Isaiah's proclamation about not lifting up swords is about pacifism, for example; we'll see in chapter 20 that, in its larger context, that wasn't what Isaiah meant.

In addition to local contexts that help us understand what individual passages mean, we also have to pay attention to the larger context of the Bible itself. One common way to distort the Bible is to quote one verse but ignore another one on the same theme. People who say the Bible commands us to "beat our swords into plowshares" are (almost) right, because those words are in Isaiah 2:4. Less well known is the prophetic counterpart in Joel 3:10: "Beat your plowshares into swords."

Some verses are quoted as, well, Gospel, like Jesus's famous antiviolence exhortation to "turn the other cheek" instead of taking revenge (Matthew 5:39, among others). But Luke 19:27 also quotes Jesus as commanding an audience to bring his enemies forth and "slaughter them in my presence."

In these cases, and many more like them, the full context of the Bible offers two (or more) different opinions, but some people, often on purpose, quote only one of them.

So we keep in mind five ways that the Bible gets distorted: ignorance, accident, culture gap, mistranslation, and misrepresentation; and two common elements that they share: misapplying tradition and missing the context.

Naturally, there's overlap among all of these, just as there are other ways of misunderstanding the Bible. So this isn't a strict framework. It's a set of guidelines that we'll use as we start exploring what the Bible originally said and how it has been so widely misunderstood.

Appropriately, we begin with "In the beginning," the very first words of the Bible.

1

IN THE BEGINNING

***Does the Bible start with "In the beginning"?* Not really.**

A book's opening words set the stage for everything that follows.

Charles Dickens's famous first lines of *A Tale of Two Cities*—"It was the best of times, it was the worst of times"—point the reader in the direction of division, which, of course, is a major aspect of his work. Even more immediately, the words "it was the worst of times" mean something completely different after "It was the best of times" than they would on their own.

Similarly, Leo Tolstoy foreshadows his theme of power by beginning his *War and Peace* with the words "Well, prince," which aren't even in Russian in the original. They are in French (*Eh bien, mon prince*), because that was the language of the upper class. With just a few words, Tolstoy frames his work.

So the nuance and detail of the first words of the Bible are important not just for what they mean, but for how they set the stage of what follows in Genesis. And unfortunately, the standard translation, "In the beginning," doesn't quite get it right.

The Hebrew there is the one word *b'reishit*. The prefix *b-* means "in" and *reishit* means "beginning," so the word itself does mean "in beginning" or "in the beginning." But the impact of the word comes from its placement in the sentence.

Hebrew phrases normally start with a verb. So in Hebrew, the ubiquitous "God spoke unto Moses" begins with the verb "spoke" (*vay'dabeir*). When something comes even before the verb, it indicates a combination of emphasis and an answer to a perhaps unasked question.

This may seem like a picayune detail to English readers, one merely of minor emphasis. But emphasis is important, and the misemphasized translation ends up as wrong as mixing up "When?" and "What?" To see how, we look at an English example, from a hypothetical court case.

A bank robber on the witness stand is asked, "When did you rob First National?" The safe answer is the neutral "I robbed First National on Tuesday." That simply answers the question. By contrast, the thief might respond, "I robbed *First National* on *Tuesday*." That is a dangerous answer, because the emphasis automatically creates an alternative set of circumstances in the mind of English speakers who hear it. Now the guy is robbing other banks on other days. He is no longer simply answering the question of when he robbed First National, but answering the broader question of which banks he robbed when.

Similarly, the English sentence "I like mustard" is neutral. Some dialects allow another, similar, sentence, "Mustard, I like." (Interestingly, while some English speakers find this a perfectly normal phrasing, others are equally convinced that it has no place in English.) Among the speakers who accept the sentence, it means the same thing as the neutral "I like mustard," but it also emphasizes "mustard" and creates a contrast. The unmistakable implication is that the person who likes mustard is ranking the condiment over something else—ketchup, perhaps.

These are the important kinds of implications that the usual translation "In the beginning" misses.

Better would be "It was in the beginning that God created . . ." or *"In the beginning* God created . . ." Or, with less pithiness, something like "In the beginning—and not any other time—God created . . ." Or, "Let's talk about when God created heaven and earth. It was in the beginning."

Obviously, these last two options don't work as translations, but they illustrate the point. Genesis in Hebrew starts by answering the question "When?"—and, in particular, when certain things happened. The English is neutral, but its most likely interpretation by English readers is that it answers the question "What?"—specifically, what happened.

The text of Genesis assumes that God created everything. In the mind-set of the day, after all, who else could possibly have done it? Of course it was God. And because the then-standard cosmological view divided the world into "earth" and "things above earth," of course God created what we now call "heaven and earth." Similarly, there was obviously a difference between land and sea, just as there were obviously three kinds of lights in the sky. (We now count at least four: sun, moon, planets, and stars. Genesis doesn't distinguish between planets and stars.) And so on.

In this light, the book of Genesis, and, therefore, the Bible, starts less with a statement about what God created than with an enumeration of the timing of events.

The question has not lost its relevance. Scientists and laypeople alike continue to be intrigued by issues surrounding the creation of the universe. To many, however, the biblical answer of "In the beginning" is particularly unsatisfying. On the other hand, though, the modern scientific answer is that the universe came into being at some point and there was nothing before that because there was no time before that. It takes longer to say (and, obviously, goes into more detail about the process afterward), but doesn't really offer more information about where everything originally came from. In both modern cosmology and Genesis, first there was nothing, then there was something.

And at any rate, we can't even probe the merits of the ancient answer of "In the beginning" without first realizing that it is indeed an answer to an unasked question. And to do that, we have to see past the standard, misleading, translation.

Another misleading translation competes with "In the beginning God created . . ." That competing suggestion is that the first verse of Genesis ("In the beginning God created heaven and earth") isn't a sentence on its own, but, rather, modifies the second verse ("The earth was without form . . ."). One instance of this is in the NRSV translation. (That is, the New Revised Standard Version translation of the Bible, which is what we'll generally use here as our baseline English translation. We'll also use the English King James Version—KJV— from the seventeenth century and some others. In addition, from time to time we'll refer to an ancient Greek translation called the Septuagint.) The NRSV adds the word "when" into Genesis: "In the beginning when God created the heavens and the earth, the earth was . . ." The editors even add a footnote, suggesting the alternative "when God began to create."

Unfortunately, this revision moves even further away from the original thrust of Genesis. Where the standard translation "In the beginning" is neutral, and fails to reflect the original emphasis on this phrase, the wording "when God began to create" actually deemphasizes the phrase "In the beginning."

To see exactly how, we again return to English. We start with the question "When did God create the world?" "In the beginning, God created . . ." works as an answer. "When God began to create . . ." does not.

This alternative phrasing with "when" is a perfect example of mixing up tradition with the original text, which is one of the five ways we noted in the introduction that the Bible gets distorted. In this case, the misleading phrasing comes from an eleventh-century Jewish Bible scholar named Solomon, son of Isaac. His Hebrew name forms an acronym by which he is best known: Rashi. Rashi left his birthplace of Troyes, France, to study in Worms (in what is now Germany) with the great Jewish scholars of his era. Then he returned to France, just in time to avoid the destruction that the Crusaders wrought on the Jewish community of Worms. All of his teachers were killed. Most of their accumulated wisdom would have been lost to time, too, except that Rashi had already left.

Rashi turned out to be extraordinarily prolific. And though he didn't always make it clear when he was conveying information he had learned and when he was providing his own opinions, it didn't take long for people to realize that Rashi preserved many hundreds of years of accumulated tradition.

Among his many writings, Rashi provides a running commentary on the Five Books of Moses. And in the context of Genesis 1:1, Rashi comments on a detail of Hebrew, even noting that the verse, as it is written, "cries out 'interpret me!'" Rashi's interpretation is based on a potential Hebrew anomaly. The word we have been translating as "the beginning" (*reishit*) looks like it actually means only "beginning," not "the beginning." If so, the full word *b'reishit* doesn't mean "in the beginning" but "in beginning," which, by itself, doesn't make much sense. Furthermore, Hebrew has a way of saying "at first," and it's not *b'reishit* but rather the related *b'rishonah*.

Rashi has a suggestion for reconciling the seemingly odd Hebrew. The details of why his suggestion solves the problem of the missing "the" are too complex to include here—readers who are interested should start by learning about a Hebrew grammatical form called *s'michut*—but Rashi's conclusion is easy to understand. The verse should be understood, he writes, as though it says "In the beginning of God's creating."

To make this work, Rashi has to change the verb "created" into the noun "creating." For many, this already undermines his analysis, because, after all, what advantage is there to a better understanding of the first word if it relies on completely changing the second?

A more substantial objection to Rashi's analysis comes in his own explanation of it. For Rashi, the problem is that the purpose of Genesis couldn't be to explain the order of creation, because the second verse refers to God's spirit on "the water." What water, Rashi wants to know? According to the text, it hasn't been created yet. Therefore, Rashi concludes, the point of the text can't be to explain the order of things, because, after all, water was created before heaven and earth.

And for that matter, Rashi adds, heaven was created from fire and water, so water had to have been created before verse 1:1 in Genesis. How does Rashi know that heaven was created from fire and water? Because the Hebrew for "heaven" is *shamayim* and the Hebrew word for "water" is *mayim*. The word for "water" is right there in "heaven." Take the *mayim* ("water") out of the *shamayim* ("heaven") and you're left with the consonantal sound *sh*, which is the sole consonantal component of the Hebrew *eish*, "fire." "Heaven," in Hebrew, is literally composed of "fire" and "water."

While this kind of wordplay forms the foundation of the kind of interpretation upon which religion is built, and while it's exactly the sort of thing that Rashi himself says the verse demands, it also demonstrates the contrast between traditional interpretation and the original text. The Hebrew word for "water" inside the Hebrew word for "heaven" doesn't demonstrate that water was created before heaven any more than we can conclude that animals were created before the earth because the English word "earth" contains the word "ear."

Furthermore, Rashi's way of reading "In the beginning, God . . ." as "When God began to create" is the second interpretation he offers. He first connects the "beginning" here to Proverbs 8:22, "The Lord possessed me in the beginning of his way." The Bible is, therefore, according to Rashi, the beginning of God's way.

Both of Rashi's analyses belong firmly in the arena of traditional interpretation. In fact, it is only in comparison to the original text that we can fully appreciate what Rashi—and many others like him—have done. We hide the evolution of Genesis when we gloss over the way that Rashi reinterpreted the text.

So to look at the fuller picture, Genesis, even according to Rashi, should no more be translated as "When God began to create . . ." than it should "In the beginning—and speaking of beginnings, the Bible is the beginning of God's way. . . ." Nor should it necessarily be translated simply as "In the beginning . . . ," because that misses the focus of the original text.

Rather, through either italics or rewording, the most accurate way to capture the original Hebrew that starts the Bible is to note that it answers not the question "What?" but rather the unasked question "When?"

For some, this makes it easier to accept the fact that the question "What?" often has contradictory answers, as we'll see next.

2

EVOLUTION

***Does Genesis contradict evolution?* No.**

God created the world in six days. Everyone knows the Bible says that.
And it does. The day-by-day stages of creation are also well known:
"the heavens and the earth" on the first day, as we just saw, along with
light and darkness. Then sky and water on the second, continents
("land") and plants on the third, and so on, culminating with God's
pièce de résistance on the sixth day: humans, created in the very image of God.

Just as familiar is the theatrical manner in which Eve was created
from Adam's very rib.

But here we have a problem, because the account regarding the rib
comes in Genesis 2:21–22: "So the Lord God caused a deep sleep to
fall upon the man, and he slept; then he took one of his ribs and closed
up its place with flesh. And the rib that the Lord God had taken from
the man he made into woman and brought her to the man." But by
Genesis 2 Adam and Eve had already been created. God created
"male and female" in his image in Genesis 1:27. And to compound

the confusion, Genesis 2:2 is clear that "God finished all the work that he had done." The woman who was created from Adam's rib had already been created several verses earlier. How is that possible?

A closer look at the details reveals even more confusion: Both "male and female" people had already been created in Genesis 1:27, and God had completed the work of creation by Genesis 2:2. But sixteen verses later in Genesis 2:18 the sole man of the earth was still "alone," which is why God had to "form every animal" in Genesis 2:19. It was in this context of a single male human with only animals for companionship that God created woman from man's rib.

In short, God took six days to create the world, including first the animals, and, finally, man and woman. Then, having finished creating everything, God rested. Then once God had rested after creating everything, man was alone with no women or animals. So God created animals. But man was still lonely, so God created woman. What's going on?

The answer is that there are in fact two separate creation stories. The first is generally the more familiar: God created the world in six days, resting on the seventh after creating everything. In the second, man comes first, then the animals, then Eve from Adam's rib. The NRSV translation acknowledges the second creation story by giving each one its own heading. The first story is captioned "Six Days of Creation and the Sabbath," and the second, "Another Account of the Creation."

The wording of the second caption is subtle. By calling it "another account" of, presumably, the "same creation," the NRSV suggests that there was only one sequence of events, even though we have two descriptions of it. And the NRSV is not alone in suggesting this solution to what seems to be a pretty fundamental problem.

Two thousand years ago, the historian Josephus summarized the first "account," as the NRSV calls it, and then characterized the second account as Moses's philosophical reflection on the first. (Josephus says that Moses wrote Genesis.) For Josephus, then, the first account is what happened; the second is what Moses thought about it.

Similarly, the Rabbis who created rabbinic Judaism, in response to this and to other apparent contradictions, declared that "there is no before and after" in the Bible. If so, it doesn't matter that Genesis 2, which obviously comes after Genesis 1, describes a state of affairs before the events in Genesis 1 were completed.

These are traditional answers. And there are others. But just as with Rashi's traditional answer about "In the beginning" in the last chapter, we don't want to confuse tradition with the original text. In this case, it doesn't take too careful a reading to suggest that there are two separate stories, not two accounts of the same story. The differences are simply too striking. There's no vegetation on the earth in Genesis 2:5, even though plants were created in Genesis 1:11–12. Adam is specifically alone without any animals in Genesis 2:18, even though Genesis 1 is equally clear that the animals were all created before Adam. (This very point was raised by the defense in the famous 1925 Scopes Monkey Trial—that is, *The State of Tennessee v. John Thomas Scopes*. Scopes was accused of teaching against the Bible by teaching evolution, and thereby violating the state's Butler Act. The defense noted that "There are two accounts in Genesis of the creation of man. They are not identical and at points differ widely. It would be difficult to say which is the teaching of the Bible.")

This is far from the only place where we find contradictions like this. We'll see in the next chapter that there are two stories of Noah's Ark, then later that there are disparate accounts of the weapon used to kill Goliath, and even of Goliath's attacker. The incongruities we see in Genesis are typical of the Bible itself, so understanding them is important to understanding the Bible.

Modern textual scholars are quick to confirm that there are two creation stories, adding that the stories were written by different people. In fact, scholars generally recognize four different authors of the Old Testament, dubbing them E, J, D, and P. The "E" stands for "Elohist," the author who uses the Hebrew word *elohim* for God. The "J" is for "Yahwist"—because in German *j* makes the sound "*y*"—who calls God "Yahweh." (We return to God's name in more detail in chapter 13.) The "D" is a "Deuteronomist" who wrote Deuteronomy, and the "P" is a priestly source who advocated for the priests. The theory also relies on a master editor (called a "redactor") who combined the material from E, J, D, and P into what we now call the Old Testament.

The theory has some flaws, particularly in the timing it demands. But its primary shortcoming comes from no fault of the theory itself but rather from the way it is used. Some people cite this theory to explain why the Bible is not consistent. But the multiple-author theory—either this specific one or another version—doesn't really do anything to explain why there are different versions of so many stories. After all, the only way different texts could have been merged is if someone (or more than one person) compiled them. This is the role of the redactor. But the redactor could equally have chosen one version over the other, as many modern readers do without knowing it. Or the redactor could have reconciled the different accounts, again as many modern readers do, following in the pattern of the Rabbis and of Josephus before them. In short, whether there were multiple authors of the multiple stories or only one author doesn't really matter nearly so much as the fact that there are different stories next to each other.

Alongside the traditional explanations of these kinds of differences, and in addition to the modern, neutral, "EJDP" theory, skeptics are quick to jump in, claiming that the disparate accounts are proof that the whole Bible is worthless. How could anyone believe any of this, they say, when it's not even internally consistent?

So the resolution of the two creation stories is not merely a question about Genesis. It's a question about the very nature of the Bible. Some traditional approaches deny the contradictions in what certainly appear to be contradictory stories. Textual scholars posit possible authors of the different stories. And skeptics see the differences as undermining the whole thing.

But these three views, in different ways, all miss the fundamental point that the stories do exist side by side. The textual scholars have to explain why the redactor—who was obviously respected enough by the community to have an authoritative voice and scholarly enough to know the different traditions—couldn't notice what any cursory read of the text reveals. The skeptics have the same problem, augmented by another: If the Bible is so badly written that it falls apart under even the most cursory of readings, why do so many people value it so highly? And the traditional explanations strike most people as contrived.

This isn't to say that the three approaches don't have value. Certainly the historical process that created the current text of the Bible is an important historical question, just as people are free to believe what they like, and to use whatever evidence they like in support of their beliefs. In particular, the traditional explanations of why the Bible isn't contradictory are part of successful religious traditions.

But we are still left with the challenge of understanding the original text with its contradictions, in this case, the two different creation stories.

The solution comes by way of stepping back from our modern, scientific view. We are now trained to think that if one claim is true, a contradictory claim cannot also be true: If heavy and light objects fall under the force of gravity at the same speed, then it cannot also be true that they fall at different speeds. Similarly, if (as it seems from Genesis 1) plants were created on a different day than people, they can't also (as it seems from Genesis 2) have been created on the same day. This basic fact about truth strikes modern readers as so obvious that any other way of looking at things seems downright silly.

But our scientific view—which has paved the way for amazing technology like medicine and communications and travel—is a modern innovation. For most of history people saw things differently. In fact, one reason we are so reluctant to give up this modern view is precisely that it is so new. As with any new toy, we are unduly captivated by it.

A direct look at Genesis, unfiltered by tradition and modern prejudices, paints a different picture. The fact that people and plants were created on different days does not conflict with the fact that they were also created on the same day. Again, our modern scientific outlook makes such a sentence seem almost absurd. But it is not.

We are even used to speaking in these terms when it comes to other endeavors. For example, one of the artist René Magritte's best-known themes comes from his series of paintings *L'empire des lumières* (*The Empire of Light*). The images depict a pleasant cloud-spotted daytime sky over a dim street at night, lit not at all by the sky, but primarily by a sole streetlight. Why isn't it light on the ground if it's daytime? Or, to flip things, the paintings might depict a night scene over which the sky has bizarrely not turned dark. Why isn't it dark in the sky if it's nighttime? These logical inconsistencies do not detract from the power of the paintings. Whatever people think of Magritte's works, their value doesn't lie in their photographic or scientific accuracy.

Or we can return to the paintings by Monet that we discussed in the introduction. Two different paintings can depict the same place differently and both be equally valid, just as two different musicians can play a Beethoven piece differently but equally well. For that matter, no one rejects Dickens's *A Tale of Two Cities* even though, as we saw in the last chapter, it starts off with as clear a contradiction as possible: "It was the best of times, it was the worst of times."

The two creation stories are just like Dickens's two opening sentences. They are two different ways of looking at the same thing, and the job of the reader is to figure out how.

Some modern readers of the Bible will object at this point, noting the obvious metaphoric language in Dickens and contrasting it with what they think is the obvious fact that two things either happened on the same day or on different days; there is no middle ground. Accounts of the past, they say, must agree factually. But in making that claim, they only reveal their prejudices about the Bible, the very misleading preconceptions that we are trying to shed here.

The creation story isn't history, and it was never meant as history.

This basic fact would have been obvious to anyone living before the scientific era. After all, right there on the page are two contradictory accounts. Of course they couldn't both have happened, not in the same sense that we use the word "happened" for things that we witness in our own lives. Why would anyone think they were meant to be historically accurate? The only reason we do so today is that we are obsessed with science.

We've taken a long time and a roundabout path to arrive at this basic statement: Parts of the Bible look like history but they are not.

The creation story obviously falls into this category. People who cite the creation story as proof that evolution is wrong, or vice versa, have radically misunderstood the text of Genesis. Right from the beginning, the creation narrative opens the door to multiple ways of understanding what happened. People who deny evolution based on Genesis err and close that door. People who force historical or scientific accuracy onto the text make the same mistake. For instance, some people, trying to make Genesis better accord with the time scale of evolution, reinterpret the words of Genesis: Maybe "day" didn't mean "day," so the six days are more like the evolutionarily plausible millions of years. But there is no evidence that "day" meant anything other than "day."

More generally, to focus on Genesis 1 to the exclusion of Genesis 2 is to ignore the context of the creation story. Or, to look at things the other way around, the biggest reason not to take the creation-in-six-days story literally is that the Bible itself contradicts it, not that modern science contradicts it.

This approach is perhaps surprising today, but was entirely run-of-the-mill during most of human history. And it provides an exciting challenge: If the text wasn't meant to be literal (and it wasn't), what is the message of the creation narrative? What does it teach us about our lives? For instance, what does it mean for woman to have been created so man wouldn't be alone, or more generally, that "people shouldn't be alone," as Genesis 2:18 posits? (We'll return to Genesis 2:18 in chapter 39.) What does it mean to have been created in the image of God? Do people rule over the animals?

But if we continue to misread the Bible, we won't even be able to ask the right questions, to say nothing of starting to answer them.

3

NOAH'S ARK

***Did the animals board Noah's Ark two by two?* Yes, but also no.**

Perhaps even more familiar than the six days of creation is Noah's Ark and the flood narrative. Its themes, from Genesis 6–8, have permeated pop culture. God plans the destruction of the earth by flood. A man named Noah is chosen to save the human race and the various species of animal by keeping them safe on a great ark. Forty days and nights of rain cover the entire earth. A dove brings back an olive branch as proof that the waters have started to recede. And God creates a rainbow as a sign that there will be no more global floods. Almost everyone is familiar with these details.

What fewer people know is that there are two flood stories, just as there are two creation stories. We get a sense of the disparity between them by comparing Genesis 6:19 and 7:8–9 (from one story) with Genesis 7:2. In 6:19, we read that Noah is to bring into the ark "two of every kind" of "every living being," an accounting reinforced in 7:8–9: "Of clean animals, and of animals that are not clean, and of birds, and of everything that creeps on the ground, two and two, male and female, went into the ark."

But Genesis 7:2 has a different enumeration. There Noah is told, "Take with you seven pairs of all clean animals, the male and its mate; and a pair of the animals that are not clean." While the animals still board in pairs, now there are seven pairs of the clean animals, not just one. Genesis 7:3 adds that Noah should gather seven pairs of every kind of bird, too.

Most people think that "clean," also commonly translated as "pure," means "kosher," according to the dietary laws of Leviticus. (Rashi, whom we met in chapter 1, says that this proves that Noah had studied the Bible. Otherwise, how would he know which animals were kosher and which were not?) But more important for us than which animals were clean or pure or kosher is the division of the animals into groups, not just in Genesis 7:2 but also in Genesis 7:8–9.

The animals have to be divided into two groups in Genesis 7:2, because there one group gets more animals on the ark than the other. But taken on its own, the division seems out of place in Genesis 7:8–9, because the clean and unclean animals are treated identically. Why would the text there bother making a distinction that had no practical purpose? On the other hand, Genesis 7:8–9 makes a lot of sense if it is refuting the tradition recorded in 7:2. What we see is two traditions about the same story, specifically differing on the details.

Some people still try to reconcile the two texts. Just because all of the animals went onto the ark in pairs—some say—doesn't necessarily mean that there weren't more pairs of some than of others. But this and similar attempts are forced, and ignore the clear context of the original text: There are two stories.

We see other evidence of two traditions: Genesis 7:17 records that "the flood continued 40 days." Following up, in Genesis 8:6, Noah opens a window on the ark and sends out a dove after those forty days. Noah's plan is to see if the bird can find land to rest on. But it does not. It returns to the ark. Noah tries again seven days later, and again the bird returns. Seven days after that the dove finally finds land. This puts the flood at not more than fifty-four days, depending on whether one counts the days of rain (40) or the days during which the land was completely covered (54).

But Genesis 7:24 says that the flood lasted for at least 150 days: "The waters swelled on the earth for 150 days." Then in 8:1–3, it seems that it was actually raining that whole time, because it wasn't until after those 150 days that "the windows of the heavens were closed" (matching the "opening" of the windows to indicate the start of the flood in Genesis 7:11) and "the rain from the heavens was restrained."

Again, a clever person can force these verses into accord. Maybe it rained really hard for forty days, flooding the earth, and then sprinkles continued for another few months, during which the water receded a bit. Or maybe there's another way.

There is yet more evidence of two stories. Genesis 7:5–7 reads: "And Noah did all that the Lord had commanded him. [6]Noah was 600 years old, and the flood was upon the earth. [7]And Noah with his sons and his wife and his sons' wives went into the ark to escape the waters of the flood." The middle line, verse 6, seems out of place. And it is. It's from the other story.

For that matter, Genesis 7:10 reads "And after seven days the waters of the flood came on the earth," contradicting the timing of Genesis 7:6. And according to Genesis 8:6, "the raven" flies back and forth "until the water dries up," while in next verse Noah sends "the dove" to see if the water has dried up.

All of these anomalies disappear when the text is split into two. In one version, the flood lasts for forty days, and more clean animals and birds are gathered on the ark than other animals. In the other version, the flood lasts, all said, for a bit longer than a year. One version has a dove, the other a raven.

Once untangled, we find two coherent stories, instead of one largely incoherent one. The following excerpt demonstrates:

Chapter 6

1 When people began to multiply on the face of the ground, and daughters were born to them,

2 the sons of God saw that they were fair; and they took wives for themselves of all that they chose.

3 Then the Lord said, "My spirit shall not abide in mortals forever, for they are flesh; their days shall be one hundred twenty years."

4 The Nephilim were on the earth in those days—and also afterward—when the sons of God went in to the daughters of humans, who bore children to them. These were the heroes that were of old, warriors of renown.

5 The Lord saw that the wickedness of humankind was great in the earth, and that every inclination of the thoughts of their hearts was only evil continually.

1

2

3

4

5

6 And the Lord was sorry that he had made humankind on the earth, and it grieved him to his heart.

7 So the Lord said, "I will blot out from the earth the human beings I have created—people together with animals and creeping things and birds of the air, for I am sorry that I have made them."

8 But Noah found favor in the sight of the Lord.

9

10

11

12

13

14

6

7

8

9 These are the descendants of Noah. Noah was a righteous man, blameless in his generation; Noah walked with God.

10 And Noah had three sons, Shem, Ham, and Japheth.

11 Now the earth was corrupt in God's sight, and the earth was filled with violence.

12 And God saw that the earth was corrupt; for all flesh had corrupted its ways upon the earth.

13 And God said to Noah, "I have determined to make an end of all flesh, for the earth is filled with violence because of them; now I am going to destroy them along with the earth.

14 Make yourself an ark of cypress wood; make rooms in the ark, and cover it inside and out with pitch.

15

16

17

18

19

20

21

15 This is how you are to make it: the length of the ark three hundred cubits, its width fifty cubits, and its height thirty cubits.

16 Make a roof for the ark, and finish it to a cubit above; and put the door of the ark in its side; make it with lower, second, and third decks.

17 For my part, I am going to bring a flood of waters on the earth, to destroy from under heaven all flesh in which is the breath of life; everything that is on the earth shall die.

18 But I will establish my covenant with you; and you shall come into the ark, you, your sons, your wife, and your sons' wives with you.

19 And of every living thing, of all flesh, you shall bring two of every kind into the ark, to keep them alive with you; they shall be male and female.

20 Of the birds according to their kinds, and of the animals according to their kinds, of every creeping thing of the ground according to its kind, two of every kind shall come in to you, to keep them alive.

21 Also take with you every kind of food that is eaten, and store it up; and it shall serve as food for you and for them."

22

22 Noah did this; he did all that God commanded him.

Chapter 7

1 Then the Lord said to Noah, "Go into the ark, you and all your household, for I have seen that you alone are righteous before me in this generation.

1

2 Take with you seven pairs of all clean animals, the male and its mate; and a pair of the animals that are not clean, the male and its mate;

2

3 and seven pairs of the birds of the air also, male and female, to keep their kind alive on the face of all the earth.

3

4 For in seven days I will send rain on the earth for forty days and forty nights; and every living thing that I have made I will blot out from the face of the ground."

4

5 And Noah did all that the Lord had commanded him.

5

6

6 Noah was six hundred years old when the flood of waters came on the earth.

7 And Noah with his sons and his wife and his sons' wives went into the ark to escape the waters of the flood.

7

8

8 Of clean animals, and of animals that are not clean, and of birds, and of everything that creeps on the ground,

9

9 two and two, male and female,
went into the ark with Noah,
as God had commanded
Noah.

10 And after seven days the waters of the flood came on the
earth.

10

11

11 In the six hundredth year of
Noah's life, in the second
month, on the seventeenth day
of the month, on that day all
the fountains of the great deep
burst forth, and the windows
of the heavens were opened.

12 The rain fell on the earth forty
days and forty nights.

12

13

13 On the very same day Noah
with his sons, Shem and Ham
and Japheth, and Noah's wife
and the three wives of his
sons entered the ark,

14

14 they and every wild animal of
every kind, and all domestic
animals of every kind, and every creeping thing that creeps
on the earth, and every bird
of every kind—every bird,
every winged creature.

15

15 They went into the ark with
Noah, two and two of all flesh in
which there was the breath of
life.

16 [. . .] and the Lord shut him in.

16 And those that entered, male
and female of all flesh, went in
as God had commanded him;
[. . .]

17 The flood continued forty days on the earth; and the waters increased, and bore up the ark, and it rose high above the earth.

17

18 The waters swelled and increased greatly on the earth; and the ark floated on the face of the waters.

18

19 The waters swelled so mightily on the earth that all the high mountains under the whole heaven were covered;

19

20 the waters swelled above the mountains, covering them fifteen cubits deep.

20

21

21 And all flesh died that moved on the earth, birds, domestic animals, wild animals, all swarming creatures that swarm on the earth, and all human beings;

22 everything on dry land in whose nostrils was the breath of life died.

22

23 He blotted out every living thing that was on the face of the ground, human beings and animals and creeping things and birds of the air; they were blotted out from the earth. Only Noah was left, and those that were with him in the ark.

23

24

24 And the waters swelled on the earth for one hundred fifty days.

Chapter 8

1

1 But God remembered Noah
and all the wild animals and all
the domestic animals that were
with him in the ark. And God
made a wind blow over the
earth, and the waters subsided;

2

2 the fountains of the deep and
the windows of the heavens
were closed, the rain from the
heavens was restrained,

3

3 and the waters gradually receded from the earth. At the
end of one hundred fifty days
the waters had abated;

4

4 and in the seventh month, on
the seventeenth day of the
month, the ark came to rest
on the mountains of Ararat.

5

5 The waters continued to abate
until the tenth month; in the
tenth month, on the first day
of the month, the tops of the
mountains appeared.

6 At the end of forty days Noah
opened the window of the ark
that he had made

6

7

7 and sent out the raven; and it
went to and fro until the waters
were dried up from the earth.

8 Then he sent out the dove from
him, to see if the waters had
subsided from the face of the
ground;

8

9 but the dove found no place to
set its foot, and it returned to

9

him to the ark, for the waters were still on the face of the whole earth. So he put out his hand and took it and brought it into the ark with him.

10 He waited another seven days, and again he sent out the dove from the ark;

11 and the dove came back to him in the evening, and there in its beak was a freshly plucked olive leaf; so Noah knew that the waters had subsided from the earth.

12 Then he waited another seven days, and sent out the dove; and it did not return to him any more.

13 [. . .] and Noah removed the covering of the ark, and looked, and saw that the face of the ground was drying.

14

15

16

17

10

11

12

13 In the six hundred first year, in the first month, on the first day of the month, the waters were dried up from the earth; [. . .]

14 In the second month, on the twenty-seventh day of the month, the earth was dry.

15 Then God said to Noah,

16 "Go out of the ark, you and your wife, and your sons and your sons' wives with you.

17 Bring out with you every living thing that is with you of all flesh—birds and animals and every creeping thing that creeps on the earth—so that they may abound on the earth, and be fruitful and multiply on the earth."

18	18 So Noah went out with his sons and his wife and his sons' wives.
19	19 And every animal, every creeping thing, and every bird, everything that moves on the earth, went out of the ark by families.
20 Then Noah built an altar to the Lord, and took of every clean animal and of every clean bird, and offered burnt offerings on the altar.	20
21 And when the Lord smelled the pleasing odor, the Lord said in his heart, "I will never again curse the ground because of humankind, for the inclination of the human heart is evil from youth; nor will I ever again destroy every living creature as I have done.	21
22 As long as the earth endures, seedtime and harvest, cold and heat, summer and winter, day and night, shall not cease."	22

We should not be surprised or concerned that these two versions offer incompatible details, because—like the two creation narratives—they focus on different aspects of the same thing.

In particular, they are part of a story that begins with the Watchers and ends with the Tower of Babel. Because this account was so well known in antiquity, the text of the Bible glosses over many of the details. (The Watchers are angels who were supposed to watch over humanity, but, according to Genesis 6:2, some of them instead mated with human women, creating evil giants. The disobedient Watchers are the now-famous fallen angels, and their half-human offspring, called "the *nephilim*" in Genesis 6:4, are the source of wickedness that led God to flood the earth.)

We have external evidence in the form of the once-widespread book of Enoch that the story of the Watchers and the giants was in fact exceedingly popular and familiar in antiquity. We also have internal evidence from the text of the Bible. The wording "the *nephilim*"—not just "*nephilim*"—reflects the fact that everyone who read Genesis was expected to know who they were.

This usage matches "the raven" and "the dove," the birds in the two different versions of Noah's Ark. People knew about the birds in the stories, too. The Noah's Ark narrative wasn't designed to tell people that there was a dove. They already knew. It was designed to tell them about the dove.

At the other end of the story arc, we have the Tower of Babel, which, the Bible tells us, was waterproofed to fulfill its purpose of inuring the people against a repeat of the flood: "they had . . . bitumen for mortar" (Genesis 11:4). (The importance of the bitumen and the purpose of the tower is often lost on modern readers, who don't know that bitumen was used for waterproofing.)

The narrative also contains extensive genealogies that serve to explain the political landscape. For instance, two of Noah's children are Shem and Ham; Ham has a son named Canaan. Shem—"Sem" in Greek—is the progenitor of the people we now call the Semites, and Canaan is the ancestor of the Canaanites, whom the Jewish Semites will conquer. This is reflected in Genesis 9:26: "Blessed by the Lord my God be Shem; and let Canaan be his slave."

Though we tend to focus on the flood, the ark, and the Tower of Babel—and to gloss over the long lists of names—the original text puts them side by side without any indication that one part is more important than another.

What we have, then, is a sequence designed to tell people about the world in which they lived. Included in it are two flood stories, a brief reference to the Watchers that prompted the flood, a quick mention of the failed tower experiment that would have protected the people against another flood, and a slew of names and genealogies that function like a geopolitical map.

All of these passages are partial answers to the sweeping question "What is the world like?" They are not answers to purely modern questions of history. We already saw that both creation stories address loneliness and the desire for people to couple up (as we saw in the last chapter, and as we'll investigate in more detail in chapter 39). Here we see that the flood stories contribute to a framework of good and evil. Noah is by and large a good person, but he is not perfect. By extension, we might learn that even good people can do bad things, or, at least, ask the question whether a single bad act disqualifies a person from being good. Equally, the world contains wickedness. Do people come in two varieties, good and evil, or maybe kind and wicked? Noah's merit in Genesis 6:9 seems to be relative to "his generation." Do we expect more from people as society progresses? Should we? These are the themes of the flood stories.

The stories are great narratives. There's a reason they have survived. And they address timeless questions. But an anachronistic focus on history hides their value. In the next chapter we'll see even more internal evidence that warns us not to read these stories as history.

4

LIFE SPANS IN THE OLD TESTAMENT

Did people really once live to be almost a thousand years old? No.

One of the most prominent features of Genesis is the seemingly impossible life spans of its major characters. Adam lives to be 930 years old. His son Seth's life was only eighteen years shorter. Noah's life lasted twenty years longer than Adam's.

Abraham's father, Terah, lived a comparatively short life of 205 years, while Abraham himself only lived to be 175. Sarah died young, at the age of 127—right at the upper edge of what we now think is biologically possible. On the other hand, she conceived a child at age ninety, so her life was not entirely within the bounds of what we now expect.

As with the creation and flood narratives of the past few chapters, people sometimes try to reconcile these numbers with modern science in two ways. One is by taking the figures literally, and assuming that science has misunderstood how long a person can live. Who's to say whether nine hundred years was possible back then? Maybe they lived healthier lives. Or maybe God is the sole arbiter of death and these ancients were granted a longer life.

The second way is by trying to massage the data. Maybe "years" in the text means half years. That would put Sarah's pregnancy in her forty-fifth year, which is possible. It would give her a life span of about sixty-three, and her husband Abraham a life span of about eighty-seven. Both of those are possible. But that would still mean that Noah lived to be 465.

To move Noah's life back toward the spectrum of scientific reality, "year" would have to be adjusted to mean about fifty-one days. Then the figure 930 attached to his life span would be only 930 units of 51 days, which is to say, 45,430 days, or about 130 years: old, but just barely possible.

By that calculus, however, Sarah became pregnant at age twelve, which is biologically possible, but inconsistent with the text of Genesis 18:11, according to which she had already entered menopause. Similarly, Abraham would have died not at age 175 but rather at age twenty-four, so verse 25:8 wouldn't make sense: "Abraham . . . died in a good old age, an old man and full of years." Worse, Isaac, who was "sixty years old" when his sons were born, would have fathered twins as a seven-year-old.

So in addition to there being no evidence that "year" means anything other than what it seems, there is no mathematically and biologically plausible candidate for what it could mean.

But that does not mean that the text is incompatible with modern science.

First off, many of the ages look like they are symbolic, though their symbolism is not always clear to modern readers.

The Bible was written in the context of Babylonian mathematics, before multiplication became easy. Most people in antiquity had no way of computing, say, 17 times 51. (Modern readers may wish to try the computation using only Roman numerals.) They could only easily multiply small numbers. So the Babylonians built a system of math based on multiples of small numbers, and these multiples—in addition to 10, 100, etc.—were perceived as round numbers.

This is why there were six days of creation (2×3), twelve tribes (3×4), and forty days of the flood in one story ($2 \times 4 \times 5$). It's also why, to this day, we have twelve hours of day and twelve hours of night, and why we have sixty ($3 \times 4 \times 5$) seconds in a minute and sixty minutes in an hour.

In this context, Adam's life span of thirty times thirty plus thirty was a nice round number. "Nine hundred thirty" years was as clearly a round number as "ten thousand and ten" is now.

More convincing is the larger pattern that emerges.

The people with the greatly exaggerated life spans (by modern standards) begin with Adam and continue through Noah's children. Then Genesis 11:10–26 traces the lineage of Abraham's father, Terah, back to Noah's son Shem, with ages progressively decreasing with each new generation. Terah at the end of that progression lives to be 205.

Then from Abraham until Moses, we have people who live about two hundred years, well short of the five-hundred- or nine-hundred-year life spans from earlier in Genesis, but still well beyond what most people expect.

Moses lives to be 120 ($2 \times 3 \times 4 \times 5$, an especially round number in antiquity).

Moses's successor Aaron lives to be 110—possible, though extreme. From King David on, people live now-normal life spans.

In other words, the ages themselves divide the text into three clear sections: many hundreds of years, a couple of hundred years, and fewer than 120 years. In addition, each of the sections addresses a different topic. The first one deals with the nature of the world and the overall political landscape, the second with the nature of the Israelites, and the third with the nature of life in Canaan for the Israelites. What we see is a tripartite division of the Old Testament marked by content and style. (In chapter 6 we'll see a similar division recorded explicitly in the New Testament book of Matthew.)

Furthermore, historians generally agree that the only historically accurate part of the Old Testament comes after the death of Moses, because historians have no historical evidence of Adam, Noah, Abraham, etc., but they do know that a kingdom was established around the time of King David.

So of the three broad divisions of the Old Testament, the part that historians think is accurate is also the part that has scientifically plausible ages.

In this context, the ages seem designed precisely to flag the non-historical sections as nonhistorical. It's as if the text is shouting, *Just to make it clear that the flood isn't the same kind of account as the destruction of Jerusalem in the year 587 b.c., we'll give the characters in the first one ages of many hundreds of years, while the people in the second one will live normal life spans. That's a sign no one can miss.*

So the ages of the characters in the Old Testament line up with everything else we've seen regarding the Garden of Eden and Noah's Ark, and a consistent picture paints itself: These stories were not meant to be historical and their value does not depend on the degree to which they are literally accurate. The ages of the characters help frame the text, and the internal details contribute to the stories' complexity.

But many readers are unable to see the message of the text. Literalists modify science to accord with the ages in the Bible, and revisionists modify the Bible to match modern science. Both groups of people miss the obvious signs that the texts were not designed to be history. Rather, they are like art, showing us new ways to see the world.

Next we'll see other apparent contradictions and incompatibilities that point in the same direction.

5

DAVID AND GOLIATH
(AND ELHANAN AND GOLIATH)

Did David kill Goliath with a slingshot? Yes, but also with a sword.
And Elhanan killed Goliath, too.

Although most of the stories with alternative versions are from Genesis, we do find them throughout the Bible. A particularly clear example comes from the familiar battle between David and Goliath, during
which, as everyone knows, David slew Goliath with a stone from his
famous slingshot.

That account comes from 1 Samuel 17, where the first verses set the
stage: "[1] The Philistines gathered their armies for battle; they were
gathered at Socoh, which belongs to Judah. [2] Saul and the Israelites
gathered . . . and formed ranks against the Philistines. [3] The Philistines stood on the mountain on the one side, and Israel stood on the
mountain on the other side, with a valley between them."

Verse 4 introduces us to Goliath, a "champion . . . whose height
was six cubits and a span." A cubit is about a foot and a half, so Goliath
was over nine feet tall. (The influential ancient Greek translation
called the Septuagint—whose earliest text dates to the third century

B.C.—records a more pedestrian height of only four cubits and a span, or about six and a half feet. But nine and a half feet, though extreme, is still right at the border of what might be possible. Guinness World Records attests to a height of 8 feet 11.1 inches, or less than an inch short of nine feet, for a man named Robert Pershing Wadlow.) The Philistine warrior is not just huge. He is well protected behind heavy armor.

Then in verse 12 we meet young David, and in verse 32 the unlikely fighter offers to battle Goliath, citing his previous experience killing wildcats and bears. Verses 38–39 augment the tension as David first dons battle armor and a sword from Saul, then removes them because he is unaccustomed to wearing such things. Goliath is not only bigger, stronger, and older than David. The Philistine is better armed.

This is why in verse 43 Goliath actually mocks David: "Have you come to me with only sticks?" David's response—one of the points of the story—is that he doesn't need advanced weaponry, because God is on his side. Still, the stage has been set for a showdown pitting the mighty and menacing Goliath against young David armed only with a slingshot.

Finally, according to verse 49, "David put his hand in his bag, took out a stone, slung it, and struck the Philistine on his forehead; the stone sank into his forehead, and he fell face down on the ground."

So far, except for an alternative translation of Goliath's height, the account is entirely consistent. And the first half of verse 50 sews things up: "So David prevailed over the Philistine with a sling and a stone, striking down the Philistine and killing him." What could be clearer?

But the second half of verse 50 reads, "there was no sword in David's hand."

This is our first sign that there's more to the story than we expect. What does the lack of a sword in David's hand have to do with the already dead Goliath? Why would anyone be talking about a nonexistent sword at this point?

Verse 51 tells us: "Then David ran and stood over the Philistine; he grasped his sword, drew it out of its sheath, and killed him." According to verse 51, David killed Goliath with a sword, not a stone. In this context, the second half of verse 50 makes sense. It's telling us— reminding us, really—that David didn't have a sword, which is why he had to take Goliath's. The second half of verse 50 combined with verse 51 would make sense, except that Goliath is already dead by the first half of verse 50.

To make matters worse, the Greek translation that put Goliath's height at less than seven feet doesn't even mention the death by slingshot.

What we clearly have is two versions of the story, one in which David kills Goliath with a slingshot, the other in which David kills him with a sword. Filling in a few lines from a hypothetical reader, we get the following dialogue from verses 50–51:

Text of the Bible: "David killed Goliath with a sling and a stone."

Hypothetical Reader: "I thought he killed him with a sword."

Text: "He had no sword."

Reader: "But he only stunned him with the stone."

Text: "Well, come to think of it, he took Goliath's sword and used that to kill him."

Reader: "Told you so."

In light of the confusion about the details, we are perhaps less surprised by a brief passage in 2 Samuel 21:19: "Elhanan, son of Jaare-oregim, the Bethlehemite, killed Goliath." This is hardly a minor detail.

It's not difficult to imagine confusion regarding the manner of an enemy's death in battle. In 1 Samuel, the Israelites were on one side of a valley, the Philistines on the other. Tensions would have been high, and the attention of spectators divided among various skirmishes. And, as we know, eyewitness accounts are notoriously unreliable. Except for the Greek translation, the text agrees that David hit Goliath with a stone. The only question was whether it was a lethal blow.

This new passage in 2 Samuel is more problematic. Here Goliath's foe isn't the famous King David, founder of Jerusalem. It's an unknown guy named Elhanan. And because this is part of the historical section of the Bible, the discrepancy is potentially more serious than the kinds of variations we saw in Genesis.

Tradition addresses the obvious contradiction here in two ways.

The book of Chronicles—like Samuel and Kings, divided into two parts—reviews a lot of the historical material in Samuel and Kings, often repeating passages word for word or, even more tellingly, revising the language of the original passages slightly. 1 Chronicles 20:5 explains that "Elhanan son of Jair killed Lahmi the brother of Goliath."

The difference between "son of Jair" here and "son of Jaare-oregim" is easy to dismiss, particularly because in Hebrew consonants are more important than vowels. Both times the name is based around the letters "JR." (The "J" in English here represents the sound "Y" in Hebrew, a convention that we saw in chapter 2 regarding abbreviation "J" for the "Yahwist" author of the Bible.) So these look like the same Elhanan. And according to Chronicles, Elhanan killed Goliath's brother, not Goliath himself. With this first explanation, then, the text of Samuel is just missing a word or two. (As modern readers, we now know, from the Dead Sea Scrolls, that our current copies of Samuel are often incomplete, missing not just a word here and there but sometimes complete passages.) The influential King James Version, from the seventeenth century, even adds the words "the brother of" to 1 Samuel, although they're not in the original text, masking the issue of the discrepancy from readers.

The second traditional way of dismissing the differences between the two passages in Samuel is to assume that Elhanan is another name for David. "Elhanan" in Hebrew means the one whom God (*el*) favored (*hanan*), so perhaps this is a nickname or epithet for David. And the second half of Elhanan's father's name in 2 Samuel, "oregim," means "weavers." So maybe the point here is "David, the one whom God favored, the weaver." And this reading of the text in 2 Samuel is what we get in another major early translation. Targum Jonathan, a translation of the later books of the Old Testament from Hebrew into Aramaic (composed, probably, in the first part of the first millennium A.D.) doesn't mention "Elhanan" in 2 Samuel 21:19, but rather "David, the weaver." And Rashi (from chapter 1) explains that "Elhanan" in 2 Samuel 21:19 means "David" and explains that "son of Jaare-oregim" means "the people from the family of weavers."

But this traditional explanation leaves other discrepancies unexplained. For instance, according to 2 Samuel, the battle occurs at a place called Gob, while in 1 Samuel it takes place in the Valley of Elah.

And there are other contradictions. David's surprising victory over Goliath in 1 Samuel 17 is how Saul comes to meet the future king, but according to 1 Samuel 16:18–23, it is David's musical skill that first attracts the attention of Saul.

All told, the various accounts of David and Goliath demonstrate both minor and major discrepancies of fact, along with more general differences about the role of the story. While it's certainly possible that real events would be distorted by various mistaken reports, more likely is that all of these accounts—even as part of the historical record of King David's rise to power—are intended as lessons, not as history.

By analogy, we might look at the qualities that define the presidency of the United States. Every schoolchild learns that a young George Washington cut down his father's cherry tree but then was forced to admit that he did so, because he "cannot tell a lie." The value of that story lies not in the details about the tree ("What kind of cherries were they?") but in the lesson it teaches about a leader (perhaps, mistakes are inevitable and honesty is important).

What was the leader of Israel supposed to be like? The two different accounts of David's rise suggest two attributes: The king was a military man who didn't even need advanced weaponry or armor. Equally, the king was a musician. In this regard, the various accounts of David are complementary, not contradictory, offering insight into history even though the details themselves are probably not historically accurate.

This is a common pattern even in the historical sections of the Old Testament, and, as we'll see next, in the New Testament, too.

6

JESUS'S LINEAGE

Was Jesus descended from Adam? No.

As we saw in chapter 1, the Old Testament starts off with an answer to an unasked question, "When?" The New Testament, too, starts off with an answer to an unasked question. And—again similar to the opening of the Old Testament—the first words set the stage for everything that follows.

Matthew, the first book of the New Testament, opens with a phrase usually translated along the lines of "an account of the genealogy of Jesus the Messiah." The English translation "genealogy" reflects the extended genealogy that takes the reader through the first seventeen verses of Matthew. But, in fact, the original Greek word extends well beyond "genealogy" to encompass a combination of "nature of" and "history of." The genealogy is only one part of the answer to a more general question about Jesus. Matthew is not merely answering "Who were Jesus's ancestors?"

Rather, Matthew's question—and, therefore, the issue with which the New Testament opens—is "Who is Jesus?" Part of the answer will come in the form of a detailed genealogy. (The next part will be a description of Jesus's birth to a virgin.) From the opening lines, the reader learns that the New Testament is about Jesus.

Matthew's genealogy connects Jesus directly to Abraham by way of three sets of fourteen generations. (Each of these set of fourteen earns the technical name "tessaradecad," also spelled "tesseradecad," a word whose use is all but confined to these sets of fourteen names.) Each tessaradecad is marked by a slightly different narrative style and represents a different period in history.

There is no doubt about the structure because Matthew explains it in verse 17: "So all the generations from Abraham to David are fourteen generations; and from David to the deportation to Babylon, fourteen generations; and from the deportation to Babylon to the Messiah, fourteen generations." (The "deportation to Babylon" is the expulsion of the Jews from Jerusalem to Babylonia in the year 587 B.C.) Matthew thus traces Jesus's lineage through Joseph (married to Mary, Jesus's mother) to other ancestors—including some famous kings of Israel—to David, and then backward even further directly to Abraham.

But there are some anomalies. A careful count reveals only forty-one names, not the forty-two that three groups of fourteen would require. One possible way of reconciling this with Matthew's own enumeration is to count David twice because he's mentioned twice, once at the end of the first list and again at the start of the second list. And in a sense, David is the most important name on the list, because Matthew saw Jesus as the Messiah, and Matthew thought that the Messiah would be a descendant of David.

Another way of reconciling the math is based on the similarity between two names that perhaps should appear in the second tessaradecad. Other sources report the following three kings: Josiah, Jehoiakim, and Jeconiah, in that order. Matthew's list jumps from

Josiah to Jeconiah. Maybe a scribe omitted Jehoiakim by accident. After all, the three names, in Greek, are Iosias, Ioakim, Iexonias. Perhaps the scribe, having already written "Iosias," glanced at the "Io . . ." of his newly written text and got mixed up. (This kind of copying error is so common that it has its own name: homoioarcton—literally, "same beginning.")

However, Jehoiakim is not the only missing generation. Matthew also skips Ahaziah, Athaliah, Jehoash, and Amaziah. There are various reasons why he might do so: Only two of these were kings of Israel, these people had reputations as evildoers, and there are other possibilities. But still, once we have established a pattern of skipping kings, the missing Jehoiakim seems less like a mistake.

By now we know what kinds of modern responses we can expect to this seemingly anomalous math. Some people will insist that the text must be literally right. For example, they note that the Greek verb that gets translated "was the father of" or "begot" in the genealogies doesn't necessarily imply direct fatherhood, just as "fathers" can mean "immediate parents" or "ancestors" more generally. That way, the text in Matthew 1:11 that skips over Jehoiakim—"Josias the father of Jeconiah"—would still be accurate. At the other end of the spectrum, some people will point to the inaccuracies as proof that the text is simply wrong, and, therefore, without value.

We know that there is a third option here: The text wasn't intended as history. This is why Matthew could take the names and organize them into fourteens, even if it meant massaging the generations.

Furthermore, there's another genealogy in the New Testament, in Luke 3:32–38. And while some of Luke's names match Matthew's, many do not. Luke begins with God, then Adam, then Seth, etc., following the list of names of Genesis up to Terah, then Abraham, then on to David, as Matthew has it. But then the lists diverge. Where Matthew lists David's son Solomon as the next in line, Luke has Nathan.

Solomon is famous, of course, and well known from the Bible to be one of David's sons. Passages like 2 Samuel 5:14 list Nathan as well: "These are the names of those who were born to David in Jerusalem: Shammua, Shobab, Nathan, Solomon, Ibhar, Elishua, Nepheg, Japhia, Elishama, Eliada, and Eliphelet."

But Jesus can't be descended directly from both of David's sons.

Once again, we find two kinds of responses.

The first tries to reconcile the two accounts. And here we find the kind of complexity and detail that usually accompanies reconciliation attempts. We'll walk through a few of them, because their details are interesting, even though we'll see shortly that the ultimate point doesn't depend directly on the mechanics of the various suggestions.

To start, perhaps Matthew meant that it wasn't Joseph but rather Mary who was descended from David through Solomon. This is a highly unlikely reading of Matthew 1:16 ("Jacob the father of Joseph the husband of Mary, of whom Jesus was born"), but at least the text of Matthew mentions Mary.

A variation on this theme is that "husband of" here—literally, "man of" (*aner*, in Greek)—means "father of," and Mary had both a father and a husband named Joseph. While this would explain the missing generation we noted above, it's an otherwise bizarre interpretation of the text. On the other hand, Luke has the simpler "Jesus was the (alleged) son of Joseph." (Technically, the quotation is "he was the (alleged) son of Joseph." We know it's Jesus from the context. In general, we'll emend quotations in this way to help focus on the issues at hand.) Luke doesn't mention Mary, so there is a tiny kernel to justify a division of labor in the lists. One traces Mary, the other Joseph. And Mary and Joseph are very distant cousins (about twenty-fifth cousins, in fact).

Yet another reconciliation achieves the same result with opposite reasoning, suggesting that Luke gives us Mary's ancestry, based on a different odd interpretation of the Greek. This time the idea is that the word "alleged" in the text—literally, "as is supposed"—should be understood differently. The full line in Greek reads that Jesus was "the alleged son of Joseph, of Heli." The usual interpretation of this is that Joseph was the son of Heli, and many translations, including the NRSV we rely so heavily upon here, render the line as "the (alleged) son of Joseph, son of Heli," specifically adding the noun "son." But maybe the parentheses, which don't appear in the Greek because Greek didn't have that kind of punctuation, should be placed differently. If so, Jesus was "the (alleged son of Joseph) son of Heli." Heli, then, could be a Greek form of Eli, which might be a nickname for one of the other people on the list, Elicim. In this way, Mary is introduced to the list by default once Joseph is eliminated.

A third reconciliation, proposed by no less than the influential theologian Saint Augustine, suggests that Joseph might have been adopted by Heli, so he would have two legitimate lineages. But then Augustine rejected his own analysis in favor of what he thought was a better one by Sextus Julius Africanus (a third-century-A.D. chronicler). Julius Africanus starts two generations before Joseph, with Matthan (from Matthew) and Matthat (from Luke). He says that a woman named Estha first married Matthan, then, when her first husband died, Matthat. Matthan's son Jacob and Matthat's son Heli were thus stepbrothers.

Then Heli died before having children, so—in accord with the tradition known as Levirate marriage, which we discuss more in chapter 32—Jacob married Heli's widow. The child of that marriage, Joseph, was biologically Jacob's but legally (according to Deuteronomy 25:6) Heli's. This is why Matthew says that Jacob "fathered" Joseph and Luke says that Joseph was "of Heli." (The situation is actually even more complicated, because Julius Africanus's text didn't have the names "Matthat" and "Levi" that come between Heli and Melchi in our copy of Luke, so his analysis was actually about Melchi, who he thought was of the same generation as our Matthan, even though Melchi is two generations older in our list. But the reasoning is the same, even if the exact names are not.)

So the first kind of response to the two different lists is to find a way of reconciling them, even at the cost of introducing otherwise unknown linguistic reasoning, in conjunction with unlikely and otherwise unattested coincidence.

Before turning to the second kind of response, it's interesting to observe how much energy in the form of mental gymnastics went into the first kind. Even the most ardent believers have to grapple with Saint Augustine's suggestion of an otherwise undocumented adoption, a scenario he abandoned in favor of an otherwise undocumented Levirate marriage. And there are other problems with the lists—like the appearance of the rare names "Zorobabel" and "Salathiel" on both lists as descendants of completely different people. Our goal is not to belittle this sort of endeavor, of course, but to note that it belongs to traditional interpretation of the text, not to the text itself. The energy some people invested in this kind of reasoning is one indication of how important it was to them.

The second kind of response rejects all of these—and other— attempts at reconciliation, and then similarly rejects both lists as meaningless because they do not agree. Another form of this second kind of response points out the nonhistorical nature of the lineages of Jesus and contrasts them with the historically accurate records of the kings of Israel. They don't belong in the same category, the naysayers claim. The next step is to deny any possibility of a person named Jesus having lived because the genealogy in the book that describes him is flawed.

But again, we know there is a third option: Neither list was supposed to be history, even if they include some historical figures.

As it happens, there's an even bigger potential problem with the genealogies. If Jesus was born to a virgin Mary, it doesn't matter who Joseph was, because even though Joseph was Mary's husband, he wasn't Jesus's father. Jesus's lineage doesn't depend on the man Mary happened to marry unless they were both his parents. Yet Jesus has to be the descendant of David.

Tradition offers two responses. (In this regard, we note that there is no legal precedent for how to trace ancestry in cases of virgin births.) This first is that Joseph adopted Jesus, so Jesus's lineage can legitimately be traced through him. The second, which many Church fathers suggest, is that Mary herself was descended from David. For instance, Saint Justin specifically writes in chapter 100 of his second-century *Dialogue with Trypho* that "the Virgin [Mary] . . . was of the family of David and Jacob, and Isaac, and Abraham." Other texts from around the same time period seem to support the same stance, though frequently the language runs along the lines of "Jesus, born to Mary, of the line of David," so we have trouble knowing for sure whether the authors meant to assert that Jesus was of the line of David or whether Mary was.

Whatever the case, the accounts of Jesus's lineage in Matthew and Luke highlight the same pattern we saw in the books of Genesis and Samuel: The literal interpretation of the text is contradictory. In response, tradition forced the texts into accord, while (usually modern) deniers reject the texts on account of the discord. By contrast, our more objective look here reinforces a vital aspect of the original texts: They were not intended to be read like scientific histories.

With this understanding of the original text, we are better able to read its message. The first part of Matthew's answer to "Who is Jesus?" is that Jesus continues the tradition of Abraham and of David. Luke agrees, underscoring an even older connection.

The answers, as is often the case, raise new questions: How is Jesus like David? (This has a pretty obvious answer, because the

Messiah is supposed to come from the line of David.) How is Jesus like Abraham? How is Jesus like Adam?

We should remember that it is the text itself that forces an honest reader to move beyond a narrow, literal interpretation of the words. Confined to a simplistic analysis, Matthew and Luke would not match, just as Genesis—with its two creation stories—would be incoherent, and Goliath would have had the misfortune of being killed at least twice, perhaps three times, by two different people in two different places.

This is one common pattern in the Bible: diverse accounts that unite to point in a single direction. We'll see another pattern next as we turn to another way the text of the Bible interacts with history.

7

JESUS'S DEATH

***Did the Jews kill Jesus?* No.**

Though the Bible isn't primarily a history lesson, certain parts of it are clearly historical. And as we saw in chapter 4, the accounts from King David onward align pretty closely with other historical evidence.

An Israelite monarchy was established in Jerusalem around the year 1,000 B.C. Various kings ruled it with various fascinating bits of palace intrigue. There were prophets who challenged those kings. A third ruling class, the priests, oversaw sacrifice, primarily as practiced at the great temple in Jerusalem. Around 587 B.C. that temple was ransacked and the Jews were exiled. The Jews returned and lived in Jerusalem until the year A.D. 70, by which time Jesus had already been born and died.

Largely because people don't focus on the historical parts of the Bible when they evaluate its accuracy, they tend to reject all of it as a reliable source of history. For instance, noting the absurdity of Adam's 930-year lifespan, they reject Adam as a historical figure—

which is what historians are supposed to do—but they also reject the Bible's account of David and Jesus. And this is a mistake.

Historians usually accept biblical accounts only when there is other material to support them—the writings of another historian, for instance, or archaeological evidence. This approach both minimizes the accounts in the Bible and unduly values some of those other reports. For example, we'll see in chapter 18 that a man named Ctesias (in the fifth century B.C.), Aristotle (in the fourth century), and Pliny the Elder (in the first century A.D.) all thought unicorns were real. To the best of our modern knowledge, they were wrong.

It's not just that ancient authors didn't have the resources that modern ones do. The whole notion of science—"just the facts," as it were—hadn't been born yet. So even ancient authors who wrote pure history also embellished their accounts. This is why Mark Twain mocked the father of history, the fifth-century-B.C. Herodotus: "Very few things happen at the right time," Twain wrote, "and the rest do not happen at all: the conscientious historian will correct these defects." Similarly, Thucydides (also from the fifth century) quotes people directly, even though he writes that he cannot "remember exactly" what they said. In other words, he made it up.

And for that matter, no one writes without a bias, both because of their own agenda and because of the circumstances of their writing. The historian Martin Cohen teaches that the most important question to ask about any historical document is "Who paid for it?" Obviously, a close second is "Who wrote it?"

Rather than arbitrarily reject the Bible as an inaccurate source and, equally arbitrarily, assume that other authors were infallible, here we'll take a more comprehensive and balanced look at the information available to us.

Along with the Bible, the most important source of information about life in Jerusalem during Jesus's time is the work of a historian named Josephus, a Jew born in Jerusalem who ultimately ingratiated himself with the Roman power structure. His skills as a historian are generally undisputed. He wasn't perfect, of course. Like his predecessors, Josephus invented some narrative (probably on purpose, in keeping with the style of the time) and even some facts (presumably by accident). And like most works from two thousand years ago, his work is available now only in translations and flawed copies of copies. But enough of what he wrote has been confirmed independently that we have reasonable confidence in most of his accounts. And he sheds invaluable light on the days of Jesus.

For example, the New Testament refers to Herod. According to Matthew 2:1, it was "in the time of King Herod" that Jesus was born. Herod (Matthew 2:13) wants to destroy Jesus, so Jesus, Joseph, and Mary flee to Egypt (Matthew 2:19) until Herod dies. Later, Herod (in Matthew 14:1) orders the death of John the Baptist. The careful reader of the Bible will wonder how the dead Herod managed to give such an order. Josephus tells us.

There were in fact four generations of Herods. The most powerful one was King Herod, who ruled Jerusalem (viciously) when Jesus was born. It was his son who had John the Baptist killed. The New Testament calls the son "Herod"—along the lines of "Herod, Jr."—while historians now generally call him Antipas. The third generation—also called Herod in the Bible—was King Herod Agrippa I; historians usually call him Agrippa I. The fourth generation was King Herod Agrippa II: "Herod" in the Bible and "Agrippa II" to historians. The primary source of this detailed information is Josephus.

So we see that, to a naive eye, the Bible is patently wrong. How could Herod die and then, after his own death, order the death of someone else? But the Bible is actually more accurate than it seems. It just used a slightly different naming convention.

In other cases, Josephus fills in background that the New Testament authors assumed its readers would know. For instance, the "time of King Herod" into which Jesus was born was a time of extreme and cruel oppression of the Jews in Jerusalem at the hands of the Romans. In this context—which the ancient reader would have known but which we as modern readers may not—the birth of a savior at the "time of King Herod" represents God's presence when it was most needed.

Another example comes from Acts 25, where Paul appears before "Agrippa and Bernice" to explain his actions. He tells the Roman leader, "I count myself lucky that you are the one I'm appearing before, King Agrippa, as I defend myself today against the accusations of the Jews, because you are especially familiar with all of the customs and controversies of the Jews." What the New Testament doesn't say—but Josephus does—is that Bernice is Agrippa's sister, with whom the magistrate is having an incestuous affair. Paul is mocking Rome's representative, sarcastically praising him for knowledge of religious law, yet belittling him for his heathenly behavior. This is another nuance we understand today only thanks to Josephus.

Keeping in mind this kind of potential complexity, we ask "Who killed Jesus?" The most widespread and widely believed answer is the simplistic "the Jews." According to Matthew 27:25, a group of Jews even takes responsibility for Jesus's death: "Let his blood be upon us and upon our children."

From that record of acceptance of responsibility by a small group of people as related in one of the four Gospels has grown a tradition of "Jewish deicide." The Jews, some say, are God killers—a notion so prevalent that when Pope Paul VI rejected it in 1965 as part of the famous Second Vatican Council document *Nostra aetate,* he assumed that his audience blamed the Jews for Jesus's death.

The charge of Jewish deicide has been coupled with a great deal of animosity and more than a little bloodshed, so it's difficult to talk about the issue in isolation. This isn't just a theoretical matter of theology and history but a practical point upon which people's lives have depended.

Still, our task here is to focus on the textual and historical aspects of the equation. Primarily, who does the Bible say killed Jesus? And then, does history support the Bible's position?

Before getting started, we note an almost paradoxical aspect of reading ancient texts. Most of them have been copied and recopied, and each successive iteration offers a new opportunity for changes, either by accident at the hands of a careless scribe, or on purpose at the direction of someone with an agenda. Unfortunately, the more pivotal the events described in a text, the more likely it is that someone with an agenda has tried to make changes to it. As a result, we often have the least faith in texts that describe the events we are most interested in.

For example, Josephus has little to say about Jesus, but at one point in the Jewish historian's work named *Jewish Antiquities,* he calls Jesus "a wise man, if it's proper to call him a man . . . He was the Christ." Josephus appears to describe Jesus's divinity. But Josephus almost certainly didn't write those words. All evidence suggests that they were added later. Josephus probably said something, but the very centrality of his opinion has erased it from our historical record as scribes changed the historian's words. We don't know what Josephus originally wrote here.

More generally, we have to be especially vigilant about the authenticity as well as the inherent bias of texts that weigh in on important controversial issues. With this in mind, we turn to the overall sociopolitical situation in Jesus's Jerusalem during roughly the first three decades of the first century A.D.

Jerusalem was the Jewish capital, as it had been for nearly a thousand continuous years. It was also occupied by vicious Roman forces who were almost universally despised by the denizens of the holy city.

King Herod (the first one), who ruled until about the year 4 B.C., was so unpopular that he needed a Roman legion to protect him from the locals. But though cruel, Herod was at least capable. Upon his death, Jerusalem—already overtaxed and oppressed—fell into near chaos.

The Romans tried to exert control by force, balancing their goal of turning Jerusalem into a Roman city like any other against their fear of rebellion. Some Jews (like, eventually, Josephus) sided with the Romans. Others fought against them with words or even with weapons. The Jews were divided religiously, as well. Some thought Jesus was the Messiah; others rejected any possibility of that being true.

With so much confusion, it is hardly surprising that, two thousand years later, we are unable to reconstruct events perfectly. But we do know the key players.

First, we have the *prefect* of Jerusalem, Pontius Pilate. A representative of Rome, he first appears in the Bible in Matthew 27:2, where a group of Jewish leaders hands Jesus over to "Pilate the governor." We also have archaeological evidence of his existence in the form of an inscription on a stone unearthed in 1961. And we know about him from Josephus, as well as from another Jewish historian, named Philo.

According to Josephus, Pilate tried to erect images of the Roman emperor Tiberius in Jerusalem, an act that, the Jews there thought, violated their second commandment. And as Pilate had done this under the cover of darkness, it was seen as a deliberate snub. But in response to overwhelming Jewish objection, Pilate took the images down. In a second episode, Pilate tried to build an aqueduct that the Jews didn't want. This time, Pilate planted plainclothes soldiers among Jewish protesters, and instructed his minions to beat the Jews, eventually forcing the locals into submission. Philo agrees that Pilate was supremely cruel, accepting bribes and carrying out arbitrary executions. None of this is particularly noteworthy in and of itself. The same qualities were attributed to most of the Roman rulers of Jerusalem.

The reason we care is that it was Pilate who oversaw the crucifixion of Jesus. According to the New Testament, the Roman was trying to save Jesus, and it was the Jews who wanted him dead.

Matthew 26 opens with Jesus predicting his own death as the Jewish holiday of Passover was approaching. (As a Jew, he would have celebrated that holiday.) Then—in one of the most familiar plots in the Western canon—Judas Iscariot, a member of Jesus's trusted inner circle, agrees to betray his Lord to the Jewish priests. Next Jesus takes part in the equally famous Last Supper. Then he takes a walk to pray. Judas interrupts those prayers when he shows up with a crowd to arrest Jesus. Jesus appears before the high priest and a Jewish body called the Sanhedrin, the official ruling body of the Jews over which the high priests presided.

This is how Jesus's fate came to depend on a group of ruling Jews.

Then, in Matthew 27, these same Jewish elders hand him over to Pontius Pilate, as we saw above. Pilate, it turns out, "was accustomed to release a prisoner to the crowd" on this festival of Passover (Matthew 27:15), and, in an apparent attempt to save Jesus, Pilate offers the crowd two choices: a criminal named Barabbas or Jesus. The crowd chooses Barabbas to be freed and demands the crucifixion of Jesus. In response, Pilate hands Jesus over to his soldiers, who kill him.

This basic account appears in the Gospels of Mark, Matthew, Luke, and John, though the details differ.

Taking this at face value, we find a group of Jews, led by the high priest, who convince the Roman Pontius Pilate, against his will, to condemn Jesus. Then Pilate tells his soldiers to kill Jesus, and they— again, from the New Testament accounts—seem all too happy to follow their orders. They gleefully mock and beat Jesus.

But there are lots of reasons not to take the account at face value.

For one thing, all four Gospels agree that it was Pilate who represented Rome, but they do not agree on who the high priest was. Mark doesn't mention any name. Matthew thinks it was Caiaphas. Like Mark, Luke doesn't mention the name of the high priest during the account of the trial. But at the outset of his Gospel, Luke offers the confusing information that "the" high priest was both Annas and Caiaphas; Luke doesn't seem to know which one it was. And John seems confused, too, sometimes (John 18:15, 18:19) using the title "High Priest" for Annas, the man before whom Jesus appeared, but also (in John 18:24) naming Caiaphas as the high priest.

Is it really likely that the name of the man who allegedly ordered Jesus killed would be lost to history? Wouldn't that man's name appear prominently in the account, the same way Pilate's name does?

Another historical problem with the account in the New Testament has to do with the custom of releasing a prisoner at Passover. In the New Testament, that practice forms the backdrop that highlights Pilate's reluctance to kill Jesus. But there was no such custom. The rituals of Passover are well documented, because Passover was even more central in antiquity than it is now. And the Jewish insistence on justice is equally clear. So the alleged practice of releasing a prisoner seems to have been invented for the purposes of this story, and seems to fly in the face of established Jewish doctrine. Even the name Barabbas suggests an allegory. The name literally means "son of a father," as if to say, "There was this guy named Ordinary Guy."

Historically, then, we find evidence of a more complex interplay between Pontius Pilate, representing Rome, and the high priest, representing the Sanhedrin and the Jews more generally. Both men contributed to Jesus's death. But divvying up exact responsibility is a difficult task. Would the Roman Pilate have taken orders from the Jewish Sanhedrin? Could he have refused to do what they wanted? Did he ask the Sanhedrin to condemn Jesus? As with most backroom deals between powerful politicians, we will probably never know the details.

Details about the group called the Sanhedrin are also lacking. We don't know the degree to which that aristocratic body represented the Jewish people of Jerusalem. We do know that the Judaism of the day was fissured into competing camps. One faction would ultimately become the Christians. Two others, the Sadducees and the Pharisees, disagreed about almost everything, as we learn from Josephus. (The New Testament often paints the Sadducees and Pharisees with the same brush, presumably because their internal differences about Judaism paled in comparison with their rejection of Jesus.) And Josephus mentions a third group, the Essenes, who may or may not have been the same as the people who moved to Qumran and preserved the Dead Sea Scrolls. So there were at least four competing schools of Jewish thought and practice at the time. Certainly the Sanhedrin—itself a body about which little is known for sure—couldn't have represented all of the Jews, because they disagreed among themselves.

So the simplest and most plausible historical answer to "Who killed Jesus?" is "the aristocracy"—both Jewish and Roman.

Then, keeping in mind the inherent biases in any writing, we are hardly surprised to find that the New Testament—even though the authors couldn't pin down the high priest responsible—blames the high priest, and with him, the Jews. They downplay Rome's role. And Matthew (in a passage of dubious authenticity) records a group of Jews as accepting blame for Jesus's death.

The Jewish aristocrat Josephus, by contrast, emphasizes Pontius Pilate's other acts of evil, and (in a passage of dubious authenticity) reports that it was "Pilate, at the suggestion of the principal men amongst us," who crucified Jesus. By "us" Josephus probably means "the Jews," but even so, Josephus downplays the role of the Jews: They may have suggested killing Jesus, but it was Pilate who actually killed him.

The complete New Testament answer, though, is nuanced. While the accounts of Jesus's trial and crucifixion blame the Jews, certainly Pontius Pilate bears some responsibility. He was the one who handed Jesus over to the (Roman) soldiers and ordered his death. On this all of the Gospels agree. The Roman soldiers are responsible, too, at least if we read the New Testament in the light of our modern ethic: We generally hold soldiers culpable for misdeeds even if they were following orders.

And for that matter, even Jesus himself could have stopped his own execution according to Matthew 26:53–54, where he chastises a follower for trying to prevent his arrest: I could appeal to my Father, who will save me, Jesus says. But to do so would violate scripture, which, Matthew reports, "says it must happen this way."

Nor does the New Testament blame all of the Jews. Quite to the contrary, it acknowledges the Jewish masses who mourned for Jesus. Luke 23:27 refers to "a great number of people" who followed behind Jesus as he was led to his death. In the next verse, Jesus addresses the women in the group as "daughters of Zion."

The simplest and most plausible biblical answer to "Who killed Jesus?" is "Some Jews and some Romans."

As in the case of Jesus's lineage in the last chapter, we see a pattern here of different accounts pointing in the same direction, though it can take some work to untangle the disparate clues. Here, all of our evidence agrees that elite Romans and elite Jews conspired to kill Jesus.

As we'll see next, sometimes the text is more straightforward. But that doesn't mean that it has always been understood accurately.

8

THE TEN COMMANDMENTS

***Do the Ten Commandments forbid coveting?* No.**

Perhaps the clearest case of a direct message from the Bible is the Ten Commandments. Before we turn to what they say, we look at what they are, because they were not originally all commandments, and traditions differ about how to number them.

The full list of ten appears twice, once in Exodus and once in Deuteronomy. They start in Exodus 20:1 with an introduction: "Then God spoke all these words," followed by the famous statement "I am the Lord your God, who brought you out of the land of Egypt, out of the house of slavery; you shall have no other gods before me" (Exodus 20:2–3).

Traditions differ about how to divvy up these opening verses. Most Protestants group verse 20:2 ("I am the Lord your God . . .") with the introduction, so for them the first actual commandment doesn't start until 20:3: "You shall have no other gods . . ." Catholics (and most Lutherans) group 20:2 not with the introduction but with 20:3, to form one long first commandment. For Jews, 20:1 is the introduction, but 20:2 and 20:3 are different commandments. So the Jewish first commandment isn't a commandment at all according to Protestants, and is only part of the Catholic first commandment.

Similarly, the numbering of the other commandments varies from tradition to tradition. This is why the commandment about honoring parents is the fifth commandment for Jews and Protestants, but the fourth for Catholics (and Lutherans).

The text of Exodus 20 doesn't even mention the number ten. We find that figure in Exodus 34:28 ("Moses wrote on the tablets the words of the covenant, the ten things"), in Deuteronomy 4:13, and in Deuteronomy 10:4.

And the Bible doesn't call them "commandments" at all (a detail we revisit in the next chapter), using instead the more general Hebrew word *davar* (plural, *d'varim*), which refers variously to words, statements, and things. This is why the NRSV translation of 34:28 refers to the "ten commandments" on the tablets, with only a footnote ("Heb. *words*") to remind the reader that it was later tradition that classified these things as commandments.

Even with all of this potential confusion, though, most of these ten things are clear. For instance, "Do not steal" (Exodus 20:15) is a prohibition against stealing, whether it's called a "commandment" or a "thing," and whether it's the seventh or eighth in the list.

The simple statement "Do not steal" in Exodus complements more complicated nuances about theft. Exodus 21:37 (also numbered 22:1) recognizes the principle of punitive damages and offers concrete examples. Someone who steals an ox owes the owner of the ox five oxen in return, while someone who steals a sheep owes the owner four sheep. Without this punitive aspect of the law, there would be little practical disincentive to steal. Thieves would have nothing to lose and everything to gain by trying to steal if the worst possible punishment were returning the stolen property. (Numbers 5:6–7 offers a different formula, prescribing punitive damages of only 20 percent of the value of whatever was taken, but the general principle is the same.)

These and other discussions of what to do about theft pose an obvious question: What's the point of the commandment in Exodus 20:15 in the context of more detailed legal discussions elsewhere? One possibility is that 20:15 is simply a summary, but given the centrality of the Ten Commandments, that seems unlikely.

A more convincing answer comes precisely from the lack of consequences in Exodus 20:15. The simple "Do not steal" suggests an absolute judgment about theft, regardless of any consequences.

We might compare modern laws about theft, which dictate various combinations of punitive damages and jail time. For instance, suppose the punishment for stealing a car is up to four years in jail. What if a man doesn't mind spending time in jail? Does that mean it's okay for him to steal the car? What if he is nearly certain that he won't get caught, so the risk-reward equation in his mind is overwhelmingly favorable? Or what if he's ill and knows he won't live long enough to see trial, let alone jail. Then is theft okay?

Modern laws don't take a stance on these vexing questions. Instead, they limit themselves to the kind of act-and-consequence discussion that we find in Exodus 21 and Numbers 5. "If you do this, here's what happens."

The Ten Commandments seem to be a list of things that are wrong no matter what. Regardless of any consequences, in spite of the odds of getting caught, and no matter the reward-to-risk ratio, Exodus 20:15 says that stealing is wrong. It's not primarily a legal statement, but a moral one.

As it happens, most modern readers agree with the moral assessment of Exodus 20:15, and are even surprised that modern laws don't address the morality of theft. Theft is different from, say, running a red light at night if there are no cars around. They may both be illegal, but only one of them is wrong. That notion of right and wrong is encoded in the Ten Commandments.

All of this brings us back to the clear nature of the messages in the Ten Commandments, and the way they contrast with, for instance, the genealogies in Matthew and Luke. The Ten Commandments are mostly a list of legal matters that, in addition to their legal status, also have moral implications. A thief must pay restitution and punitive damages. In addition, theft is wrong. (We'll dive into more detail about the commandment regarding killing in chapter 38.)

Even these clear and direct statements are not beyond the reach of revisionism. The clearest case is the commandment variously numbered 9, or 9 and 10: "Do not covet." The Hebrew verb there (*chamad*) does not actually mean "covet" but rather means "take." However, a related verb, *nechmad*—which shares the Hebrew root Ch.M.D—means "desirable." Some people therefore thought that *chamad,* too, should have something direct to do with desire. But that's not how language works. (For instance, "host" and "hostile" share a root in English, but a host doesn't have to be hostile.) And other instances of the verb *chamad* clearly point in the direction of "take."

We don't know for sure how "taking" is different from "stealing," but one reasonable guess is that "stealing" is taking with no intent to return the stolen property, while someone who "takes" might plan on giving it back, perhaps before the owner notices that it is gone. In English, people sometimes dub this kind of taking "borrowing," using their fingers to put the word in quotes. Often, these people find more justification in this kind of illicit "borrowing" than they do in outright theft. And our modern laws often recognize a difference between outright theft and taking with intent to return, with, for example, lesser punishments for "joyriding" (taking a car with the intent of returning it) than for "grand theft auto" (taking a car with the intent of keeping it).

Whatever the nuance of "taking," though, it was clearly an overt action. But tradition quickly changed the meaning of the last (or last two) commandments, turning the focus away from action and stressing an emotional state instead.

In the context of moral right and wrong, this is no small difference. The Ten Commandments as tradition has them include mostly actions but also indicate that merely desiring something can be morally wrong. By contrast, the original text takes no stance on internal states of being, only on overt actions. Even a clear and direct statement was thus mangled over the course of time.

Though the Ten Commandments are the most obvious case of direct statements in the Bible, they are far from the only place the Bible offers direct guidance, and, equally, far from the only place these direct statements are misunderstood today.

9

COMMANDMENTS

Does the Bible contain Ten Commandments? No.

Before we turn to other instances of direct statements in the Bible, let's look a little more closely at the terminology surrounding the famous Ten Commandments. Exodus 20, as we just saw, doesn't contain the number "ten" or the word "commandment."

What we know directly from Exodus 20 is just that there are some unnumbered "things." The Hebrew word there, as we saw in the last chapter, is *davar,* and it's a general term that refers both to words and things. Just for example, in Exodus 4:15 God puts words in Moses's mouth, and the Hebrew term for those words is *davar.* Similarly, the Hebrew phrase for "after these things," that is to say, "what happened next," is "after these *davar*s." (In English, too, we use the word "thing" ambiguously for physical objects and for spoken words. Someone can see three things or say three things. So we are not surprised by the generality of the term in Hebrew.)

The influential ancient Greek translation called the Septuagint renders the Hebrew word in Exodus 20 as *logos,* a word with a similarly wide range of meaning. (This is the source of the technical English name for the Ten Commandments, the Decalogue: "deca" is the English spelling of the Greek *deka*, "ten," and "logue" comes from *logos*.) In Latin the word there is *sermo*, which also indicates speech of some sort. (This is where we get our English word "sermon," but unlike sermons, which are generally religious in nature, the Latin word was more general.)

We also know that these ancient translations updated the text as they saw necessary. The Hebrew verb for "take" that we saw in the last chapter becomes "desire" in the Septuagint.

Though we don't see it here, Hebrew does have a word for "commandment" (*mitzvah*) that appears throughout the Old Testament. It's such a common word, in fact, that we find it in an elaboration of one of the first commandments. In Exodus 20:6, in the context of not making idols or bowing down to them, God promises good things to "those who love me and keep my commandments." So we see that the Hebrew text could have called these ten things commandments, and so could other ancient translations. But they did not.

However, Mark 10:19, in the New Testament, refers to at least five of the things from Exodus as "commandments," or, in Greek, *entoligi*. The Latin translation gives us *praeceptum*. Related to our word "precepts," the word meant "teaching." Mark actually lists six commandments: "Do not murder," "Do not commit adultery," "Do not steal," "Do not bear false witness," "Do not defraud," and "Honor your father and mother."

Of these, five are clearly from the Ten Commandments as we know them. "Do not defraud" does not seem to belong. A similar list in Luke 18:20 changes the order slightly and omits "Do not defraud."

These texts suggest that there may have been a list of "Five Commandments" that now forms the second half of our list of "Ten Commandments," spanning "Honor your mother and father" to "Do not bear false witness," currently either the fifth through ninth or the fourth through eighth commandments, depending on who does the counting.

So far, at most, we have an observation that some of the Ten Commandments, along with lots of other things in the Bible, are commandments.

We get the number ten from three places that describe the two tablets that contain the covenant that Moses received from God. (In spite of popular depictions, we don't know if they were the now-familiar single stone comprising two columns, each with a rounded top—also now envisioned as two connected stones with rounded tops. It's just as likely that the whole thing was written twice, on two different tablets. Pacts in antiquity were commonly written in duplicate, there being no carbon paper or photocopying technology yet.) Exodus 34:28 explains that Moses spent forty days and forty nights with God, neither eating nor drinking. That was when he "wrote on the tablets the words of the covenant, the ten *davar*s." Deuteronomy 4:13 agrees, clarifying that there were "two stone tablets." Moses smashed his first set of tablets after seeing the idol that the people of Israel had created in the form of the infamous Golden Calf. Recounting Moses's second transcription of the pact, Deuteronomy 10:4 mentions the tablets and the "ten" things on them.

But even though those three verses give us the number "ten," they do not use the word "commandment" in Hebrew, a fact concealed by the many English translations that nonetheless render the Hebrew there as "Ten Commandments." As with Exodus 20, the Greek and Latin, like the original Hebrew, mention only "ten things" or "ten words."

So, surprisingly, we do not see any reference in the Bible to "Ten Commandments." There was an important collection of ten things, and at least some of them were commandments, but the Ten Commandments that are so famous now are actually a result of later interpretation.

10

GOD SO LOVED THE WORLD

Does the Bible say that "God so loved the world"? No.

We'll return to the Ten Commandments later, when we talk about killing in chapter 38, but because the issue of killing is so complicated in the Bible, we turn to other, clearer direct statements first, continuing in the direction we started in chapter 8. Not surprisingly, the Bible has direct statements not just about our actions ("Do not steal") but also about theology.

Perhaps the most famous such theological statement comes from John 3:16, very widely quoted as "God so loved the world that he gave his only begotten son." But that turns out to be a mistranslation.

The problem in this case is the changing nature of English. The familiar phrase "God so loved" comes from the four-hundred-year-old King James Version, an edition so central that it continues to define many aspects of Bible translation to this day. In that influential work, the English word "so" was meant to translate the Greek word *houtos*.

The word *houtos* appears throughout the Bible, and its meaning is pretty clearly "in this way." For instance, the word appears in Jesus's introduction of what we now call the Lord's Prayer in Matthew 6:9–13: "Our Father in heaven, hallowed be your name." Before those words, which comprise the start of the Lord's Prayer, Jesus says, "Pray then in this way" or "This is how you should pray." In Greek, that's *"houtos."*

In other words, in both John 3:16 and in Matthew 6:9, we find the same Greek word *houtos,* meaning "in this way."

Four hundred years ago, the word "so" before a verb meant "like this" or "in this way," a usage that still persists in a few isolated instances. For example, the English expression "so help me God" asks God to help "in this way," just as "I do so declare" means I declare "in this way." The word "so" used to be a perfect way to translate *houtos.*

However, usually the word "so" in today's English means "very" or "so much." This is why "I'm so happy" means "I'm very happy," not "This is how I'm happy." The modern-English "so" does not mean the same thing as the four-hundred-year-old "so" or the Greek *houtos.* So the once-correct translation in the King James Version is no longer accurate. It used to mean "this is how God loved the world" (which is what the Greek means) and now the phrasing wrongly suggests that John 3:16 is about how much God loved the world.

In short, the common phrasing "God so loved the world" misses the point of John 3:16, which is: "This is how God loved the world. . . ." In other words, John 3:16, in its original form, answers the question "How did God love the world?" The four-hundred-year-old common translation now gives the false impression that the verse answers the question "How much did God love the world?"

Still, in spite of the now-misleading common translation, the statement is direct and clear. One way God loved the world was by giving his son. Once we get past the wrong translation, we don't need to guess what this verse was supposed to be about.

This doesn't mean that there are no unanswered questions regarding John 3:16. We don't want to confuse clarity with simplicity. John 3:16 is clear even if it is not simple. One might wonder what it means for God to have given his son, what it means for God to love, who is part of "the world," or, for that matter, what we mean by "God." But those are questions that arise from the direct statement about how God loved the world, a statement whose original nature has been concealed by changing patterns in English.

This isn't the only place that outdated translations have survived to mislead modern readers. In Song of Solomon, the King James Version talks about a "turtle" in verse 2:12. The same animal appears in Jeremiah 8:7. But in both places it's a dove, sometimes called a "turtledove" today. Psalm 59:10 advises that "the God of my mercy shall prevent me," because "prevent" four hundred years ago meant "walk in front of." And when Matthew in verse 3:15 says that Jesus "suffered," he means that Jesus consented, just as when Isaiah asks in verse 43:13 "who shall let it?" the prophet means "who shall prevent it?"

Still, once we retranslate these verses into modern English, they become straightforward, and it's clear what they are about.

As we'll see in a few chapters, we don't always have this kind of clarity. Before we get there, though, let's look at some other direct theological statements, because outdated translations aren't the only way statements in the Bible get distorted.

11

THE TRUTH WILL SET YOU FREE

Does the Bible say that the truth will set you free? No.

"You will know the truth, and the truth will set you free" (John 8:32) is among the best-known lines from the Bible, and is even the unofficial motto of the United States Central Intelligence Agency. And unlike the concepts in "this is how God loved the world" from the last chapter or in other statements of deep theology, the concepts here are pretty commonplace. Most people are used to talking about truth and most people are used to talking about freedom. The impact of John 8:32 seems to come from the way these two familiar concepts are combined. But the common translation in fact misses the major impact of the original Greek line, which wasn't meant merely as a statement of fact.

The context of the line is Jesus addressing Jews who believe in him: "Then Jesus said to the Jews who had believed in him, 'If you continue in my word, you are truly my disciples; and you will know the truth, and the truth will make you free.'" Except for the odd English expression "continue in my word" (presumably, "follow what

I preach"), this passage seems pretty straightforward. But there's much more going on than the English suggests.

To see the depth of the line we take a quick detour through the surprising power of wordplays.

In English, we have an expression "A stitch in time saves nine." The imagery is in fact antiquated, and based on the notion of fixing fraying clothes by sewing them up. The idea is that if a sock, say, develops a hole, it's better to fix it right away than to wait, because the hole will get bigger with wear, and demand more work later. That's why one stitch before it's too late ("in time") saves more stitches later.

But why nine? Why not ten, or five, or two, or one hundred? The answer is that "nine" (almost) rhymes with "time," and people naturally value things that rhyme. The phrase "A stitch in time saves nine" sounds cool, and people therefore take it more seriously.

Another example comes from the expression "Birds of a feather flock together," which has nothing to do with birds, feathers, or flocks. It means more generally that similar people tend to associate with each other. "Birds of a feather" is an odd way to refer to "similar birds," and birds are not usually symbols of human behavior. The words in this case were not chosen for their specific meanings, but rather because "feather" rhymes with "together." Then "birds" came into play because they are the animals that have feathers. It would, of course, be a mistake to tie the meaning of the expression too closely to the details of the words. Its power comes from the rhetoric.

Yet another example comes from the English "rhyme or reason." "There's no rhyme or reason to it" doesn't usually have anything to do with rhymes. It's just an emphatic way of saying "There's no reason for it." So why is the word "rhyme" in the phrase? Because both "rhyme" and "reason" start with the same sound. (Shakespeare uses the phrase more than once in his plays. In *As You Like It*, Rosalind asks Orlando, "But are you so much in love as your rhymes speak?"

Orlando answers, "Neither rhyme nor reason can express how much." Orlando cleverly combines the literal and idiomatic meanings of the phrase.)

Because this phrase is based on the way the words sound, we cannot substitute other words that mean nearly the same thing. For instance, "There's no meter or rationale to it" doesn't mean "There's no rhyme or reason," despite the close connection between "meter" and "rhyme" and between "rationale" and "reason." Similarly, the expression "part and parcel" in English means "an integral part of." So, "Raising money is part and parcel of modern politics." "Part" and "portion" are nearly synonymous, as are "parcel" and "division." But that doesn't mean that we can use "portion and division" the same way we use "part and parcel." "Raising money is portion and division . . ." doesn't make any sense in English.

We see the same thing with the English expression "You are what you eat." There's no poetry in the line in English, but it comes from a German expression: "One is what one eats." The German for "one" is *man* and the German for "what" is *was* (pronounced "vass"), which is similarly not poetic. But the German words for "is" and "eats" sound the same, though they are spelled differently. The German expression is *Man ist was man isst.* The rationale behind the saying is that the words for "is" and "eats" sound the same. This similarity of sound helped propel the expression into common consciousness. Most people believe that food has more impact on the self than science suggests, all because of two words that sound the same in German.

A final example comes from the O. J. Simpson trial, in which defending attorney Johnnie Cochran tried to convince a jury that his client, Simpson, couldn't have committed the murder that the prosecution charged him with, because the evidence didn't match.

A trial normally has lots of minor details that don't match perfectly, but Cochran repeatedly told the jury, "If it doesn't fit, you must acquit."

(Cochran was also highlighting one particular bit of evidence that presented both a figurative and literal misfit: a glove from the prosecution's case that was too small for Simpson's large hand.) Because "fit" and "acquit" rhyme, the jury latched on to the phrase and—many people believe—acquitted Simpson as a result.

Cochran knew that people don't just pay attention to what words mean. They focus on how they sound. Rhymes (like "fit"/"acquit" or "time"/"nine"), alliteration ("part"/"parcel" or "rhyme"/"reason"), and so on are not merely incidental aspects of language. They are an elemental part of the way humans make sense of the world.

Or to look at things the other way around, it's just a mistake to focus too closely on the number "nine" in the expression "A stitch in time saves nine." Even though the word "nine" is part of the saying, it just means "more stitches." There's no particular importance to what "nine" means, only to how "nine" sounds, just as the importance of "birds" and "feathers" above stems from their sounds, not their meaning.

These examples, and many more like them, demonstrate that it is insufficient to look only at what the words in a text mean. The wordplay is just as important.

We should not be surprised to find this kind of wordplay in the Bible, too. And this brings us back to John 8:32, because the power of the line comes from the way two Greek words are similar.

The Greek for the noun "truth" is *alitheia,* and for the verb "set free," *eleutherow.* Like "part" and "parcel" in English, they sound similar, both consisting of vowels surrounding the consonant sequence L-TH. The power of the line comes not just from the meaning of the two words, but from their sound. So the English "truth . . . set you free" is just as misleading as it would be to change "part and parcel," as we saw above, into "portion and division."

And, again taking a cue from the English examples, it's a mistake to focus too closely on what "truth" and "set free" mean in John, just as it's a mistake to focus only on what "time" and "nine" mean in the English expression.

In other words, the English translation "the truth will set you free" translates only one aspect of the line, and not even the most important aspect. The text's original power lies in the way it combines a message about truth and freedom with a wordplay.

Because we live in the scientific era, it's easy to dismiss the wordplay as mere play and focus only on the meaning, which seems like the crux of the message. But it would be a serious mistake to do so. Even more, to deny the power of the wordplay here is tantamount to denying any purpose to poetry or music. And as further evidence we need only keep in mind that a man was acquitted in part because of a wordplay, and people decide what to eat in part because of a wordplay.

As it happens, we see more evidence of the wordplays in John 8:32, in the previous verse. The English translation "continue in my word . . . truly my disciples" contains no hint of similar-sounding words, but the Greek phrasing cleverly transforms an *m* and a *t* in *meinite* ("continue") into *mathitai* ("disciples"). So we have a weak wordplay followed by a stronger one, and they are connected by the shared root of "true": "truly" in 8:31 and "truth" in 8:32.

Unfortunately, we usually have no way to capture the combination of a message and a wordplay in translation. The translations that most people read completely destroy the wordplay, while efforts to capture the wordplay usually miss the nuances of the meaning: "deliberation leads to liberation," for instance, is nicely repetitive, but "deliberation" doesn't mean the same thing as "truth." But we should be clear. "Deliberation leads to liberation" is certainly as close to the original Greek as "the truth shall set you free," and is perhaps even closer. One translation captures one part of the original message; the other captures another. Neither translation captures them both.

Even without a good translation, we can recognize the dual qualities of the original Greek text. What we have is more than simply a statement, because it's augmented by art, albeit art that we have trouble re-creating in English. As with a song we can't hear, though, or a painting we can't see, we at least know that the message is only part of the original impact.

And we can even identify much of what the artistry in Greek conveys. The sentence is not just about what truth will do. It conveys the impression that truth and freedom are two sides of the same coin, similar in unexplored ways. The verse doesn't just answer "What will truth do?" or "What will free you?" It answers "How are truth and freedom related?"

By posing the unasked question in this way, the text asserts that truth and freedom are alike, and the reader comes to see both concepts differently, newly connected to each other.

The very fact that we need such a long discussion here to explore what might look like a simple line underscores the power of poetry: It conveys in only a few words what would otherwise require paragraphs of prose.

And this is far from the only such case. Next we'll see a parable with important messages conveyed only through the poetry.

12

HEALING A WITHERED HAND

Is the parable of the withered hand primarily about healing? No.

Jesus in Matthew 12:9–14 heals a man with a withered hand. This account, repeated in the Gospels of Mark and Luke, is one of a set of parables that form an ongoing theme in the New Testament (and, as it happens, outside of it).

The plot of this short episode is simple. One Sabbath, Jesus enters a synagogue where there turns out to be a man with a hand in need of healing. The people in the synagogue ask Jesus if the act of healing is permitted on the Sabbath. (Jewish custom at the time prohibited working on the Sabbath, but the definition of "work" was in flux.) Jesus responds by asking whether one would save a sheep that had fallen into a pit on the Sabbath. Assuming the answer to be yes, Jesus explains that people are more valuable than animals, so of course it's okay to heal a person on the Sabbath. And with that, Jesus heals the man's hand. In response, members of a group called the Pharisees plot against Jesus.

Here's the NRSV rendition of Matthew 12:9–14:

[9] He left that place and entered their synagogue; [10] a man was there with a withered hand, and they asked him, "Is it lawful to cure on the sabbath?" so that they might accuse him. [11] He said to them, "Suppose one of you has only one sheep and it falls into a pit on the sabbath; will you not lay hold of it and lift it out? [12] How much more valuable is a human being than a sheep! So it is lawful to do good on the sabbath." [13] Then he said to the man, "Stretch out your hand." He stretched it out, and it was restored, as sound as the other. [14] But the Pharisees went out and conspired against him, how to destroy him.

There are obvious political overtones to the story that explain the last line. The Pharisees were one established religious-political faction (another being the Sadducees). Jesus's actions fanned the fire of conflict. We also know from the Dead Sea Scrolls that some groups ruled it forbidden to raise an animal from a pit on the Sabbath. So we see a common debate from Jesus's day woven into the plot. And of course, the matter of Jesus's healing power is prominent.

So just to judge from the translation, there's a legal message, namely, that practicing medicine is permissible on the Sabbath. There's a moral message: People are more valuable than sheep. And there's a religious message: Jesus can heal.

But the rhetoric in Greek introduces teachings that are hidden in English. To understand them, we look first at the Greek word *anthropos,* which means both "man" and "person."

Greek, like many languages, has different categories of words, commonly but misleadingly called "masculine," "feminine," and "neuter." Much less confusing would be "Class 1," "Class 2," and "Class 3," or some other set of less charged terms. But because the words that describe men tend to be of one sort and the words that describe women tend to be of another, the terms "masculine" and "feminine" have stuck, often with hugely misleading consequences. People—especially speakers of English, which doesn't have this kind of grammatical distinction—wrongly assume that "masculine" language must refer to men. It does not. In terms of the magnitude of the error, this mistake is a lot like thinking that a short word can refer only to a short thing.

It doesn't take much searching to demonstrate that the overlap between masculine/feminine/neuter words and people is only partial. And we don't have to use ancient Greek to do it. We can look at, say, modern German, which has the advantage of still having native speakers around whom we can ask to make sure we've correctly understood how the language works. There are two German words for "person," *Mensch* and *Person*. One is masculine, the other feminine. The word for "girl" (*Mädchen*) is neuter. None of these grammatical facts has anything to do with the genders of people generally or girls specifically in Germany.

In fact, Mark Twain poked fun at this misunderstanding about how German works in his essay "The Awful German Language." For instance, he offered the following translation snippet:

> "*Gretchen*. Wilhelm, where is the turnip?
> "*Wilhelm*. She has gone to the kitchen.
> "*Gretchen*. Where is the accomplished and beautiful English
>   maiden?
> "*Wilhelm*. It has gone to the opera."

Bill Watterson, too, in his successful *Calvin and Hobbes* comic, drew attention to how easy it is for English speakers to misunderstand gender in foreign languages. His elementary-school-aged character Calvin asks his teacher to teach the class whether "desk" and "chair" are masculine or feminine. After all, he argues, students overseas are learning that material, and America has to stay competitive. (The punch line is that Calvin demands sex education.)

All of this is to say that it takes a lot of theory to help Americans ignore the evidence from their own experience with English and properly understand how the single Greek word *anthropos* can mean both "person" and "man."

As it happens, many English dialects use the word "man" both for "male human" and for "human" more generally, but, equally, in many dialects it is considered insulting to use "man" in a general sense. And because the role of women in society is in flux (it was just last century that women were granted the legal right to vote in the United States, for example), it's easy to let social and societal debates about how people do and should live color linguistic investigation.

But we will resist that temptation, and, at the same time, skip any long theoretical excursion into language and gender. We'll just note that the correct translation of *anthropos* is sometimes "man" and sometimes "person." (This important issue will come up again in chapter 28.)

And here is the problem, because the parable of Jesus healing the man with the withered hand depends centrally on various contrasting senses of the word *anthropos*.

Here's the story again, with the words that translate *anthropos* italicized so we can identify them:

[9] He left that place and entered their synagogue; [10] a *man* was there with a withered hand, and they asked him, "Is it lawful to cure on the sabbath?" so that they might accuse him. [11] He said to them, "Suppose *one of you* has only one sheep and it falls into a pit on the sabbath; will you not lay hold of it and lift it out? [12] How much more valuable is a *human being* than a sheep! So it is lawful to do good on the sabbath." [13] Then he said to the *man*, "Stretch out your hand." He stretched it out,

and it was restored, as sound as the other. [14] But the Pharisees went out and conspired against him, how to destroy him.

The repetition of *anthropos* to refer first to the man with the hand
in need of healing ("a man/person with a withered hand") and then to
the people asking about him (literally, "which one of you men/peo-
ple . . . ?") adds an ironic element to the text. The people in the tale
don't realize how similar they are to the man in need of healing, but
the Greek reader does, because the text uses the same word for them
both. From this repetition comes a fourth message of the parable:
People are all the same. All of us are the people in the synagogue, just
as we are all the one in need of healing.

This message of universality is reinforced when the text calls the
man *anthropos,* which here might be explained as "a person who just
happens to be a man but could equally well have been a woman." Greek
has a different word (*aner*) for a man as opposed to a woman. So the
Greek text is about all people, both men and women. But because
people are either men or women, the story has to reference one or
the other.

This choice of a man to represent people is no different linguisti-
cally or stylistically than using a sheep to represent other animals:
surely the message of the story extends beyond sheep to, say, cows,
dogs, cats, etc. But it's more powerful to choose a specific animal to
talk about. (And we saw in chapter 8 how the Old Testament uses
specific animals to demonstrate the general principle of punitive
damages.) Similarly, according to the Greek text, this is a story
about people, with one particular person augmenting the impact of the
words.

So in addition to the three messages that are apparent from the
English (practicing medicine is permissible on the Sabbath, people
are more valuable than sheep, and Jesus can heal), the rhetoric

highlights a forth: The message is universal, and all people are fundamentally the same.

In the last chapter we saw how rhetoric adds nuance and depth to what would otherwise be a simple message about truth and freedom. Here we see the same thing in a longer passage. In chapter 14 we'll see how this innate human desire for linguistic artistry actually created a widespread misimpression about what the Bible says. Before we do, we'll take one more look at wordplay in the Bible, and, this time, how it got confused with God's actual name.

13

GOD'S NAME

Was God's name in Hebrew Yahweh? No.

In chapter 2, we looked briefly at a theory of the Bible that posits multiple authors, one of whom called God *elohim* in Hebrew, another of whom used *yahweh* instead. Which is it? What was God's name originally? Where does "Jehovah" come from? And why do we call God "the Lord" now?

There are two main Hebrew names for God in the Bible. To understand them, and how they've been massively misinterpreted over three thousand years, we take a quick detour through, of all things, the invention of the alphabet.

Writing itself goes back more than five thousand years to Uruk, in what is now southern Iraq, when people starting drawing common objects on clay tablets. Unlike art (which goes back much further), these images are more basic and seem to have been designed to convey information. We have not yet been able to decipher their exact meaning, but we do notice that they are stylized representations of plants, animals, people, and more. The drawings seem to be an early way of writing down words.

The idea of agreeing on a symbol to represent what a word means was a good one, so good that we still use it today. For instance, we use a triangle on top of a square to mean "house," even though there are no houses that look like that. And we use a leaflike shape for both "heart" and "love," even though, again, there are no hearts that look like that; if nothing else, hearts have four chambers, while the symbol has but two. But it doesn't matter. That's the beauty of the system. These stylized symbols are called "icons," and the meaning-based writing systems that use them are called iconic writing.

The Egyptians expanded and modified this kind of iconic writing to develop what we now call hieroglyphics. Their writing—and the communication across time and space that it permitted—was one foundation of their great society. But their system, with its thousands of symbols and intricate way of combining them, was so complex that only professional scribes could master it. This is why a four-thousand-year-old Egyptian text proclaims that "there is no greater calling than to be a scribe." Of course, that was written by a scribe, so we don't know for sure how everyone else back then felt, but the scribe was right. Hieroglyphics paved the way for Egypt's success. But though powerful, that ancient system was imperfect. It required thousands of symbols, and even with that massive inventory, the range of what could be written down was limited.

The next advance in writing came when people discovered that they could write down the sounds of their words instead of the meaning. The Sumerians, about five thousand years ago, were the first to do this, and they chose to focus on the syllables that formed their words. This gave the world the now-famous cuneiform writing, which required only hundreds of symbols, far fewer than the Egyptian system. And it was more flexible. Still, the system also relied on professional scribes, because most people couldn't master all of the symbols.

Next, in the second millennium B.C., a group of people called the Phoenicians created a writing system that required fewer than thirty symbols. Still based on sound and not meaning, their system recorded only the consonants, leaving the reader to infer the vowels. But this task of filling in the vowels meant that Phoenician writing, too, was beyond the reach of the average reader.

Finally we get to the Israelites around the start of the first millennium B.C., when King David was establishing Jerusalem as his capital. The Israelites modified the Phoenician system, doubling up three consonants—*yud, heh,* and *vav,* or the equivalents of *y, h,* and *w*—for use as vowels to help people read. Though the original spelling patterns three thousand years ago didn't record all of the vowels, this was the first time a concise writing system allowed people to record consonants and vowels.

The hints provided by the occasional vocalic *yud, heh,* and *vav* opened the doors of widespread literacy. The Hebrew collection of only two dozen symbols could be used to write anything down, and anyone could master the system. (Much later, toward the end of the first millennium A.D., more systematic vowels would be added to Hebrew. These are "the vowels" of Hebrew. Because ancient Hebrew didn't have them, it's common to say that ancient Hebrew didn't have vowels. But in fact it did have a few, because *yud, heh,* and *vav* could be used as vowels. We'll see more about the newer vowel system immediately below.)

The Israelite system—called the alphabet, because the first two letters were *aleph* and *bet*—became Greek, then Latin, and spread around the world. The alphabets used today in the Americas, Europe, India, and the Middle East all trace their roots to this Israelite experiment in writing three thousand years ago.

Of course, this new technology gave the world not only its most successful system of writing, but also its all-time-best-selling book: the Bible. By contrast, even though most people have heard of the Phoenicians, few have read any of their writings.

The Israelites seem to have appreciated the awesome power of their invention, which made widespread written communication possible, and, specifically, let everyone read scripture. The key to the alphabet—the aspect that made it so much better than the nearly identical Phoenician system—was the double use of three letters.

As we've seen, those letters are *heh* (like our modern *h*), *yud* (like our modern *y*), and *vav* (now pronounced like a *v* but originally like our modern *w*). In English we use the letter *h* as a consonant (as in "hello," for instance) and also to indicate the vowel sound /a/, as in "say aahh." The Israelites are the ones who first made that connection. Their *heh* was used for the consonant sound /h/, in keeping with the Phoenician system, and also for the vowel sound /a/, a practice the Israelites invented. Similarly, the *yud* was used for the vowel sounds /e/ and /i/, and the *vav* for the sounds /o/ and /u/.

The /a/ sound, represented by their letter *heh,* was particularly central, because Hebrew used the final /a/ sound for a variety of linguistic purposes, including distinguishing masculine and feminine words.

The reason all of this matters is that the Israelites used these "magic vowel letters"—*heh, yud,* and *vav*—not just for writing down words but also symbolically. The first monotheist's name was originally Abram, which means roughly "tribal elder" and comes from the words *ab* ("father") and *ram* ("exalted"). When he became a Jew in Genesis 17:5, his name was changed to Abraham, which, in Hebrew, is the same as his old name with the addition of the Israelites' magic *heh* right in the middle. Similarly, Sarai (which may be related to the word for "princess") also added a *heh,* to become Sarah. The patriarch and matriarch of the Jews get their names from ordinary words with a *heh* added to them.

In addition, there was an ancient word, *elim,* which meant "gods." Following the same pattern that turned Abram into Abraham and Sarai into Sarah, Elim became Elohim, the Jewish God. This is the first Hebrew name for God in the Bible, and this is how the name of the Israelite God is connected to the invention of the alphabet.

There's another name for God, too, and it's also derived from the Israelites' "magic" vowel letters. This name is composed entirely and only of the three magic letters, with the especially important *heh* doubled up: *yud-heh-vav-heh.* This appears to have been a purely symbolic way of writing God's name. It didn't even have a pronunciation. How could it? It was just a symbolic collection of vowels.

Later tradition would report that this four-letter name for God— technically called the tetragrammaton ("four-lettered" in Greek) and conveniently written Y-H-W-H in English—was used only by the priests, and, with the decline of the priestly caste, the name was forgotten. However, it seems all but impossible for a society devoted to the worship of God to forget God's name. It's far more reasonable to assume that this combination never had a pronunciation because it was intended to be purely symbolic.

Tradition turned this unpronounceable tetragrammaton into "the Lord," or, in Hebrew, *adonai,* a word that literally means "my lords." This is why in English we have two ways of referring to the deity of the Bible: "God" (matching *elohim*) and "the Lord" (matching *adonai*).

Some people, however, not recognizing the symbolic nature of Y-H-W-H, tried to pronounce it like an ordinary word. This is where we get the most common wrong name for God as originally pronounced: Yahweh. This mistaken pronunciation erroneously assumes that the vowel letters in the word are consonants, and then fills in vowels to make them into a word.

Another mistaken name for God comes from a misunderstanding of another innovation in writing.

Toward the end of the first century A.D., a group of people called the Tiberian Masoretes took it upon themselves to mark all of the vowel sounds in the Hebrew of the Bible—whether or not those sounds were originally written down. The Masoretes kept the original letters in place, adding dots and dashes around the letters to indicate the rest of the vowels, the ones the ancient writers didn't bother to include. When these Tiberian Masoretes got to Y-H-W-H, they had a problem, because this word didn't have a pronunciation. What vowel symbols should they add? They decided to use the vowel symbols from *adonai,* so as to remind the reader of the word's pronunciation without changing the way the word was written.

Alas, as this combination made its way into English—variously as *iohouah* or *jehovah,* among other spellings—its symbolic nature was lost and it came to be pronounced. At first, everyone knew that the *j* was the same as the *i* (like the *j* in "hallelujah"). Then, as even this bit of information was lost, people starting calling God "Jehovah." And this is the second common wrong name for God's original name.

Of course, no one uses the exact original name for God. The English "God" and "the Lord" are translations, as were the Latin *deus* and *dominus* before them, and the Greek *theos* and *kurios* before them. Even people who use *elohim* in Hebrew substitute their own modern accent for the (now-lost) ancient one; and although *adonai* for Y-H-W-H is ancient, it was still a first-century-B.C. innovation that veered away from the original. But people who say "God" usually know they are using a modern name, while these same people often don't know that "Jehovah" is just as modern.

In addition to Yahweh and Jehovah, a third mistaken name for God pops up, this one based on Exodus 3. There, Moses plans ahead for the day when the Israelites will ask him what God's name is. "What should I tell them" when they ask, Moses wants to know (Exodus 3:13).

Cryptically, God answers in Exodus 3:14 *ehyeh asher ehyeh,* or, in English, variously "I am what I am" or "I will be what I will be." Both are reasonable interpretations of the Hebrew, because the Hebrew tense system works differently from the English one. Similarly, "I am who I am" and "I will be who I will be" are just as likely, because Hebrew doesn't distinguish between "what" and "who" in this context. Then, in the second half of the verse, God uses the first part of that phrase as though it's a name: Tell the Israelites *"ehyeh* sent me to you."

Because Moses has just asked what God's name is, and because God uses the first word of the answer as a name, some translations assume that God's name here is *ehyeh asher ahyeh,* with, perhaps, a short form or nickname of just *ehyeh.* This is why the NRSV translates Exodus 3:14 like this:

> *God said to Moses, "I AM WHO I AM." He said further, "Thus you shall say to the Israelites, 'I AM has sent me to you.'"*

But what we seem to have here is a wordplay. The word for "I am" (*ehyeh*) bears some resemblance to the tetragrammaton. The first is spelled A-H-Y-H, the second Y-H-W-H. In both words, the second and fourth letters are a *heh.* Both words contain a *yud* (in different places). And the A (*aleph* in Hebrew) is, like the *vav,* sometimes used to represent a vowel. It's an ideal wordplay. But it is not God's name, and it is not God's final answer.

In fact, the very next verse repeats the syntax of the previous one, offering another answer to Moses's question. According to Exodus 3:15:

God also said to Moses, "Thus you shall say to the Israelites, 'The Lord [Y-H-W-H], the God of your ancestors, the God of Abraham, the God of Isaac, and the God of Jacob, has sent me to you': This is my name forever, and this is my title for all generations."

The emphatic nature of Exodus 3:15 underscores the incompleteness of Exodus 3:14. But, taken by itself, 3:14 offers the third wrong ancient name for God. Variations on "I am what I am" thus join "Yahweh" and "Jehovah" as distortions of God's original names.

So in addition to masking the power of some of the Bible's messages, unappreciated wordplay ended up distorting God's name.

Next we'll see yet another example of how wordplays influence our understanding of the Bible.

14

LIVE BY THE SWORD,
DIE BY THE SWORD

***Does the Bible say that those who live by the sword will die by the
sword? No.***

Around the year 1800, the US statesman Mr. Gouverneur Morris
(Gouverneur is his first name) wrote in the context of global politics
that it was insufficient "to quote the text, 'Those who live by the sword
shall perish by the sword.'" His words, recorded in the second volume
of *The Diary and Letters of Gouverneur Morris,* reference a phrase so
familiar that it appears in contexts ranging from essays like his to *The
New York Times,* which used the metaphor of "live by the sword, die
by the sword" in its 1857 analysis of the then-recent economic crisis
(called a "panic" back then).

The phrase is so common that it naturally mutates into related
forms. In 1601, the British writer Anthony Munday's character Oxford
in *The Death of Robert Earl of Huntington* laments that "those that live
by blood, in blood they die," an obvious reference to living and dying
by the sword. Semipermanent protest signs erected by the activist
William Thomas Hallenback, Jr., in front of the White House in the

1980s carried the slogan "Live by the Bomb, Die by the Bomb"—a clear antinuclear-weapon slogan. And in 1997, when rapper Christopher George Latore Wallace (the Notorious B.I.G.) was shot to death in Los Angeles a couple months shy of his twenty-fifth birthday, *New York Times* reporter Todd S. Purdum quoted one of Wallace's fans: "when you live by the gun, you die by the gun."

Even just the first part of the line is enough to evoke the entire sentiment, which is why Gus Russo titled his 1998 book about Castro and JFK *Live by the Sword*. Everyone understands the implications. And in 2007, Mary Tannen wrote a piece for *The New York Times* about a new class at her gym that taught Forza—an Italian variant of the Japanese *iaido* swordsmanship technique—as a way of staying fit. Tannen called her essay "Diet by the Sword" and bracketed the pun with the closing words, "You must live by the sword."

Yet for all its fame, the phrase "live by the sword, die by the sword" does not appear in the Bible. It's a misquote.

The original text that gets misquoted so frequently is from Matthew 26, in the context of Judas coming to arrest Jesus (as we discussed in chapter 7). In verse 46, Jesus tells his disciples that his betrayer is at hand, and then in verse 47 Judas arrives with a large crowd of people carrying swords and clubs. When these people grab hold of Jesus to arrest him, one of Jesus's supporters draws a sword and cuts off the ear of a Jewish high priest's slave, who was presumably among those detaining Jesus. In response, Jesus chastises his supporter and tells him to put his sword away, because "all those who take the sword will perish by the sword." Even the KJV from 1611 gets this right: "for all they that take the sword shall perish with the sword."

So even though Mr. Morris in the early 1800s thought he was quoting the Bible, he was not, and neither were the people after him (and possibly before him), or those who turned the sword into a gun or a bomb or whatever.

In its original context in Matthew 26:52, the sword might literally be a sword. After all, Jesus's follower has just used a sword to attack and wound a slave, and we know from earlier in the text that the people arresting Jesus are also carrying swords. And Jesus is not directing his words here at the reader, but rather at another person who was with him at the time. This isn't necessarily meant to be a general moral message.

On the other hand, we know that swords are used throughout the Bible as symbols of warfare, as in Isaiah's claim that "Nation shall not lift up sword against nation," which we'll return to in chapter 20. And when Jesus goes beyond a simple request for his follower to put away his sword and cites a universal rationale ("all those who take the sword . . ."), it seems that Jesus is providing a lesson that everyone is supposed to learn from.

So even though we cannot be sure, Matthew 26:52 does look like a lesson about violence. But the message has nothing to do with living by violence. It involves *using* violence, potentially any violence. And this is a big difference, for two reasons.

First, most people draw a distinction between different kinds of force—attacking and defending, say. Certainly those two are different in the eyes of modern law, which generally condemns unprovoked aggression along with retaliation, but permits even lethal force in self-defense. (We'll look at what the Bible says about self-defense in more detail in chapter 38.) Matthew 26:52—if it is indeed more than an instruction to a single person—seems to be about any sort of violence.

Secondly, most people recognize the possibility of exceptional circumstances. A normally peaceful person may decide that force is called for to battle a particularly egregious enemy, for instance. The phrase "live by" tends to suggest a way of life. Someone who "lives by deceit" is a deceitful person. But what about a generally honest person who uses deceit for a good purpose, say, to obtain medicine for a child from a corrupt doctor? To say that such a person lives by deceit seems like an overstatement.

Similarly, "live by the sword" tends to suggest a way of life, which is why it was so appropriate in the context of the death of the rapper we saw above, who was accused of systematic violence and of dealing drugs; the phrase would be less apt if, say, a pacifist folksinger had picked up a gun only once to defend his family and been shot to death in return.

So Jesus's original words were about using violence, and the misquotation shifts them toward a lifelong pattern of violence.

Yet the misquote has intuitive appeal, because it so clearly contrasts "live" and "die." In chapters 11 and 12 we saw the power of rhetoric, and how important it is to learn from it when it forms part of the original text of the Bible. Here we see the opposite pattern. A misquote has such powerful rhetoric that it has become more common than the original text.

And the force of the symmetry between "live" and "die" suggests a message about more than violence, a universal karma-like observation that the way one lives—violently, peacefully, deceitfully, egotistically, whatever—influences the way one dies.

The misquote, then, aligns in meaning with "what goes around comes around" and specifically focuses on living a life of violence. Neither of those are the theme of Matthew 26:52, which on the one hand deals more narrowly with violence alone, and on the other addresses any sort of violence, not just a life of violence.

This is exactly how the great theologian Origen explained the verse. He thought there was religious allegory to be drawn out of the words, but he also thought they expressed a very clear point, to be careful not to unsheathe a sword even if prompted to do so by some particular happenstance, like being in the army, or for self-defense, or really any reason, because—Origen explains—Christ teaches in the Gospels that all of these uses of the sword are abominations.

Still—perhaps because of the appeal of the misquotation, perhaps for more general ethical reasons—people are quick to ignore the differences between drawing a sword (perhaps only once) and living by violence more generally, and most people, inaccurately, wrongly think that Matthew 26:52 is about the karmic way in which a violent life leads to a violent death.

This kind of widespread misquotation of a single verse is relatively rare, especially now, because we have such convenient access to the text of the Bible. Usually when people misquote the Bible, they are at least accurately quoting a mistranslation, as we saw in chapter 10 with "God so loved the world." Here the error again attests to the power and importance of rhetoric, so we return to that theme in the next chapter, looking at more ways that we as modern readers miss the messages conveyed by the Bible's original language and phrasing.

15

DUST AND ASHES

Does the Bible say that people are but dust and ashes? No.

In Genesis 18:27, according to most translations, Abraham expresses his humility before God by referring to himself as mere "dust and ashes." In this and other biblical contexts, the phrase builds on Genesis 2:7, where God creates the first man of dust from the earth, and on Genesis 3:19, according to which dying is becoming dust again.

In other contexts, the phrase "dust and ashes" refers to extreme disappointment, a usage that has its roots in Josephus's "apple of Sodom" or "Sodom apple"—also called a "Dead Sea apple" or "Dead Sea fruit," because Sodom is located by the Dead Sea. These fruits looked enticing but would turn to dust when someone tried to pick them. (Debate continues over whether Josephus had a particular species in mind.)

So "dust" is humility. As it happens, the original Hebrew word, *afar*, probably means "dirt" and not "dust." For most people, "dust" refers to especially fine-grained particles, while the Hebrew probably intended the soil that is normally on the ground. But "dust" is certainly close enough to convey the main point of the original.

However, "ashes" is completely wrong in a translation of Genesis 18:27, because the whole point of the pair "dust" and "ashes" in Hebrew is that they sound almost the same—so close, in fact, that our normal way of writing the words in English barely distinguishes them. The Hebrew for "dust and ashes" in Genesis 18:27 is *afar* and *efer*. Because vowels exert less influence over a Hebrew word than consonants, these words are almost identical. (As it happens, the consonants are not exactly identical. The word that becomes "dust" starts with the Hebrew letter *ayin*, while "ashes" in Hebrew starts with an *aleph*. The *aleph* probably represented a glottal stop in Hebrew. That sound is rare in standard American English, but we do hear it between the "uh" and the "oh" of "uh-oh." In some dialects of British English it takes the place of "t" and other consonants, as in "wa'er" for "water." The *ayin*, on the other hand, is currently the same as the *aleph* in most dialects of Hebrew, but in the days of the Bible it probably had a more pronounced guttural sound. But even though they were different, they were closely related.)

The point of adding *efer* to *afar* is to augment the first word ("dirt" or "dust") with another, similar one. Unfortunately, "ashes" sounds nothing like the word "dust" in English. We have seen repeatedly in the past few chapters how important the sounds of words can be. Here we have a near repetition of sounds in Hebrew, but that rhetorical device is lost in English translation.

We don't have any successful way of translating the *afar-efer* pair into English—though "earth and ashes" at least does a better job than "dust and ashes"—but we get a sense of what we lose by comparing similar pairs in English. For instance, the "sticks and stones" of aphorism fame are a much more compelling pair than, say, "sticks and rocks," just as "might makes right" is more convincing than "power makes right."

Abraham took a word already used in connection with humility and added another, similar word to it to express extreme humility. The English translation, in addition to getting the nuances of the words wrong, misses the whole progression.

Then, once "dust" and "ashes" became accepted as a translation, the phrase "ashes to ashes, dust to dust" was coined as part of the official funeral liturgy in the Anglican Book of Common Prayer. That phrase wasn't supposed to directly translate anything in the Bible. Rather, it was designed to convey a biblical notion of mortality, based on the dust to which Adam returns after he dies, and the combination of "dust" with "ashes." But it is based on a translation that misses the point of the original text of the Bible.

This isn't the only place where the Bible purposely puts similar sounding words together. Another instance comes from the first half of Genesis 1:2: "And the earth was without form, and void," according to the KJV. The Hebrew there, again, offers two rhyming words: *tohu* for what becomes "without form" and *vohu* for "void." The latter word, *vohu,* only appears in the Bible in connection with *tohu,* and its point—like *efer* after *afar*—seems tied up with its relation to *tohu.*

Frustratingly, we don't know exactly what *tohu* or *vohu* meant in Genesis 1:2, just as we don't know the exact meaning of *afar.* But even if we did, the point of these words was not their meaning in isolation but rather the way they work together, and we won't get a better sense of the original text simply by learning more about the nuances of *afar* and *efer* or of *tohu* and *vohu.*

Yet again, we find the power of rhetoric, and the way a failure to recognize it has distorted the original meaning of the biblical text.

16

PSALM 23

Does the Bible say that the Lord is a shepherd? No.

For the past several chapters we've looked at direct statements in the Bible and the ways that they can be misunderstood today. We continue now in that theme, both because of the immediate results that we get and because it will help us better understand other, indirect ways that the Bible gets interpreted.

Here we turn to the opening of one of the most famous psalms: "The Lord is my shepherd."

Right off the bat, we know that this isn't meant to be taken literally. It's clearly imagery. God is like a shepherd, says the psalm, forcing us to ask, "How is God like a shepherd?"

To drive home the difference between literal and figurative meanings, it's helpful to consider some of the obviously wrong answers to what it means for God to "be my shepherd." Perhaps the clearest one relates to someone who actually owns flocks and has what we might call a "real" shepherd, called, say, "Bill." "Bill is my shepherd" is a different kind of sentence than "The Lord is my shepherd." Another wrong answer comes from the reasonable assumption that a shepherd is in charge of nonhuman animals; that's not what God is in Psalm 23. And an even worse answer presents itself in light of the observation that shepherds generally guard at least part of their flocks only long enough for the animals to be brought to slaughter.

Readers of the Bible—and readers in general—often don't like to admit the existence of figurative speech, because it can seem less precise than literal meanings, and there's a certain satisfaction in precision. But most language is figurative, and it's frequently so clear that we don't even notice the figures of speech.

We might imagine someone running for president whose combination of disarming personality and movie-star looks makes him popular with voters. He's not literally running; he's behaving like someone who runs a race. There are no weapons involved, so there's no one to disarm; he's behaving like someone who ratchets down a conflict (even though there are no real ratchets involved). And he doesn't necessarily look exactly like a real movie star; he looks good.

By way of a second example, this candidate might want to stay above the political fray, so he hires a consultant to be his pit bull for him.

The "pit bull" image is particularly helpful here, because it shows us how this kind of language works. What we mean is that the consultant shares only some qualities of a pit bull; we completely ignore other qualities. He is fierce (as pit bulls are perceived to be), but not small (as pit bulls usually are). For that matter, pit bulls, like all dogs, only very rarely make it past their twentieth birthday; but we don't mean that the candidate hired a teenager.

Even though they are based on metaphor, all of these sentences are precise and clear. We similarly have no trouble understanding what it means for new drugs to be coming down the pipeline (there's no pipe), for someone to pin down details (there's no pin), for rocket fire to blanket a city (which is different from smothering, even though blankets can smother), or for education and initiative to be the building blocks of a productive society.

A whole different kind of example comes from Shakespeare's *Romeo and Juliet:* "But soft, what light through yonder window breaks? It is the east, and Juliet is the sun." What does it mean that "Juliet is the sun"? Any reader of English knows that it means that she is pretty and desirable. But the sun causes sunburns and skin cancer. (This is why the sun was a symbol of danger in the Bible: "The sun will not harm you by day," reads Psalm 121:6.) Obviously, though, Romeo doesn't mean that Juliet is carcinogenic or otherwise dangerous.

Similarly, "The Lord is my shepherd" had a clear, precise meaning in the Bible. But to find it, we have to ask what aspects of the ancient "shepherd" are relevant. And here's where the misunderstanding comes from.

The problem is that the image of "shepherd" has changed radically since the days of the Bible. Nowadays, the qualities that often describe a shepherd include: peaceful, unkempt, weak, poorly dressed, carrying a staff (technically called a "crook"), bearded, interpersonally awkward, and probably old. Not every shepherd has all of these, of course, and there might be exceptions. But someone who describes a man as "looking like a shepherd" conveys many of these attributes.

The shepherds of the Bible were very different. David, in an attempt to convince Saul to let him fight Goliath, brags "I'm a shepherd" (1 Samuel 17:34). Shepherds were supposed to be strong and brave enough to successfully wrestle a wildcat, grabbing the members of their flocks from the jaws of a feline attacker. David said he was in the habit of doing so, as we saw in chapter 5. Amos 3:12 mirrors the gruesome imagery: "As a shepherd rescues two legs and a bit of ear from the mouth of a wildcat, that is how Israel will be saved." Shepherds were convened to defend a village, as in Micah 5:5: "If the Assyrians come into our land and tread upon our soil, we will raise shepherds against them." And in Nahum 3:18, we see that sleeping shepherds are a sign of lax defense: "Your shepherds are asleep, O king of Assyria; your nobles slumber."

The shepherd of the Bible was a brawny, fierce, brave fighter, nothing at all like our modern image of shepherd. Accordingly, Psalm 23 starts off with an image of God as a mighty warrior—nothing at all like the modern conception. Psalm 23 matches Exodus 15:3: "The Lord is a man of war." And that is why, as the opening line of the psalm continues, "I lack nothing." Nothing could possibly hurt me, the psalm asserts, with the great power of God watching my back. (The common translation of the second half of the line, "I shall not want," reflects an unusual meaning of the verb "want." It doesn't express desire but rather lack. This is why some versions prefer "I shall lack nothing.")

In fact, the poetic beauty of the psalm consists of the contrast between the first line and the second, which reads, ". . . he leads me to restful water."

According to the common, modern misunderstanding of Psalm 23, the opening image of "shepherd" conveys quiet, calm, meek work outdoors. And this matches the second line, which is also about peace and nature. It's poetry of matching. But that is not the original poetry of Psalm 23.

Unlike in Exodus 15 ("The Lord is a man of war"), where God's might results in the defeat of the Egyptian army, here God's might produces serenity and peace. And that was the original intent of the psalm.

Psalm 23, then, isn't about shepherds at all, certainly not modern shepherds, but not really about ancient shepherds, either. The shepherd is just a convenient metaphor for might, and the Psalm is about God's might producing feelings of satisfaction, safety, and tranquillity in the Psalmist.

We naturally focus now on the shepherd precisely because

shepherds nowadays are rare, so the shepherd jumps off the page. But in an era when shepherds were as common as taxi drivers are in a major city, or doctors in a hospital, the ancient reader would have known to look elsewhere for the impact of the psalm.

By analogy, we can imagine a modern story that begins, "I still remember the first time I landed behind the Iron Curtain." For a modern reader, this sets the stage for an account of East versus West, the Cold War, communism, and so forth. But if some magical technology let us transport that opening line back to the days of the Bible, readers would focus on only one thing: "landed." A human was *flying*? Surely that, they would think, must be more important than where this astonishing flight terminated. They would, of course, be wrong, just as we are wrong to focus too closely on the actual shepherd in Psalm 23 at the expense of the imagery that the word represents.

So the opening verse of Psalm 23, like the passages we've seen in the past few chapters, asserts a theology, but it is not the theology that most people think, because changing imagery has hidden the original intent of the ancient words. This is far from the only case of a metaphor mismatch between modernity and antiquity. We see another one next.

17

HEART AND SOUL

***Does the Bible say to love God with all of one's heart and soul?* No.**

According to most translations, Jesus says in the Gospels that the most important commandment is to "love the Lord your God with all your heart, all your soul, and all your mind" (Matthew 22:37, Mark 12:30, and Luke 10:27). Jesus is quoting Deuteronomy 6:5, which was considered one of the most important lines in the Old Testament two thousand years ago.

While the Old Testament itself doesn't afford the passage any particularly elevated status, Deuteronomy 6:5 has been incorporated not just into the New Testament but also into the core of Jewish prayer services. And it's one of the verses that gets included in the Jewish ceremonial doorway markers known as *m'zuzot* (singular, *m'zuzah*) and the prayer boxes known as *t'filin* in Hebrew, or, unhelpfully, as "phylacteries" in English. (The word "phylacteries" shares an etymology with "prophylactic," and, like medicine taken prophylactically to ward off a disease in the future, *t'filin* were conceived as a way of preventing future misfortune.) And the members of Qumran who gave us the famous Dead Sea Scrolls also thought that Deuteronomy 6:5 was pivotal. They quote it in the preamble of the Community Rule, one of their defining documents.

Yet for all its fame and centrality, the line as it's currently translated misses the original point. It's about much more than hearts, and it's not about souls at all.

It's easy to see how the mistake was made. The Hebrew word in Deuteronomy 6:5 that becomes "heart" in translation (*levav*) does refer to the organ we call a "heart" in English. So does the Greek word (*kardia*) that translates the Hebrew in the Gospels, a fact reflected in our English "cardiac," "electrocardiogram" (EKG or ECG), and even, indirectly, "heart," all of which trace their roots to the Greek. But once again, literalism has masked a message that is based on imagery.

In English, we use the word "heart" not just for the organ that pumps our blood, but also metaphorically to indicate "emotion." This is why "have a heart" means "to care," and why "heartbroken" is a state of sorrow, not a medical condition, just like a "sweetheart" is someone beloved.

Furthermore, people who "think with their hearts" behave not just emotionally but also irrationally. This shows us that the heart in English represents emotion, and more specifically emotion to the exclusion of intellect. In this sense "heart" is the opposite of "brain" or "mind."

Because English speakers so naturally associate "heart" with both the organ and with emotion, it's easy for them to miss the fact that other languages work differently. In this case, the Hebrew word *levav* and the Greek *kardia* include both emotion and intellect. The Hebrew and Greek "heart" is the seat of love, hatred, etc. (as in English), but also of cogitation, planning, daydreaming, wondering, etc.

So the English translation "heart" starts off by rejecting rational thought in favor of emotion, while the original starts off by specifically including both.

The word "soul" in English similarly has a range of connotations.

For some people, it's the part of being alive that continues after death. (This is true even for those who don't believe in the soul. What they often mean by "not believing in a soul" is that they don't believe that any part of a person survives death.) Or the soul complements the body and forms a complete person, so people have both a body and a soul. The body is the part that we can see and feel. The soul is everything else. This is why Thoreau wrote. "Good for the body is the work of the body and good for the soul is the work of the soul." He was describing two parts of being alive. In this sense, soul is the opposite of body in English, just as the heart is the opposite of the brain.

But, surprisingly, the original Hebrew word in Deuteronomy 6:5 (*nefesh*) doesn't mean soul at all. It's a general term that includes "flesh," "blood," and "breath." In other words, the Hebrew word that we usually translate as "soul" is just the opposite of "soul." It's the body and the blood and the breath and everything else about being alive that is tangible.

Based on its core meaning, this Old Testament word for the physical elements of the body came to mean not just the parts but also the entire person.

As it happens, this pattern of using part of something to mean the entire thing is common enough that it has its own technical term: synecdoche. And we see it frequently in English. The phrase "not a soul was left in the room" doesn't refer to a gathering of soulless corpses, but rather a room in which all of the people have left. "Soul" here means "people who have a soul." Another example of synecdoche is the captain who shouts "all hands on deck" when, obviously, he wants the people to whom the hands are attached.

There was barely any concept of life after death in most of the Old Testament, and there was nothing comparable to today's notion of "soul." Then, as the modern notion of a death-surviving soul became more popular—probably about two thousand years ago—a word was needed for it. While the Hebrew *nefesh* meant practically the opposite of "soul," it was also commonly being used for "person." This may be why the word was able to shift to mean not the body that a person has but something else that a person has: a soul.

Or perhaps it was the perceived connection between "breath" and "soul" that helped *nefesh* migrate in meaning. One of the things that *nefesh* included, along with flesh and blood, was, as we just saw, the breath. But unlike flesh and unlike blood, breath is mostly invisible. And breath always leaves a person who dies. So it wasn't hard to imagine that the soul was in the breath.

In fact, this is exactly what happened with the Greek parallel to the Hebrew *nefesh*. The Greek root meaning "breath" is *psyche-*, a form that created the ancient Greek verb "to breathe" (*psychen*) and also the noun "breath" (*psyche*). Then over time, the Greek word for "breath" shifted to mean "soul." ("Psyche" is also the name of the woman whom the Greek god Cupid courted.)

At any rate, words that originally meant physical parts of a body ended up meaning the body more generally, then the nonphysical soul of a body. Unfortunately, translators translated the newer meaning of the words, instead of focusing on what the words meant when they were written. This is how "soul" came to be used as a translation for what should be "body."

Taken together, these two translation mistakes—of "heart" and of "soul"—give us an English translation that describes only part of earthly existence (emotion, connected to heart) and an otherworldly existence (the soul). Worse, the modern translation excludes things like thinking and the physical body, two things that the ancient text specifically included.

The original biblical text, in fact, was based on a perception that there are two parts to being alive: the internal proceedings of a person's mind and heart, and the external manifestation of the body.

We don't have convenient words for these exact concepts in English, but they are remarkably similar to the way we define computers in terms of "software" and "hardware." The software is the part that we cannot see or touch, while the hardware is both visible and tangible. (Or, as some say, the software is the part you can't kick.)

The English phrase "software and hardware" gives us a sense of what the ancient text had in mind. The point was to include the two different kinds of things that make people alive. (Even people who don't care about the biblical exhortation may be intrigued by this ancient understanding of what it means to be human.)

Taken together, these two ancient words—*nefesh* and *levav* in Hebrew or *kardia* and *psyche* in Greek—combine to express the entirety of human existence, even stressing the observation that we all have parts that are visible and parts that are not.

As it happens, the combination of these two concepts appears not just in Deuteronomy 6:5 and the places that cite it. It was a common expression throughout the Old Testament, and it reflected a specific view of what it meant to be human.

But it's only in Deuteronomy 6:5 and the Gospels that quote it that the pair gets a third word, which often becomes "might" or "mind" in English. Unfortunately, we don't know what that third word means.

Still, we do know that the first two words have little to do with the heart and nothing to do with the soul. Deuteronomy 6:5, Matthew 22:37, Mark 12:30, and Luke 10:27 are not about which parts of our humanity should be used to love God. They are about loving God with everything that makes us human.

This question about what makes us human is part of a more general question: "What is the world made of?" As we'll see next, sometimes the answers are surprising.

18

UNICORNS AND DRAGONS

Are there imaginary animals in the Bible? No.

Isaiah 34:7 mentions unicorns as part of the judgment on the nations.
The previous verse sets the stage with "the sword of the Lord is
filled with blood . . . the blood of lambs and goats." Then, according
to the KJV, "the unicorns shall come down with them, and the bull-
ocks with the bulls; and their land shall be soaked with blood."

And this is not the only place we find unicorns. According to Numbers 23:22, God has the strength of "a unicorn" (or, as the KJV so
quaintly phrases it, "an unicorn"). In Psalm 22:21, the psalmist asks
for deliverance from the lion's mouth and from the unicorns' horns. All
in all, the unicorn makes nine appearances in the Old Testament.

What's going on?

These unicorns all come from the Greek translation of the Bible in
the Septuagint; the original Hebrew word is *r'em*. While the Hebrew
itself gives us no direct indication of what kind of animal it is, the Greek
monokeros means "single" (*mono*) "horn" (*keros*), so it certainly looks
like a unicorn. (The English word "unicorn" similarly comes from

words that mean "single" and "horn," in this case, the Latin *uni* and *cornu*.)

The King James Version, based on the clear meaning of the Greek, therefore translates the Hebrew *r'em* as "unicorn."

As early as the fifth century B.C. people were writing about unicorns. The Greek physician and historian Ctesias of Cnidus reported that "there are wild asses in India the size of horses and even bigger. They have a white body, crimson head, and deep blue eyes. They have a horn in the middle of their brow." (Our information about Ctesias and his writings is fragmentary, and at this point based mostly on secondhand reports, primarily from the ninth-century-A.D. patriarch Photios I of Constantinople, who summarized Ctesias's writings. So when we note that Ctesias was a physician and historian who wrote something, we normally mean that other people later said so.) The horn, it turns out, is tricolored, ranging from bright white at the base to bright red at the sharp tip; the rest is black. People who drink from the horn are immune to various ailments and inured against poison.

So there you have it. Unicorns.

On the other hand, Ctesias also reports four-footed birds the size of wolves with legs and claws like a lion: griffins. These red-breasted, black-bodied beasts inhabit the large mountains where the Indian gold lies. "Because of these creatures," Ctesias says, "it is hard to obtain the gold from the mountains, although it exists in large quantities." And for that matter, according to Ctesias there are people with "ears big enough to cover their arms as far as the elbow and their entire back at the same time; one ear can touch another." Ctesias hardly seems like a reliable source. (Still, as late as 1652, a Scottish writer and clergyman named Alexander Ross wrote in a work titled *Arcana Microcosmi* and subtitled "A Refutation of Thomas Browne's Vulgar Errors" that griffins were certainly real. The reason we never see them is that, quite naturally, they generally hang out in remote places where they might better guard their gold.)

In spite of Ctesias's dubious reliability in general, Aristotle (fourth century B.C.) writes in his *On the Parts of Animals* (book 3, part 2) that the "Indian ass" has but a single horn, unlike most animals, which have either two or none. And the first-century-A.D. Roman author and naturalist Pliny the Elder (whose full name was Gaius Plinius Secundus) also wrote about an animal called the *monokeros* ("single-horn"), noting that certain Indians hunt down "a very fierce animal called the unicorn, which has the head of a stag, the feet of an elephant, and the tail of a boar, while the rest of the body is like that of a horse; it makes a deep animal noise, and has a single black horn, which projects from the middle of its forehead . . . This animal, it is said, cannot be taken alive." (*Natural History,* book 8, chapter 31.) Pliny's detail that "it cannot be taken alive" suggests that he was basing his report on Ctesias's account, and other details in Pliny's work suggest that he was also responding to Aristotle. In particular, Pliny, like Aristotle, notes that animals with foreteeth in the upper jaw don't have horns. Pliny argues against those who say that the substance of foreteeth is expanded into horns. Aristotle was the one who made that claim.

Pliny mentions unicorns again in book 11, chapter 45, where he observes that no toed or solid-hoofed animals have horns "with the sole exception of the Indian ass, which is armed with a single horn." (This taxonomy of animals according to the shape of their hoof seems to have been widespread. We'll see in chapter 29 that the dietary laws of the Old Testament identify animals by the shape of their hoof.)

In the fourteenth century A.D., the Italian explorer Marco Polo wrote of unicorns that are barely smaller than elephants and have a single large, black horn in the middle of their forehead. But they are not what he expects. They have the hair of a buffalo and elephantine feet. And they attack with their long, spiny tongue, not with their horn. They spend their time wallowing in mud and slime. They are ugly. "They are not at all like we describe them when we say that they let themselves be captured by virgins." For that matter, in the sixteenth century the Swiss naturalist Konrad Gesner included the unicorn in his compendium of living animals, *Historiae animalium*.

Additionally, two chained unicorns adorn the original Scottish royal coat of arms, which was in use until the Union of the Crowns in 1603. To this day, the royal coat of arms of the United Kingdom has a lion on the left to represent England and a chained unicorn on the right to represent Scotland. (The unicorns are chained because free unicorns are so dangerous.)

Clearly, people until fairly recently thought that unicorns were real animals no different from horses, deer, or lions.

Marco Polo's "unicorn" is widely believed to be a rhinoceros, which, after all, does have a horn on its nose. (The name "rhinoceros" comes from the Greek words for "nose" and "horn.") Other parts of his description match the rhino perfectly: huge, indelicate animals barely smaller than elephants that have rough tongues and wallow in the mud. King Ptolemy II—the third-century-B.C. ruler of Egypt credited with commissioning the Septuagint—had all manner of exotic animals in his court, including, apparently, a rhinoceros, so the Septuagint could have been referring to a rhinoceros with the word *monokeros*.

The white body and colored horn that Ctesias describes doesn't seem like a rhinoceros, but his observation that the horn has particular power when used as a drinking vessel matches myths about the rhinoceros. Some people think that Ctesias combined two animals into one description. Other people think that Ctesias's other accounts are so bizarre that there's little point in trying to match this one up to reality.

Still, particularly because Ptolemy had rhinoceroses, the most prevalent opinion is that the "unicorn" of the Septuagint is a rhino.

That doesn't help us with the original Hebrew *r'em*. The Hebrew word—unlike the Greek *monokeros* and the English "unicorn"—gives us no direct information about what the animal might be. And from Deuteronomy 33:17, which talks about "the horns of the *r'em*," it seems as though the animal had more than one horn (presumably two). Based on the little evidence we have, most people think the *r'em* was a bovine of some sort, which is why modern renditions tend toward "wild ox" for a translation. Supporting this view is the parallelism in Psalm 29:6, which juxtaposes "calf" and *r'em/monokeros*, suggesting that they are similar. Another possibility is that the *r'em* was some variety of antelope, perhaps the beautiful oryx, whose straight black horns, from a distance and viewed at the right angle, might even create the impression of a single horn. Furthermore, the horns of the oryx don't regenerate, so if an animal loses one of its horns—fighting off another animal, perhaps—it ends up with just one.

So what we have is a Hebrew text with an animal whose species we no longer know for sure, and guidance from the Septuagint—the text that was used as the foundation of Christianity—that the animal is a unicorn.

Does this mean that the Bible says unicorns are real? Not necessarily, because animals generally carry some sort of specific, culturally dependent imagery.

In English, for instance, an eagle is generally good while a vulture is bad. People who behave like vultures are improperly preying on the weak and defenseless. That imagery is consistent with vultures' reputation as scavengers. Yet eagles are scavengers, too. But there's no similar English expression about behaving like an eagle.

We do have "eagle-eyed," which refers to acute eyesight or to a watchful eye. While eagles' eyes are certainly several times more powerful than human eyes, so, too, are vultures' eyes. Yet "vulture-eyed"—a common expression in English—indicates cruelty or vicious-ness, not visual acuity. Eagles and vultures represent different things, even though most people can't even correctly identify a vulture versus an eagle.

Hawks, like vultures, are used to represent violence, but generally in the context of war. "Hawkish" is the rough opposite of "diplomatic" or "peaceful," while the imagery of vultures contrasts instead with kindness. And again, these differences in English don't come from the animals themselves. Hawks are like vultures and like eagles. In many dialects, in fact, the same bird is called both a "hawk" and a "vulture," at least colloquially.

In the Bible, horses represent arrogance and war, while donkeys represent humility and peace. This is why Moses sends his family back to Egypt on donkeys in Exodus 4:20, while the evil Haman in the book of Esther wants the king's honor in the form of "royal robes which the king has worn and a horse that the king has ridden" (Esther 6:8).

And this is why Jesus in Matthew 21 arrives in Jerusalem on a donkey, with text that echos Zechariah 9:9: "Your king comes to you, triumphant and victorious, humble and riding on a donkey." Matthew specifically notes the prophet's words, "humble, and mounted on a donkey." When John relates the same entry into Jerusalem (John 12:12–19), he just mentions the donkey. He doesn't need to repeat "humble," because his readers would have known that donkeys represented humility.

The problem for us as modern readers is that we associate different characteristics with these animals. Donkeys in English represent stupidity and stubbornness, and the synonym "ass" suggests indifferent or cruel behavior.

So when we see animals in the Bible, we have two questions: "What species were they?" And, "What did they represent?" And depending on context, one question will take precedence over the other. In chapter 29, we'll see that some birds are, according to the Bible, not to be eaten. In that case, most people want to know which species the text means. (As it happens, it's almost impossible to know, but that doesn't lessen the importance of the question.) By contrast, in Exodus 19:4 God carries the people of Israel "on eagle's wings," using the Hebrew word *nesher* for the bird. What that originally meant depends on the imagery of the bird, not the species. The same Hebrew word appears in Proverbs 30:17, which condemns a mocking eye to the fate of being pecked out by one kind of bird and eaten by a *nesher*. There, the NRSV calls the *nesher* a vulture, because vultures more than eagles connote aggression. That is, the NRSV uses different translations for the same bird called a *nesher* in Hebrew to better capture the imagery in English.

In the case of the unicorns (according to the Greek in the Septuagint and the King James Version) or the wild oxen (according to one understanding of the Hebrew), our primary concern is their imagery, not their identity. It's not hard to understand how a rhinoceros or wild ox would come to be considered a symbol of power.

Like the raptors in the original text that become variously eagles and vultures, the *r'em* of the Hebrew and the *monokeros* represent power and might, even though we don't know what species the first one is, and even though we now know that the second one doesn't exist.

All of this brings us to the sea monsters and dragons in the Bible. According to Genesis 1:21, God created the "great sea monsters." The prophet Nehemiah (in verse 2:13) describes how he walked by the "Valley Gate" past the "Dragon Spring." According to Psalm 74:13, God broke the heads of the "dragons" in the water. And the book of Revelation has a "great red dragon with seven heads and ten horns, and seven crowns upon his heads" (12:3).

Both the "sea monsters" and the "dragons" in our English translations of the Old Testament come from the same Hebrew word, *tanin*. (Elsewhere that word gets translated as "snake" or "serpent," as in Exodus 7:9–10, when Moses turns his staff into a snake.)

Dragons and sea monsters in antiquity—and even not too long ago—were like unicorns (and griffins). They were magnificent animals that most people thought probably existed somewhere. Furthermore, the Greek word *drakon,* which gives us our English "dragon," meant both "snake" and "dragon." (Even in English, a "dragon" used to be a kind of snake.) So, once again, we find that the Greek translation in the Septuagint colors how people understand the original Hebrew.

And in this case, people often misunderstand the Greek, too. In Exodus 7, for instance, the transition from staff to *tanin* in Hebrew or *drakon* in Greek is obviously to a snake, not a dragon. And because these animals almost always live in the water, they seem to be water snakes and other water creatures. The word didn't apply only to one species, just as, in English, lots of animals—snakes and eels, for instance—might be called "serpents."

Once again, we understand the text by looking for the symbolism of these animals. In Revelation, the beast is mythic and unlike anything observed in the natural world; its seven heads are obviously inconsistent with nature. (The seven crowned heads probably represent complete dominion over everything, in accord with a cosmology that envisioned seven heavens.) So there, "dragon" is appropriate in English. In the Old Testament, "snake" or "serpent" better conveys the general intent, though many translations get this wrong. The "dragons" of Psalm 74:13 are water creatures—snakes, serpents, or even whales—not the fire-breathing flying creatures that we call dragons in English.

More generally, we find a huge culture gap between the days of the Bible and modernity. Now we have detailed taxonomies of animals—

identified by kingdom, phylum, class, etc.—and we like to believe that we have discovered all of the major kinds of animals that inhabit the earth. So for us, animals come in two varieties: "real" and "imaginary." The ancient view was different. Animals still came in two varieties, but they were "common" and "extraordinary."

In terms of imagery, "real" loosely aligns with "common," and "imaginary" with "extraordinary." Dogs and cats and pigeons fall into the first category in both cases. Zebras and rhinos (for those of us who don't live in Africa) and giant squids fall into the second.

Equally, there are obviously big differences, the most important being that the imagery of the ancient extraordinary animals gets overshadowed by their modern imaginariness. We saw above how modern translations use "eagle" and "vulture" for the same ancient animal, the better to reflect the original imagery. "Eagle" and "vulture," both being real birds, easily convey both literal and metaphoric meaning to people who read the Bible in English. By contrast, it's all but impossible for modern readers to think about unicorns or dragons and ignore their most obvious feature: They don't exist.

Yet to correctly understand the ancient text, we modern readers have to do just that. We have to ignore the (modern) distinction between real and imaginary, and focus on the ancient impact of unicorns and dragons.

This important lesson helps us understand the otherwise odd animals that we find in the Bible. Next we'll see that it also helps us understand one of the most common themes in the bible: kings.

19

KINGS

***Are there kings in the Bible?* Not really.**

The word "king" appears nearly three thousand times in the Bible. There's King David, naturally, and King Solomon, along with Jehoshaphat and Uzziah and Hezekiah and other lesser-known kings of Israel. There's King Herod. And Jesus's cross bore the inscription "King of the Jews."

Because we still have kings today, it's tempting to think that we know what "king" meant in the Bible just because we know what "king" now means. But, surprisingly for many, we find some of the same issues with "king" that we found with "unicorn." The problem is that the role of king has changed so dramatically.

Today's kings are people like Carl XVI Gustaf of Sweden, who personally hands out Nobel Prizes. Like many kings, he traces his position to a founding father, Eric the Victorious in his case, from the tenth century. (As it happens, Eric the Victorious is the earliest historical Swedish king, but since the seventeenth century the Swedes have also entertained a mythical royal lineage that goes all the way back to the biblical Magog, son of Japheth. Because of this dual reckoning, Carl XVI—that is, "Carl the Sixteenth"—is only the tenth Swedish king to bear the name Carl.)

Britain has a queen, but in principle could just as well have a king; the next monarch will probably be a king. The currently reigning Queen Elizabeth II traces her monarchy directly back to Queen Anne in 1707 (when England merged with Scotland), and before that, monarchs dating to the end of the first millennium A.D. ruled England and Scotland. According to the official website of the British monarchy, the "British Sovereign no longer has a political or executive role." Like the role of the king of Sweden, who hands out prizes, the queen's role is largely ceremonial, though she does make some decisions. (For instance, the influential KJV translation of the Bible was commissioned by King James for the Crown. Even though the translation is over four hundred years old, it is still under something called Crown copyright. The queen or her successor gets to decide who uses her translation. As of 2016, Queen Elizabeth delegates this control to Cambridge University Press.)

We see two patterns emerge regarding royalty: The lineage is important and the monarchs are largely figureheads.

Furthermore, our modern cultural world is awash with various kinds of imaginary or semihistorical kings. King Arthur of round-table fame, despite not being historical, is certainly more famous in the English-speaking world than King Carl Gustaf. So is King Henry VIII of wife-beheading fame. More generally, the European medieval system of knights and kings and castles is still part of the Western modern psyche, so the word "king," like "knight," conjures images of jousts, castles, maidens, and chivalry. Even though some of these impressions of medieval life are inaccurate, they still influence many people's concept of "king."

So when people read "king" in the Bible, they automatically start with preconceptions based on modern powerless figureheads, on long lineages, and on chivalry. Right off the bat, people misunderstand the word "king" in the Bible.

Kings in the Bible lived long before chivalry, so that modern influence is completely misleading. Some kings—particularly those who ruled Israel as recorded in the historical sections of the Bible—earned their rule in part by virtue of their lineage, but other kings in the Bible show up with no mention of their history at all. And certainly "powerless figurehead" was the opposite of "king" in the Bible. The kings wielded ultimate and absolute power. The figureheads were the prophets, whose only influence came from their personal power of persuasion. In some ways the kings of the Bible were more like dictators, and in other ways more like presidents or prime ministers; in some ways they were like modern generals.

For that matter, kings nowadays rule over countries, but there weren't even any countries in the Bible. There were cities and collections of cities. In that sense, kings in the Bible were like mayors or governors.

For instance, Genesis 14 sets the stage for Lot's captivity and rescue with "in the days of King Amraphel of Sinar, King Arioch of Ellasar, King Chedorlaomer of Elam, and King Tidal of Goiim," who waged war against five other kings. We don't see any sign of lineages here. Far from being powerless, these kings are military commanders, but they command tiny cities, not countries. They are nothing like most people's perceptions of modern or medieval kings.

In chapter 5 we met King David, who (in addition to another) slew Goliath. One of David's defining qualities was his musical talent—a quality unlikely to define a modern king.

By analogy, we might consider "birds." When most people think of a bird, a sparrow comes to mind, or a hawk, or a seagull, or maybe just a nondescript small flying animal. And if an animal is "like a bird," it is probably like one of those animals. It is probably not like a penguin or an emu, even though those are both birds.

In the last three chapters, we saw how imagery and metaphor are always in play, even when the text doesn't overtly tell the reader so. The phrase "heart and soul" means "like the way the heart is understood and like the way the soul is understood," just as "unicorns" means "similar to the way that unicorns are understood." And the shepherds of the Bible are not at all like what the modern word "shepherd" conveys. In just the same way, when we read that someone is a "king," we automatically start assigning properties to that person based on our modern conception of kings, and that misleads us.

In the case of kings, it frequently doesn't matter all that much. The kings in Genesis 14 are bit players, and we can understand the events in Genesis even if we misunderstand who those nine kings are.

King David is more important. If we read the whole text, we find sufficient detail to overcome our inaccurate modern prejudices. He is a multifaceted leader: a talented musician and poet as well as a fighter. The throne is also the seat of justice. But if we read only parts of the text—for instance, David's famous encounter with Goliath—we end up misunderstanding the pivotal character.

King David's qualities are not unimportant. Jews and Christians agree that the Messiah will come from the Davidic line, and the New Testament (as we saw in chapter 6) ties Jesus directly to David. Certainly descendants are not always the same as their ancestors, but our default assumption is that specific families have specific attributes. To come from a family of musicians, now, is different than to come from a family of warriors, which is different again than coming from a family of lawyers. To be part of the Davidic line is to be all three.

This pattern of roles that have changed in the past two to three thousand years extends beyond the people (like kings and shepherds), animals (like unicorns), and body parts (like hearts) that we've seen so far. One particularly devious category in this regard is religious terms, because they were once new and now they form the basis of thousands of years of tradition.

For instance, we read of "John the Baptist," but when he lived there was no baptism as we know it now. Today's baptism is an ancient practice; John's was a modern innovation. (There are other differences, as well.) So in one sense, a more accurate modern description would be "John the Dunker" or some other phrase that would avoid the impression that what John was doing was the same as our modern baptism. On the other hand, that more accurate description also masks the evolving connection between baptism in its various forms and John's original practice.

The same kinds of considerations apply to kings. We might want to call them "rulers" more generally, to avoid the impression that they are like our kings as they are now perceived. We see support for this kind of approach in Genesis 41:46, where the text calls Pharaoh the "king" of Egypt, even though we don't generally use the term "king" for a pharaoh, preferring instead "ruler." Similarly, we don't usually use the title "king" for Alexander the Great, even though he, too, was technically a king.

So in spite of the word "king" that appears in every modern Bible translation, the rulers in the Bible were generally different from what we now think of as a king.

This is one more example of how difficult it is in modernity—even with translations—to understand the text of the Bible (or any other ancient document). Next we'll see that even when we understand the basic words, we don't always appreciate their impact.

20

NATIONS, SWORDS, AND PLOWSHARES

Does the Bible say nations shouldn't take up swords against each other? No.

In the past few chapters, we've looked at how translation errors, unappreciated rhetoric, and more contributed to widespread misunderstandings of some of the Bible's most important direct statements: the ethical instructions in the Ten Commandments (even though they weren't originally commandments); theological positions, like God's might, as expressed by comparison to a shepherd; the tangible and intangible aspects of being human; and so on. Just as often, what we now think of as a direct statement started as something completely different. This is what we find in Isaiah's well known "statement" about turning swords into plowshares.

The famous Isaiah 2:4 reads, "And they shall beat their swords into plowshares, and their spears into pruning hooks; nation shall not lift up sword against nation, nor shall they learn war any more." We now know that we have to interpret "swords," "plowshares," "spears," and so on as poetic imagery. This is obviously not merely a statement about swords and plowshares.

A plowshare—now unfamiliar to most industrial readers in the West—is a sharp edge used to till the land. (The word "share" comes from an original root meaning "to cut," an etymological history we see in the related word "shear," as well. A "share" was an instrument for cutting, especially the part of a plow that cuts the earth. From its relation to cutting, a share came to mean also the parts of something that was cut up, which is where we get stock shares. And the verb "to share" in the sense of "divvy up" comes from allocating those parts.) And a sword, of course, is a sharp-edged blade used for violence, especially battle. So turning swords into plowshares involves taking a sharp blade that was used for war and repurposing it as a sharp blade used to provide food.

The imagery is beautiful and striking, which is one reason the passage is so famous today, even in an era where swords are generally ceremonial and plowshares all but unheard of. Spears and pruning hooks match in the same way. Spears are sharp edges used for war, while pruning hooks (sharp edges used to cut away unwanted vines or branches so the rest will grow better) are sharp edges that help society better provide food. As it happens, we don't know for sure if "plowshare," "spear," and "pruning hook" are the exact right translations, but the metaphor of turning implements of war into implements of farming is exceedingly clear.

And the next line continues the theme: "Nation shall not lift up sword against nation" obviously refers to war, again using "sword" to represent military violence. And just in case there was any doubt, the ending refers to war specifically: "they shall not study war any more."

The text we have here seems to be a clear and impassioned statement promoting pacifism. But it is not, because we quoted the text here—as most people do—completely out of context, starting right in the middle of a verse. Verse 2:4 does not begin with the imagery of peace and war but rather with a prophecy about God as final arbiter: "God will judge between the nations and shall arbitrate for many peoples," and only then "will they beat their swords into plowshares."

In other words, the day will come when God will decide disputes among nations, so that war won't be necessary anymore. *But that day isn't here yet.* This whole passage is a vision about the future. Isaiah even tells us so himself in the verses that open that chapter: "This is what Isaiah prophesied . . . In days to come, the mountain of the Lord's house will be established . . . and all nations will stream to it." Verse 2:4 is about what will happen "in days to come." This is why the NRSV captions the entire passage "the future house of God."

Isaiah's vision here is just one of many about the future. In the next chapter, the prophet turns his attention to the demise of the arrogant ruling class: "The Lord . . . will remove . . . support and staff—all support of bread, and all support of water—warrior and soldier, judge and prophet, diviner and elder, military captain and dignitary . . ." Obviously, this is high poetry, and we don't know if we have correctly understood the nuances of each word, but the point is clear. An upheaval is on the way.

Verse 3:5 describes one aspect of that upcoming shift: "The people will be oppressed, everyone by another and everyone by a neighbor; the young will bully the old, and the despicable will bully the honorable." Obviously, this part of Isaiah's visions is not something to look forward to. Hopefully, it will just be the catalyst that helps move things along. But it's still right there in the vision.

Furthermore, Isaiah's prophecy is only about Israel. The full text of verse 2:1 reads, "This is what Isaiah prophesied about Judah and Jerusalem," with the common combination "Judah" and "Jerusalem" referring to God's people in Israel. Chapter 3 similarly opens with "The Lord will remove from Jerusalem and from Judah . . ."

In short, the famous "antiwar" passage from Isaiah—which, as it happens, also appears in Micah 4—is only one tiny part of one prophecy in a series of prophecies about what will happen to Israel in the future.

Certainly, one way to interpret Isaiah's prophecy here is that we should work to build the ideal that the ancient prophet envisions. We should take the first steps and start dismantling our weapons. However, an equally compelling way to read the text is that we should keep building swords and other weapons until God's role as arbiter is finally established, because these instruments of war are necessary parts of civilization until God takes over and makes them irrelevant. Though this second reading strikes many people as less satisfactory, it has just as much basis in the text.

For that matter, if we let ourselves lop off the context of Isaiah's vision, we might cite just the part about the upheaval: "the young will bully the old, and the despicable will bully the honorable." Here—as is often the case—the young, like the despicable, represent people who are inexperienced, who lack authority, who are driven by the wrong goals, or who are otherwise undeserving. And while we're not sure about the translation "bully," this is clearly a case of things going awry. Isaiah doesn't command pacifism any more than he commands us to replace wise leaders with foolish ones. Both themes are part of his prophecy.

This is not to say that the traditional interpretation is wrong. Religious traditions that use these lines to promote peace over war have every right to do so, and people who read or sing these ancient words to protest violence are aligning themselves with solid religious tradition. But let us be clear: This is a matter of tradition, not "what Isaiah says" and certainly not "what the Bible says."

In its original context, this famous passage is just part of a vision of what Israel will be like when God establishes a cosmic court of justice. What we do until then is up to us.

Still, as part of his more general theology, Isaiah connects peaceful use of sharp objects with God's ultimate dominion, and belligerent uses with the imperfect times that we currently experience. So even if Isaiah isn't promoting pacifism here, he does seem to take the position that peace is better than war. But he leaves open the possibility that peace might not always be an option, that war—though undesirable—might still be better than alternatives like injustice or defeat. We'll return to these themes when we talk about violence in chapter 35.

For now, we focus both on the details of Isaiah and the broader pattern we see: Mainstream religious traditions take verses out of context to change what they mean. Once again, this is a problem only for people who don't understand religious endeavors. The same process of painting things in a new light applies, sometimes literally, to art, but art isn't condemned for it. Similarly, the pattern of recontextualizing text lies at the core of religious textual interpretation.

This is precisely why we draw a line between what the Bible originally said and what its words have been made to say. Both are important, and both are interesting. As modern readers living in the scientific era, we—probably for the first time—are also interested in distinguishing the two approaches.

In this case of Isaiah here, it was pretty easy to find the original prophetic message and contrast it with the traditional pacifistic one. It's even easy to see how one turned into the other.

In other cases, as we'll see next, it's harder to draw such a clear line.

21

IF NOT BY BREAD ALONE, THEN BY WHAT DO PEOPLE LIVE?

If we don't live by bread alone, do we live by every word from God's mouth? Yes, but also no.

Matthew 4 recounts what is commonly known as "the temptation of Jesus" by Satan. God leads Jesus into the wilderness, where he fasts for forty days and forty nights (numbers that are clearly symbolic, as we saw above). Famished, Jesus encounters Satan, who taunts him, asking why he doesn't turn stones into bread. And Jesus answers with the famous passage from Matthew 4:4: "One does not live by bread alone, but by every word that comes from the mouth of God." We find an abridged version of the same account in Luke 4:4: "It is written, 'One does not live by bread alone.'" The phrase was apparently so well known that Luke didn't even have to finish the quotation.

Matthew 4:4 (along with Luke 4:4) actually begins with an indication that Jesus is quoting scripture in his response to Satan. "He answered, 'It is written.'" Because the only scripture around at the time was the Old Testament, we expect to find the same text in the Old Testament.

And we almost do.

The text of Matthew and Luke is quoting Deuteronomy 8:3. There we find the same introductory thought: "One does not live by bread alone." But then things get more complicated, because Deuteronomy 8:3 has a different alternative to bread: ". . . but on anything that the Lord decrees."

The context in Deuteronomy is Moses reviewing the saga that brought the people of Israel to the border of the Promised Land. In verse 8:2 Moses tells the people to "remember the long way that the Lord your God has led you these forty years in the wilderness, in order to humble you, testing you to know what was in your heart, whether or not you would keep his commandments." So, as in Matthew 4:4, this is a test. But unlike in Matthew, it is the people of Israel being tested, not Jesus.

In the context of a test and of remembering the journey, Moses follows up with Deuteronomy 8:3: "He humbled you by letting you know hunger, then by feeding you with manna." The manna, of course, is the amazing food substitute that sustained the people during their arduous journey. Exodus 18:35 explains that "the Israelites ate manna forty years, until they came to a habitable land; they ate manna, until they came to the border of the Land of Canaan." In John 6:25, a crowd challenges Jesus, recalling that their "ancestors ate the manna in the wilderness."

Still in Deuteronomy, Moses follows up with more about the manna. According to the text, the point of the manna was to make the people understand that they can live on anything the Lord says: bread, certainly, but also something they've never even considered. To express this thought, the Old Testament text uses the expression "whatever comes out of the Lord's mouth," or, in Hebrew, every *motza* of God, where *motza* means "something that comes out." (The word is unrelated to the similar-sounding *matzah*.) According to Deuteronomy 8:3, "one does not live on bread alone, but on anything that God says."

It is common to use the same language to describe words and what they mean, so common, in fact, that we don't usually notice. We see this in the English expressions "I give you my word" and "I always keep my word." Both have to do with what my words mean, not the words themselves. Or I might agree to "do whatever you say" and, just to make sure I don't forget, "write down what you say." But "what you say" in the first case refers to the meaning of your words, and in the second, to the words themselves. Similarly, the Hebrew expression "*motza* of one's mouth" is usually the same as the English "whatever one says."

And in the case of Deuteronomy 8:3, we're lucky to have the entire context of the manna, which makes it clear that the "*motza* of God's mouth" is the manna. Deuteronomy 8:3 is simple and clear: People can live not just on bread but on anything that God says people can live on, including, for example, manna. (The use of "bread" here is similar to the English "break bread with," and refers to food in general, in exactly the way that "sword" refers to weaponry in general, as we saw in the last chapter.)

If our only goal were to understand Deuteronomy 8:3, we wouldn't need to analyze the Hebrew language here. We could leave that to a class on biblical Hebrew. But we started with the goal of understanding Matthew 4:4. Matthew 4:4, remember, quoting Deuteronomy 8:3, says that people can live on God's words. But Deuteronomy 8:3 doesn't say that!

This is a case of something that is actually very common. The New Testament is quoting the Old Testament out of context. Here the leap from "whatever God says" to "God's words" is explained by the expression "*motza* of God's mouth," which normally means "whatever God says" but which, out of context, might mean "God's actual words." A passage that started off by asserting that one can live on any food that

God declares edible morphed into a statement about living on God's very declarations.

Then the hugely influential Greek translation called the Septuagint made this leap easier, because the Greek word for *motza* is usually based on some variation of "go out," in keeping with the literal meaning of the Hebrew word. But in Deuteronomy 8:3, the Greek uses the word *rima* for *motza,* and that Greek word means "word." The Greek translation of Deuteronomy 8:3 says "every word that comes out of God's mouth" instead of the more general "every thing that comes out of God's mouth." The meaning is essentially the same, and both the Hebrew and the Greek phrases refer to manna. But the appearance of the Greek *rima* ("word") means that Matthew can quote the text accurately and still change the meaning completely.

Matthew's revision of the Old Testament to fit his new context in the New Testament is exactly like the better-known case of revising Isaiah's words to make them about pacifism, as we saw in the last chapter. Revising text is what religion does. But it's not just cynics who don't understand this central element of how religious text works.

In particular, Bible translators, too, sometimes think that Deuteronomy 8:3 and Matthew 4:4 must match exactly, so they change their translation of Deuteronomy 8:3. This is why the NRSV translation of Deuteronomy 8:3 reads, "one does not live by bread alone, but by every word that comes from the mouth of the Lord," relegating the more accurate "by anything that the Lord decrees" to a footnote. The motivation seems to have been to make Deuteronomy and Matthew match more closely than they actually do. But the editors have thus done a terrible disservice to their readers. The translation—and most others—hides the way that Matthew cites the text of the Old Testament.

The authors of the New Testament were not alone in reinterpreting religious texts to suit new purposes. Matthew, of course, was Jewish, though he belonged to a stream of Judaism that would eventually become Christianity, and Christianity has continued breathing new life into old words. The reclusive Jews at Qumran who created the now-famous Dead Sea Scrolls read text in exactly the same way, looking not just at what it originally meant but at what it could be made to mean. And the great Rabbis who forged the path that would eventually lead to Judaism as we now know it also reinterpreted their texts. Interpreting and reinterpreting scripture is as old as scripture itself.

But because Bible translations hide this central facet of reading text, many modern readers of the Bible either assume that textual citations must match exactly, or that any mismatch must have been a mistake.

An example from rabbinic Judaism helps demonstrate the point. The daily Jewish liturgy, created by the Rabbis in the aftermath of the Jewish exile from Jerusalem in the year A.D. 70, emphasizes God's merciful and gracious nature. A famous prayer passage starts, "The Lord, the Lord: God is merciful and gracious, slow to anger," and ends with the words "forgiving sin." The line quotes Exodus 34:7. But even a cursory look at Exodus 34:7 shows that the Rabbis left a word out. And the word is "not"! The original biblical text reads, ". . . not forgiving sin," and then goes on to explain, "but visiting the iniquity of the parents upon the children and the children's children, to the third and the fourth generation." (Because of a quirk of Hebrew grammar, the shorter version without "not" is not technically a misquote, but only an abridged quotation. It would be like a passage in English that started off as "forgiving sin under no circumstances" and ended up as "forgiving sin.")

In spite of the shorter version with the opposite meaning in the prayer service, the Jewish Torah—the Five Books of Moses as written, to this day, by hand on parchment—still contains the original text. The

Torah is the focal point of many worship services, and it is the Torah from which scripture is ceremonially read during those services. The original text in Exodus and the revised text (with an opposite meaning) in the liturgy survive side by side.

It is only as modern readers that we sometimes question the validity of this kind of approach, either trying to wipe away the inconsistencies (though that hardly seems possible when the missing word in the quotation is "not") or using the mismatch to discredit the entire endeavor. But when we do either of these, we are shoving our modern scientific viewpoint into realms where it does not belong. We are, once again, making the same kind of mistake that we saw regarding Genesis in chapter 2. There we used the analogy of judging Magritte's paintings of daytime skies over a nighttime street. The critic who observes that daytime skies cast more light than Magritte drew and the viewer who wonders if maybe this isn't a miraculous dissipation of light have both missed the point. So too, here.

The matter is of considerable importance. It helps us understand the text of the New Testament in Matthew 4:4, as well as in other places, as we'll see in the next few chapters. It also helps us put traditional interpretations into the right context, better enabling us to understand why tradition does not always reflect the original meaning of the text. And it helps us put other reinterpretations—like the repositioning of Isaiah as a text urging pacifism—into their proper context.

22

WHO IS THE VOICE CRYING
IN THE WILDERNESS?

Does the Bible talk about a voice crying in the wilderness? Yes, but
also no.

The Bible's image of a voice crying in the wilderness is so powerful
that in addition to its religious use, it has given rise to a common secular expression in English, referring to someone who expresses a dis-
senting or unpopular opinion.

The imagery has its origins in the New Testament, where that voice
is John the Baptist. In John 1:23, he tells us so, answering people who
want to know who he is with the quotation "I am the voice of one
crying out in the wilderness, 'Make straight the way of the Lord,'"
adding that he is quoting the prophet Isaiah. Matthew (3:1–3), Mark
(1:3–4), and Luke (3:2–4) agree. ("Wilderness" is sometimes translated
as "desert.")

John the Baptist's unpopular role as the herald of Jesus and Christianity forms the basis of the secular expression. And the notion that
God can be found in the desert remains a powerful religious concept.

But Isaiah doesn't talk about a voice in the desert or wilderness.

Like the reference in Matthew 4:4 to Deuteronomy 8:3 that we saw in the last chapter, the New Testament quotes Isaiah out of context. And again, as with Matthew's repurposing of Deuteronomy, the new meaning is based on an innovative reading of the old words.

In this case, Isaiah 40:3 opens as follows: "A voice crying out in the wilderness prepare the way of the Lord." Because the original Hebrew didn't have punctuation, this first half of verse 40:3 might refer either to a voice in the wilderness crying out, "Prepare the way of the Lord," or, alternatively, to a voice crying out, "In the wilderness, prepare the way of the Lord." That is, the voice might be in the desert, where it talks about preparing a way for the Lord; or the voice might be anywhere, talking about preparing a way in the desert for the Lord. But the second half of the verse in Isaiah makes it clear that it's the way, not the voice, that is in the desert: "make straight in the desert a highway for our God."

This is typical parallel structure, one of the most widespread biblical literary devices. We find it, for example, in Isaiah 1:2, the first poetic line of the book of Isaiah. (Isaiah 1:1 is an introduction, closer to what we would now call a title.) The text there reads, "Hear, O heavens, and listen, O earth." We find two parallel verbs ("hear" and "listen") and two parallel subjects ("heavens" and "earth"). Here the verbs mean the same thing, and the subjects express what is technically called a merism, that is, using two extremes of a spectrum to represent the entire spectrum. (The clearest English example of a merism is the phrase "young and old," which includes not just children and the elderly but everyone in between.)

The next verse, Isaiah 1:3, continues with the same poetic device: "The ox knows its owner, and the donkey its master's crib." The double parallelism puts "ox" and "donkey" together, and also "owner" and "master's crib." And again in Isaiah 1:4, we find "Ah, sinful nation, people laden with iniquity, offspring who do evil, children who deal corruptly." The sinful nation is parallel to the people laden with iniquity; the offspring are the children; and doing evil is like dealing corruptly.

So when we see "in the wilderness"/"way of the Lord" followed by "in the desert"/"highway for our God" in Isaiah 40:3, we are confident that the "voice" called out two parallel things, and that it was the way of the Lord that was in the wilderness, not the voice itself. These facts are so clear from the text, in fact, that most translations render Isaiah 40:3 in the Old Testament differently from the verses that quote it in the New Testament.

We also have to assume that John, Matthew, etc., were aware of this original reading of the text. It would have been all but impossible for them to miss the obvious parallel structure with which any ancient reader of the Old Testament would have been familiar. The authors of the New Testament didn't care that they were reinterpreting the text. This is more confirmation of the pattern we started looking at in the last chapter: The New Testament sometimes quotes the words of the Old Testament but gives them new meaning.

On the one hand, because the text quotes the right words, this is an accurate quotation. On the other hand, we are tempted nowadays to cry foul, because the quotation misrepresents the original meaning. The reader may remember the example in the introduction about the reporter who quotes an economist as judging the economy to be "good," when the economist actually said it was "not good." It's technically an accurate quotation. The economist used the word "good." But that's not how we judge accuracy today. This is why, in other cases—regarding the creation story above, for example, or homosexuality in the Bible, below—we demand that an answer to "What does the Bible say?" take into account the full context of the Bible, not an abridged context purposely designed to misrepresent. If so, how can we acknowledge and accept this exact kind of narrow quotation in the New Testament?

The answer is that in cases like these the New Testament is not purporting to convey the original message of the Old Testament any more than other purposely out-of-context quotations. The answer to "What does the Old Testament say?" cannot be limited to the way the New Testament understands it. But, equally, we do not criticize the New Testament for the way it creates a religious tradition, any more than we reject the pacifistic interpretation of Isaiah based on the (mis-) quotation about turning swords into plowshares. This is, in fact, part of our more general pattern of differentiating between the original meaning of the text and the way it has been interpreted as part of religious traditions.

If quoting words out of context on purpose strikes the modern reader as odd, it is only more confirmation of a culture gap between modernity and antiquity. This kind of accurate-but-out-of-context quotation is a central feature of the New Testament, and understanding it is part of understanding not just Christianity but also rabbinic Judaism and other, lesser-known traditions like the Qumran Cult that gave us the Dead Sea Scrolls.

In the end, the question "Who is the voice crying in the wilderness?" has three answers: In the Old Testament, there is no such voice, because the voice isn't in the wilderness. In the New Testament, the voice is John the Baptist. And in the context of Christianity, it's again John the Baptist.

Because the pattern of Old Testament quotations in the New Testament is so important—here, as we just saw, and in the last chapter, as well—we continue with more examples next.

23

OLD TESTAMENT PROPHECIES FULFILLED IN THE NEW TESTAMENT

Does the New Testament say that it fulfills prophecies from the Old Testament? No.

One of the most widespread misconceptions about the New Testament comes from the kind of misquotation of text that we saw in the last two chapters. There's one pattern, in particular, that plays a central role in connecting the Old Testament to the New Testament. Unfortunately, it's widely misunderstood.

To get a sense of what goes wrong, and why it is so important, we start with a pivotal theological passage from James 2. Starting in verse 14, the text deals with the question of salvation, and whether it is achieved merely by believing, or whether some action is required, too. Going back to the KJV translation, the two potential parts of salvation earn the names "faith" and "works," so the question is whether faith alone can save, or whether faith requires works, too.

In verse 26, James concludes that "faith without works is dead." He's repeating the proposition that he put forth in verse 17: "Faith by itself, if it has no works, is dead." Understanding how James creates his argument will help us better understand the New Testament more generally.

In verse 20, James offers to demonstrate that "faith apart from works is barren." (He opens the verse by prejudicing the issue. The full line reads, "Do you want to be shown, you senseless person, that faith apart from works is barren?") His proof is Abraham, whose faith was accompanied by the most dramatic of works, the binding of his own son Isaac on an altar of sacrifice. "Wasn't our ancestor Abraham justified by works when he offered his son Isaac on the altar?" James asks rhetorically. "Faith was brought to completion by the works," James adds. His point is that it wasn't enough for Abraham to believe in God. He had to act on his belief, too.

As further proof, James quotes Genesis 15:6 of the Old Testament: "Abraham's faith in God was credited to him as righteousness." Most translations, unfortunately, mask the connection between James and Genesis. They use the terms "faith" and "works" in James, but translate Genesis 15:6, as quoted by James, with the word "believe." For instance, the NRSV offers "Abraham believed God, and it was reckoned to him as righteousness" in James, and the similar "And he believed the Lord; and the Lord reckoned it to him as righteousness" in Genesis itself. But in Hebrew and Greek, "belief" and "faith" are the same word. James quotes Genesis 15:6 because it contains the word "faith," and therefore matches the "faith" that he is talking about. So the English reader sees "believed" in one case, and "faith" in the other, while the ancient Greek reader would have seen the same root in both places.

Genesis 15:6 describes Abraham long before he nearly sacrifices his son Isaac. Abraham is still childless in Genesis 15, and he still goes by the name "Abram," not having yet changed his name as part of his pact with God. In verses 7–21, Abraham will experience one major part of that pact, the famous and exotic covenant of the split pieces, according to which he earns a future as the progenitor of a great nation. Right before that, God promises Abraham that his descendants will be as numerous as the stars, and Abraham believes him. God credits Abraham with this leap of faith. That's what Genesis 15:6 means by "and he believed the Lord; and the Lord reckoned it to him as righteousness."

The only connection between Genesis 15:6 and James's argument is the shared word "faith." Taken in isolation, Genesis 15:6 even seems to disprove James's thesis, because in Genesis 15, Abraham has yet to take any action. But that doesn't matter. The point is the word "faith."

To indicate why he is quoting Genesis 15:6 here, James uses a commonly mistranslated technical word in Greek: *plirow* (pli-RO-oh). A bit of investigation will show us what it really means and why it is so important.

According to James 2:22–23, "You see that faith was active along with Abraham's works, and faith was brought to completion by the works. [23] Thus the scripture was *plirow*'d that says, 'Abraham had faith. . . .'"

Because nowadays we don't usually cite text just because of a shared word, we don't have an exact English way of translating *plirow*. But, as we saw in the last two chapters, this shared-word sort of quotation was a central theme in the New Testament (and more widely in the ancient religious world), so we are not surprised that Greek had a term for it, even though English does not.

We can come pretty close to a translation with the English word "match," even though "match" is more general. The point in James is that his discussion of faith matches Abraham's faith. Unfortunately, a more common translation of *plirow* misleads the English reader.

In other contexts, the word *plirow* just means "fill." This might suggest an English translation of "fill in the blanks" when the word applies to Old Testament citations, except that it's naive to try to look too literally at a word when translating it. (We see what can go wrong by comparing the English words "host" and "hostile," which share the root "host" but are otherwise unconnected; or, for that matter, "strip-tease" and "strip mall.") Another naive translation of *plirow*, based on another superficial similarity, is the English word "fulfill." Alas, this is what the KJV translators chose.

Normally "fulfill" in English is itself pretty vague in meaning. Things that can be fulfilled range from duties to promises to obligations. So even though "fulfill" is the wrong translation for *plirow*, by itself it's vague enough that it doesn't do too much damage. However, one other thing that can be fulfilled is a prophecy. And the wrong translation "fulfill" combines with the prevalent spirit of prophecies to create the radical misimpression that *plirow* means "to fulfill a prophecy."

We know that that cannot be right. After all, the text that James cites here ("Abraham believed the Lord") isn't a prophecy at all. It's a simple statement in the past tense about what happened, not a prediction about what will happen. And James's point is precisely that it already happened. This bears no more resemblance to a prophecy than does any other simple statement about the past, say, "It rained yesterday."

Continuing that example, someone who observes that "it's raining today, which is interesting, because it rained yesterday" is not turning the previous day's rain into a prophecy or prediction of any sort, just observing that two things match. James was doing the same kind of thing. He was talking about faith, and his discussion matched Abraham's faith in Genesis.

Yet most translations stick with the hugely misleading and naive rendition from the KJV. So the NRSV text of James 2:23 reads, "Thus the scripture was fulfilled that says, 'Abraham believed . . . ,'" even though this is not how we usually use "fulfill" in English, and, worse, even though it creates the false image of a prophecy in the mind of the reader.

We see another example of the same kind of translation gaffe in the translation of how John 19:24 cites Psalm 22:18, in the context of Jesus's crucifixion. James writes that the Roman soldiers, after they had crucified Jesus, took his clothes and also his tunic. Then "they said to one another, 'let us not tear it, but cast lots to see who will get it.' This was to fulfill what the scripture says, 'They divided my clothes among themselves, and for my clothing they cast lots.'"

The quotation is from Psalm 22, which begins with the famous "My god, my god, why have you forsaken me?" (Mark 15:34 and Matthew 27:46 record that Jesus quoted this line.) Psalm 22 presents an impassioned plea by an anonymous person in tremendous pain—probably someone suffering from illness, to judge from verses 14–15 (also numbered 15–16): "my bones are out of joint . . . my tongue sticks to the top of my mouth." The psalm has a complex dramatic form that weaves together the subject's suffering and despair with notes of hope and gratitude. Following the poignant descriptions in verses 14–15, we find "save my life from the sword . . . save me from the mouth of the lion" and then, in verse 27, "All the ends of the earth will remember and turn to the Lord," which leads into the triumphant ending that "God has acted."

Amid the graphic depictions of his body falling apart, the subject of Psalm 22 compares a group of people mocking him to a pack of dogs circling him and closing in, nipping at his limbs. They "divide my clothes among themselves, casting lots for my garments." And this is the connection to John 19:24.

By reference, then, John incorporates the vivid language of suffering from Psalm 22 into his account of Jesus's crucifixion. The ancient reader familiar with Psalms would have recalled the ailing body, the despair, and the mocking onlookers behaving like a pack of dogs. The crucifixion of Jesus matches Psalm 22.

But the bulk of Psalm 22 is certainly not a prophecy (though the ending of the psalm to the effect that future generations will serve God might potentially have been). There is nothing here to be fulfilled. And John is not saying that Psalm 22 was written about Jesus. Rather, his point is more powerful. We can convey it by fixing the erroneous word "fulfill" to give us a better translation: "This matches what scripture says, 'They divided my clothes among themselves, and for my clothing they cast lots . . .'" or "This is like . . ."

This pattern of reference is widespread in the New Testament, and we find numerous examples in addition to Genesis 15:6 in James 2:23 and Psalm 22:18 in John 19:24. Time and again, statements in the Old Testament—whether about the past, the present, or the future—are taken out of context and inserted directly into New Testament accounts to enhance their detail, vividness, and impact.

In common speech today, we often quote only part of a line to refer to a whole set of circumstances. "*Et tu, Brute?*" conjures a complex image of betrayal at the hands of a trusted adviser. " 'Tis better to have loved and lost" automatically references the second line of the famous quotation, "Than never to have loved at all," and thereby offers (dubious) advice to the lovesick. The pithy "Other than that, Mrs. Lincoln?" represents a longer, mocking, hypothetical question—"Other than that, Mrs. Lincoln, how did you enjoy the play?"—and with it a general if ill-timed query about setting aside true tragedy to find superficial pleasure.

The Old Testament citations were similar to these snippets, but also much more powerful, because in addition to using only a few words to create a complex image in the mind of the reader, the quotations were of holy scripture. By bringing them into the New Testament (which wasn't scripture yet), the authors incorporated the divine into their work. This is why the Jews did the same thing with their early-first-millennium-A.D. texts like the Midrash and worship services—the difference being that for the Jews their secondary texts were never considered on a par with the Old Testament. (This is why some Jews object to the implications of the term "Old Testament," there being, for them, just one testament.)

So we see an innovative and complex literary technique at work, and we learn about the nature of religion two thousand years ago. That is our silver lining for giving up "fulfillment of prophecy," which we now recognize as a complete misunderstanding of the original intention of the text. Where our translations say "fulfills"—based on a naive four-hundred-year-old understanding of language—we should read "matches."

One such instance of matching is so pivotal that it deserves its own detailed treatment, so we turn to it next.

24

THE VIRGIN BIRTH

Was there really a virgin birth in the Bible? **No and yes, in that order.**

The virgin birth of Jesus to Mary is a cornerstone of Christian belief, and has been for nearly two thousand years. Yet for all its centrality, it remains a matter of controversy not just because of the boldness of the claim that a virgin woman conceived and gave birth, but because of two different kinds of confusion about the text. The result is that some people (wrongly) claim that both the Old Testament and the New Testament refer to Jesus's birth to a virgin Mary, while other people (wrongly) claim that the virgin birth is just a mistranslation. The truth is more nuanced and more interesting.

On one hand, the Gospels of Matthew and Luke are clear on the matter.

According to Matthew 1:18, Jesus is born to Mary, who becomes pregnant before having sex with her betrothed, Joseph: "When Jesus's mother Mary had been engaged to Joseph, but before they lived together, she was found to be with child from the Holy Spirit." We recall from our chapter 6 that this is the second part of Matthew's answer to the unasked question "Who is Jesus?"

The literal translation of the language here, from the NRSV, in theory leaves open various possible interpretations: for instance maybe Mary and Joseph were having sex before they lived together. So do other common translations, including the KJV, which attributes Mary's pregnancy to the time before she and Joseph "came together." But the text is clear, in spite of the euphemism for sex. Joseph and Mary had not yet had sex when Mary became pregnant.

To drive home the point, Matthew 1:19–20 explains that Joseph worried about marrying the now-pregnant Mary, but an angel explains to him that he shouldn't be concerned, because the "child conceived in her is from the Holy Spirit." Again, this leaves open the technical possibility that the child, though not Joseph's, belonged to another man, but only if the angel was lying. And we find nothing in the text to support that suggestion.

Luke is even more direct. Luke 1:27 indicates specifically that Mary is a virgin. In verse 31, a visiting angel tells Mary that she will conceive, and she wonders, in verse 34, how that is possible since she is still a virgin—literally, "has not known a man." The angel assures her in the following verses that she will conceive by power of the "Holy Spirit," and, furthermore, that unlikely pregnancies are well attested, because nothing is too difficult for God. It's still possible to try to find an out: Mary is a virgin when the angel visits, but maybe she doesn't stay a virgin; maybe "know a man" isn't exactly the same thing as having sex; and more. But these are clear attempts to force a reading onto the text that isn't there. This is a passage about a virgin giving birth.

So that part is clear. Both Gospels report that Jesus was born to a virgin Mary.

The confusion starts with the continuation of Matthew's account.

As the NRSV has it, "All this took place to fulfill what had been spo-ken by the Lord through the prophet: 'Look, the virgin shall conceive and bear a son, and they shall name him Emmanuel,' which means 'God is with us.'" We already know, from the last chapter, that we should replace the word "fulfill" here with the more accurate "match." Matthew is matching his account of Jesus's virgin birth with part of the Old Testament.

The part he has in mind is Isaiah 7:14. And this is the first source of confusion, because Isaiah isn't originally about a virgin. It's about a young woman. The Hebrew word for the woman who gets pregnant in Isaiah 7:14 is *alma,* and we know from elsewhere that the word doesn't mean "virgin," but rather "young woman."

How, then, could Matthew quote Isaiah? We saw in the last three chapters that the point of aligning two texts was that the words had to match up, even if the meanings did not. What matches here? In this case, the Greek translation called the Septuagint provides the bridge between Isaiah and Matthew, in the form of one tiny translation mis-take. Where the Hebrew talks about a young woman (*alma*) in Isaiah, the Greek there refers to a virgin (*parthenos*).

Though it seems like a pretty big goof now, in antiquity most young women were virgins and most female virgins were young women, so translating one as the other was a pretty good approximation. We have lots of pairs of words now that are similar enough that mixing them up would be reasonable in most circumstances. One example is "village" and "town"; there are technical distinctions between the two (some people insist that a town has to have a market, while a village only needs a church), but they are mostly interchangeable. In a place where everyone drives a car, "automobile" and "vehicle" can be used in place of each other. For most people, "teenager" and "high-schooler" mean roughly the same thing, even though there are teenagers who are not in high school and high-schoolers who are not teenagers. Similar to these modern pairs, "virgin" and "young woman" in antiquity were close enough for most purposes.

Many modern readers are surprised that the hugely influential Septuagint would make do with "good enough" or "close enough" or "almost" for its translation. But the goal of the Septuagint was never just to mimic the Hebrew exactly, and we frequently find rough or imprecise translations. For instance, the Hebrew of Genesis 24:16 describes a "young woman who was a virgin," but the Septuagint, content with near matches for vocabulary, inadvertently changed that into the silly "a virgin who was a virgin." It didn't matter. The point was still clear.

There is, though, one case in which the difference between a young woman in general and a virgin specifically is crucial, and that is when she is pregnant. The Hebrew of Isaiah 7:14 reads, "Therefore the Lord himself will give you a sign. Look, the young woman is with child and shall bear a son, and shall name him Emmanuel." But the Greek turns that into "a virgin is with child." The Greek version of Isaiah 7:14 is a mistranslation of the Hebrew.

So it's true that Isaiah 7:14 is about a sign, but—in spite of the Greek—the sign is certainly not a virgin birth. It's not even clear that the sign is the birth at all. The sign might be the child's name, "Emmanuel," which means "God is with us." Or, based on the next verse, the sign might be the child's diet: "He shall eat curds and honey by the time he knows how to reject evil and choose good." And the text doesn't indicate when the sign will appear.

The only thing that is clear, from this passage and from the larger context, is that the prophet Isaiah intercedes during a spat between God and a king named Ahaz. Starting in verse 10, God and Ahaz engage in verbal sparring over whether Ahaz needs to ask for a sign from God: God taunts Ahaz, "Go ahead, ask for a sign." The king replies, "I don't need a sign; I trust you." This is when Isaiah intervenes and tells Ahaz not to worry. God isn't helpless. God will take the initiative and "give you a sign." (This is why the NRSV says, "the Lord himself"—to indicate "of his own accord," similar to the way a parent might chastise a child: "I shouldn't have to tell you to do your chores. You should know to do them yourself.") The sign—whatever it is—is from God for King Ahaz.

The Greek mistranslation of Isaiah 7:14 that turned a pregnant young woman into a pregnant virgin is unfortunate, but hardly a matter for too much concern. There are far worse mistranslations in the Greek Septuagint. (We already saw in our chapter 9 that the Greek turned the Hebrew verb "take" in the Ten Commandments into "desire," and in our chapter 21 we noted that the Greek added the word "word" to Deuteronomy 8:3, making it easier for Matthew to quote that text to mean that we can subsist on God's word alone.)

Many English translations, misunderstanding the way Old Testament passages are quoted in the New Testament, insist on rendering the Hebrew of Isaiah 7:14 as "virgin," even though it's clear that the original word there means "young woman." Frequently, the motivation behind this purposeful mistranslation is to bolster the account in Matthew, reinforcing Jesus's virgin birth.

But the reasoning is faulty. We already know that the same words in the Old Testament and the New Testament can mean different things. This is the pattern we saw with "what God says" that became "God's word" and with the voice crying about the wilderness that became a voice in the wilderness. Quoting out of context was acceptable and even desirable. Furthermore, there are other inconsistencies between Matthew and Isaiah. Most obviously, the child in Isaiah is named "Emmanuel" while the child in Matthew is named "Jesus." And as we saw above, Matthew even quotes the part of Isaiah that mentions Emmanuel's name ("All this took place to fulfill what had been spoken by the Lord through the prophet: 'Look, the virgin shall conceive and bear a son, and they shall name him Emmanuel' ").

Some people look at the text of Matthew and conclude that the writer just made a mistake based on the faulty Greek translation in the Septuagint. But in light of all of the evidence, this doesn't seem likely. It's not just that the children have different names and the contexts don't match. Matthew would certainly have known Hebrew. And this is not the only place where Matthew quotes an Old Testament passage completely out of context.

Rather, the Greek mistranslation opened the door for Matthew to connect the virgin birth in the New Testament to an otherwise unrelated passage in the Old Testament, which, in its new context, provided commentary on Jesus's life as Matthew understood it.

So originally there was no virgin birth in the Old Testament. Then a mistranslation created one. And there was a virgin birth in the New Testament all along.

In this case, the misunderstanding comes from two sources: a general misconception about the Greek word *plirow* (as we saw in the last chapter) and a specific translation error in the ancient Greek Septuagint. But at least we are able to identify the mistakes clearly. Other times, as we'll see next, we're unsure what the best translation should be.

25

MOSES'S HORNS

Did Moses have horns? Maybe.

Michelangelo's famous statue of Moses in the church of San Pietro in Vincoli in Rome features prominent horns extending from Moses's head. So does the bas-relief of Moses in the House Chamber in the US Capitol. These and many other works going back nearly a thousand years represent the once-common way of understanding Moses: He had horns.

This horned Moses is now closely connected to anti-Semitism, along with a belief—born variously of similar anti-Semitism or sometimes of ignorance—that all Jews have horns. After all, the Devil, too, has horns. This vicious aspect can make it difficult to talk about where Moses's horns come from, but here we ignore the social implications and jump right to the heart of the matter.

Exodus 34 details Moses's descent from Mount Sinai after he received the Ten Commandments from God. Verse 29 reads, "Moses came down from Mount Sinai. As he came down from the mountain with the two tablets of the covenant in his hand, Moses did not know that the skin of his face shone because he had been talking with God."

Then verse 35 explains that "the Israelites would see the face of Moses, that the skin of his face was shining." This has essentially been the understanding of the text going back at least as far as the KJV, which—except for now-archaic verbs like "wist" for "know"—agrees with our translation here from the NRSV. So far, there's nothing about horns.

However, the Hebrew verb for "shine" (*karan*) is more general than its English counterpart. It refers variously to anything that starts small and gets larger. One obvious such thing is a ray of light. So *karan* means "shone," and the related noun *keren* means "ray of light."

But light is not the only thing that follows this pattern. Metaphorically, investment funds also start small and grow (or at least they're supposed to). This is why the Hebrew word *keren* refers both specifically to "principal" and more generally to "fund." We see the former meaning in a passage from the early-first-millennium compendium of Jewish law called the Talmud (in Shabbat 127a), which compares commandments to investments. Those who follow them earn interest on them in this world, while the principal investment, the *keren*, is safely squirreled away for use in the world to come. We see the latter meaning of "fund" more generally in the Hebrew name of the global real-estate project called the Jewish National Fund. In Hebrew, that's the "Ongoing *keren* for Israel" (*keren kayemet l'yisra'el*).

There is another, much more ubiquitous object that starts small and grows: a horn. (Technically a horn, while still attached to an animal, may start large and shrink, the larger end being the one that is attached to the animal. But when detached from the animal and used as a musical or other instrument, the horn starts small, near the mouth of the trumpeter, and grows.) So *keren* in Hebrew also means "horn." And because verbs and nouns are closely related, the verb *karan* can mean "was horned" in addition to "glowed." (Based on the imagery of something that resembles a horn, *keren* by association also sometimes indicates strength in general and male fertility in particular.)

So when we see Moses's face described with the verb *karan* in Exodus, we know that the text refers either literally to something that starts small and grows, or figuratively to something related to such a physical object. The Septuagint thinks that the verb *karan* here means "was glorified." The glory, presumably, came from Moses's recent encounter with God. The influential Latin translation by Saint Jerome called the Vulgate (from around the end of the fourth century A.D.), by contrast, thinks that Moses's face was "horned." Our English translations agree on "glowed." Because of the broad semantic range of the Hebrew *karan*, all of these are reasonable interpretations of the text.

Furthermore, horns used to have a primarily positive connotation, which is why they graced everything from royal ceremonial headdresses across the world, including the Ancient Near East, to the altar of the great temple as described, for instance, in Leviticus 4:7: "The priest shall put some of the blood of the sacrifice on the horns of the altar." Coins from the late fourth century B.C. depict a horned Alexander the Great. Mesopotamian gods wore horned hats. And so forth. Light was similarly a positive image, the way it is today. We've already seen, in our discussion of the nuances of "heart" and "shepherd," that words almost always come with metaphoric implications. "Light," "glowing," and "horned" are no different. In particular, all three were good things.

Light continues to be a positive image today, which is why the proverbial light at the end of the tunnel is a good thing, and why Juliet (as we saw in chapter 16) is compared to light and to the sun. As it happens, even though the sun used to be considered dangerous, light was always positive. This is why "light" in the book of Esther is part of the sequence "light, gladness, joy, and honor" (8:16) that marks the victory of the Jews over their evil oppressors.

Horns, however, are now negative, connoting evil in general or the Devil more specifically. This is why "horned" and "glowing" are now practically opposites, even though they used to mean roughly the same thing.

Against all of this background, we can ask, but not fully answer, "What did the text originally mean? Does the text give Moses horns or rays of light?" The important part of the answer is that it doesn't matter. Either way, the point was that Moses was graced with a positive indication that conveyed his closeness to the divine. Both horns and light would have been appropriate. So we know what the text means.

The less important part of the question is whether Moses would have been visualized with light or with horns. Unfortunately, we really don't know. It has become popular to blithely assume that *karan* obviously meant "glowing," and that Saint Jerome obviously blew it. But neither part of that claim is obvious. Among other possibilities, Moses may have had horns of light, in which case both "horned" and "glowing" would be right. Or he may have been glowing, but only in a good sense, along the lines of "radiant," obviously not in the negative sense of "radioactive." Or he may have had horns, but again, in the good sense, even though it is difficult for us to appreciate it now.

So this is not just a potential mistranslation mistake from the fourth century. It may not have been a mistake at all, but even if it was, it shows us yet again that we have to take culture into account when looking at what the text of the Bible means. If Michelangelo's statue is misleading, it's only because the implications of horns have changed.

The past several chapters have exposed various ways the text of the Bible can be misunderstood, as everything from translation mistakes to cultural mismatches hide what the text used to mean. In addition, sometimes the line between what the Bible says and what people say about the Bible becomes so blurred that things that aren't even in the Bible masquerade as direct statements. We saw one example of this in chapter 14. Perhaps the most widespread example takes us right back to Genesis, as we see next.

26

THE APPLE FROM THE
GARDEN OF EDEN

***Was the forbidden fruit in the garden of Eden an apple?* No.**

Few biblical images are more familiar than the famous forbidden apple from the Tree of Knowledge in the Garden of Eden. Adam and Eve weren't supposed to eat it, but the snake convinced Eve to disobey God. She took a bite, then offered some to Adam, paving the way for the first couple's downfall and, according to modern Christian theology, the state of fallenness in which humans still live. All because of an apple.

The story, and, in particular, the snake and the apple, are so well known that a drawing of a snake and an apple is enough to evoke the entire saga.

But the Bible doesn't say it was an apple. In fact, there aren't even any mainstream translations that refer to it as an apple. (For all their popularity, the images of the snake and the apple are, in fact, doubly inaccurate, because the snake in the Garden of Eden still walks on feet, locomotion on its belly being the result of God's punishment only after it gives the non-apple fruit to Eve.)

There was a Tree of Knowledge, more fully called the Tree of

Knowledge of Good and Evil (or the Tree of Knowing Good and Evil). And it had fruit, from which Eve ate at the snake's urging. But the Bible doesn't specify what kind of fruit it was.

This popular misconception that the fruit was an apple actually comes from a Latin coincidence (like the jubilation of the "jubilee year" coming up next). The Latin word for "evil" is *malus*. Like most Latin words, it changes its form depending on how it is used in a sentence. So in the "Tree of Knowledge of Good and Evil," the Latin word for "evil" is *mali*. In the similar expression "knowing good and evil," the Latin word is *malum*. As it happens, *malum* in Latin also means "apple." So by coincidence, "evil" and "apple" often sound the same in Latin.

At least, *malum* means "apple" in the general sense of an apple-like fruit. Pomegranates were a kind of a *malum*, for example.

For that matter, the English word "apple" used to be pretty vague, too, used for any round, fleshy fruit. The most common kind of "apples" according to this broader usage were what we would now call "crab apples," but they were rarely fit for human consumption. (They were, however, excellent bases from which to make booze, which is how John "Johnny Appleseed" Chapman was able to make a business out of his crab-apple trees.)

We still see remnants of this older English usage in words like "pineapple," which, of course, isn't an apple but is a wholly different fruit. The pomegranate used to be known as the "apple Punic." And some English dialects know of an "earth apple," which is actually a potato. French still calls potatoes *pommes de terre,* literally, "apples of the earth," as do many other languages.

It wasn't until grafting was perfected that we were able to create the modern apples that are reliably edible, because the genetic variation in apple seeds is so great that the fruit of a tree grown from one seldom resembles the original. For example, the seeds of a Golden Delicious apple are unlikely to produce a Golden Delicious apple tree. So certainly the fruit of the tree in the Bible wasn't a modern apple.

But it probably wasn't even an apple of any sort. Ancient sources like the hugely popular book of Enoch record the fruit as being a kind of grape. The Talmud (in Berachot 40a and Sanhedrin 70a–70b) from the first half of the first millennium A.D. records a debate about the fruit, with opinions ranging from grape to fig to wheat. And the Midrash from roughly the same time period suggests that the fruit may have been a citron, also known by its Hebrew name, *etrog.*

The grape was appropriate, according to Rabbi Meir in the Talmud, because nothing makes a man weep the way wine can. Wine was even Noah's downfall. (According to Genesis 9:21–22, Noah got drunk and embarrassed himself in front of his children.) The rationale behind the fig is that Adam and Eve fashioned clothing from fig leaves. What better poetic justice than for them to use the instrument of their downfall to cover themselves up? And wheat made sense because of the ancient view that an important stage in children's maturation is the ability to eat solid food, made from grain, which can come from wheat; and eating from the Tree of Knowledge was a kind of maturation. All of these, and the citron, have the benefit of growing in the Ancient Near East, unlike apple-like fruit.

Of course, grapes grow on vines, not trees, and wheat, which also doesn't grow on a tree, isn't even a fruit. The Rabbis found ways around these objections, such as the possibility that the "tree" was actually a huge wheat stalk. None of the debate would have possible, though, if there had been any consensus about the species of fruit from the tree. We see very clearly that they didn't know what the fruit was.

Discussions like these also show us an older way of answering the question "What kind of fruit was it?" Nowadays, we might ask scientists or historians. But in antiquity, they asked what the fruit *should* be: something with poetic justice (like the fig) or broader implications (like the grape). In this context, the similarity of the original Latin words for "evil" and "apple" would have been particularly compelling.

Returning to modernity—and basing an answer not on wishful thinking but on history—we have, in fact, two questions: "In antiquity, what did they think the fruit was?" And "What was the fruit really?"

We've already answered the first question. Opinions varied, but did not include the apple.

In terms of the second question, the fruit may have been metaphoric. Or, if it was intended as a specific variety, what we know is this: The fruit had to exist in antiquity (ruling out the modern apple). It had to grow in that part of the world, which is to say, the Ancient Near East (all but ruling out most forms of crab apples and other applelike fruit). It had to grow on trees (so it wasn't wheat or grapes.) This leaves a couple of guesses, which, while not particularly informed, are the best we have. And at the top of the list is the pomegranate.

This isn't the only place Latin coincidences distort the original meaning of the Bible. We see another one next.

27

THE JUBILEE YEAR

Is there a year of jubilation in the Bible? No.

According to Leviticus 25:10, every fiftieth year is a special celebration: "And you shall hallow the fiftieth year and you shall proclaim liberty throughout the land to all its inhabitants. It shall be a jubilee for you." The word "jubilee" occurs thirteen more times before chapter 25 ends, and then chapter 27 returns to the theme, so this jubilation was obviously a matter of some importance.

Leviticus 25:10 is most famous today for its proclamation of liberty, and its words appear on the famous Liberty Bell, in Pennsylvania: "Proclaim LIBERTY throughout all the Land unto all the Inhabitants thereof." The Liberty Bell was designed to commemorate the fiftieth anniversary of the state's original constitution, William Penn's Charter of Privileges in 1701. So it was probably not a coincidence that Leviticus 25:10, whose text demands the sanctification of the fiftieth year, was chosen to appear on the bell. (Abolitionists in the 1800s are the ones who dubbed the bell the "Liberty Bell.")

These two notions of freedom and celebration are so intertwined that it's easy to read Leviticus 25:10 as an instruction to combine liberty and jubilation every fifty years. But that's not at all what Leviticus means here.

The first part of Leviticus 25 details the "sabbatical" year, so called because it is a year of rest that comes around every seven years, just as the Sabbath is a day of rest on every seventh day. Every seven years, according to Leviticus 25:4, "there shall be a complete rest for the land, a sabbath for the Lord: you shall not sow your field or prune your vineyard." The commandment appears earlier, too, in Exodus 23:10–11: "For six years you shall sow your land and gather its yield; [11] but the seventh year you shall let it rest and lie fallow, so that the poor of your people may eat; and what they leave the wild animals may eat." This language matches what the text says next about the Sabbath itself: "Six days you shall do your work, but on the seventh day you shall rest."

The fiftieth year is the natural culmination of seven sets of sabbatical years, and this is how it is explained in Leviticus 25:8: "You shall count off seven Sabbaths of years, seven times seven years." Reinforcing the theme of sevens, verse 9 instructs that a trumpet be sounded in the seventh month to mark the occasion. (Counting was an inexact science in antiquity, and what we would now call the forty-ninth year was sometimes called the fiftieth year back then. The confusion comes from where one starts counting. The time period between now and one year from now includes two years, this year and next year, so one year from now was sometimes called the first year, sometimes the second. According to the latter reckoning, the seventh sabbatical year would fall in the fiftieth year, not the forty-ninth.) So the fiftieth year was like a super-sabbatical year.

Letting the land lie fallow every seven years seems to be good farming practice. And the text of the exodus story emphasizes Joseph's skill in storing food. So the sabbatical year may have been a real practice in the ancient world.

There is less evidence about the jubilee year, and the Rabbis of the first millennium A.D. record in the Talmud that the jubilee year was not practiced at the end of the first millennium B.C., during the days of the great temple. However, other ancient societies enforced a fifty-year cycle designed to bolster financial and political stability: Every fifty years debts would be canceled in order to minimize gaps in power and wealth, those gaps being considered destabilizing forces. So this may have been an actual practice in ancient Israel.

Though our translations talk about "freedom" being proclaimed in the jubilee year, better would be "release." Servants are released from servitude, and the land released from ownership. The text even addresses details of how real-estate deals interact with the jubilee year. This focus on release as opposed to freedom in general is our first hint that our perceived connection between "freedom" and "jubilation" might be deceptive.

And it is. Because the idea of dubbing the year the "jubilee year" comes from a Latin coincidence. In Hebrew, the year is called the "*yovel* year," and it looks like *yovel* refers in general to a ram and more specifically to a ram's horn. The "*yovel* year" got its name, probably, from the tradition of sounding a trumpet of some sort to inaugurate it (in the seventh month, as we just saw). It turns out that there's a Latin root *jubil-* (or *iubil-*) that sounds remarkably like the Latinized form of the Hebrew *yovel*, which is *jobel-* (or *iobel-*). The Latin root *jubil*, which is the source of our English word "jubilation," just happens to refer to celebration. This similarity of sound between *jubil* and *jobel* prompted English translators to render what should have been "the *jobel* year" as "the jubilee year."

The original text made no mention of celebration or jubilation at all. This is how a fifty-year cycle of release as marked by the sounding of trumpets became a year of jubilation and freedom.

We saw in the last chapter that the fruit on the Tree of Knowledge came to be known as an apple because the Latin for "apple" and the Latin for "evil" sound the same. But at least there, translations didn't start using the word "apple." So a curious reader could check an English translation to see whether the fruit was called an apple or not. Here we have a more severe problem, because English translations going back to the King James Version (when "jubile" was spelled with only one "e") force a connection between the fiftieth year and celebration that is entirely absent in the original text.

In the end, the difference between a fiftieth year of jubilation and a fiftieth year of sounding a horn is a relatively unimportant one. As we'll see next, errors also plague central theological matters like Jesus's titles.

28

THE SON OF MAN AND
THE SON OF GOD

Does the Bible call Jesus the "son of man"? No.
Does the Bible call Jesus the "son of God"? No, but also yes.

According to most New Testament translations, one common term for
Jesus is "son of man," and because this is considered a divine title, the
phrase is often capitalized as "Son of Man." For instance, Matthew 9:6
explains Jesus's authority to forgive sins: "the Son of Man has authority on earth to forgive sins." Yet the English "son of man" doesn't convey the original intent of the text.

On one hand, it's easy to see where the traditional translation comes
from. Greek has a common phrase *huios anthropou*. One literal translation for *huios* is "son," and for *anthropou*, "of man." (*Anthropou*
comes from the word *anthropos*, which we encountered in chapter 12.
The change from -*os* at the end to -*ou* is the equivalent of the English
word "of.")

A related phrase adds the Greek word *tou*, which means "the." So
one literal translation of that longer phrase—*huios tou anthropou*—is
"son of the man." But a quirk of English correctly eliminates the word

"the" in that context. (The quirk itself is interesting. Normally in English, we use the word "the" for two purposes. The first is to refer to one specific thing. The difference between "a snake" and "the snake" is that we use "the snake" to refer to a specific snake. The second use is to refer to the species itself. For example, "The coyote is gradually returning to Yellowstone Park" means that coyotes in general are returning, not that one lone animal is making a trek. We might therefore expect that "the man" could refer both to a single human and also to humankind. In English it does not, but in Greek it does.)

The original text of the Bible didn't have capitalization, so as we render the ancient text in English, we have to decide what to capitalize. Names like "Abraham" and "Matthew" are normally capitalized, because names always get initial capital letters in English. In addition, words referring to God are often capitalized. This is why almost every translation uses a capital "G" in the word "god" even when the word is generic, as, for example, in Isaiah 30:18: "For the Lord is a God of justice." (For other reasons, some translations print "Lord" in all caps: "LORD.") Some translations even capitalize the pronouns that refer to God, again as in Isaiah 30:18: "Happy are all who wait for Him."

So just as it's easy to see how the Greek phrases *huios anthropou* and *huios tou anthropou* became "son of man," we understand how those phrases came to be capitalized as "Son of Man" when they refer to Jesus.

But in spite of the logic that led to it, this translation does more to mislead than to inform. There are three problems.

First, both words of the phrase in Greek are more general than they are in English. The Greek word *huios* means "member (of a group)" in addition to "son" or "child." For instance, Matthew 9:15 talks about "wedding guests" using a Greek phrase that literally means "sons of the wedding-hall." Obviously, though, "sons" makes no sense in this context, because that English word is much more specific than the Greek *huios*. And the Greek word *anthropos* refers to humankind. In some English dialects, "man" has a similarly broad meaning, but for many speakers, "man" is more limited than the general "humankind" or "human."

Secondly, both *huios* and *anthropos* in Greek are gender-neutral, referring equally to men and women. So we don't know if those wedding guests in Matthew 9:15 are men or women, and we already saw in chapter 12 that the plural of *anthropos* means "people." So even though *huios anthropou* literally means "son of man," it also literally means "child of a person."

From these first two problems, we see that "member of the human race" is just as literal a translation of the Greek as is "son of man." This is why the Common English Bible in 2011 decided to substitute "Human One" for "Son of Man."

There's a third problem with "son of man" as a translation. The phrase *huios anthropou* is actually pretty common in both the New Testament and the Old Testament. In the Old Testament, it is the translation of the Hebrew *ben adam*. The Hebrew word *ben* is parallel to the Greek *huios,* referring variously to "son," "child," or "member." And the Hebrew word *adam* means "person" (and happens also to be Adam's name in Hebrew).

For instance, in Psalm 80:17 we find the word *ish* ("person") in parallel with *ben adam*. (In chapter 22 we saw how useful parallel structure can be for figuring out what ancient words mean.) The NRSV, recognizing that both *ish* and *ben adam* mean "person," translates both as "the one": "But let your hand be upon the one [*ish*] at your right hand, the one [*ben adam*] whom you made strong for yourself." Numbers 23:19 asserts that God is divine, not human—that is, not a *ben adam*. In both cases the Greek translation of the Hebrew phrase is *huios anthropou*. Genesis 11:5 deals with the Tower of

Babel that "the humans" built, putting "the *ben adam*" in the plural, which, because of complicated aspects of Hebrew grammar, becomes *b'nai ha-adam.* There the Greek is the plural of the three-word phrase, literally, "sons of the man," clearly a reference to just "humans" or "mortals." Mark 3:28 deals with people who will be forgiven for their sins, and the Greek phrase for "people" is, once again, the plural of *huios tou anthropou.*

So we see that the Hebrew *ben adam* and the Greek *huios anthropou*—even though they both literally mean "son of man"—usually simply mean "human."

This common phrase is used to special effect in the book of Ezekiel, where that prophet frequently quotes God as addressing him not by name but rather as *ben adam* in Hebrew, which of course becomes *huios anthropou* in Greek. For example, Ezekiel 2:1 reads, "God said to me: O mortal [*ben adam*], stand up on your feet, and I will speak with you."

Then in the New Testament, we find a subtle distinction: the shorter *huios anthropou* ("son of man") appears only four times, and of those, the only case where the author clearly means Jesus is John 5:27. But the longer *huios tou anthropou* ("son of the man") refers to Jesus almost exclusively (or perhaps even exclusively—the metaphoric nature of some of the texts leaves room for uncertainty).

This creates a progression of sorts. We have "a human one" or "a mortal" or, much less accurately, "a son of man" throughout the Old Testament, referring variously to people in general or to specific people. Then, in the New Testament, we have "the human one" or "the mortal" or (again, less accurately) "the son of man" referring to Jesus. The real key seems to be the addition of the word "the," as if to say, "Jesus is *the* human."

Unfortunately, the translation "Son of Man" hides this aspect of the original Greek as well. The standard translation isn't just too narrow, wrongly gender-specific, and too exotic; it masks what seems to be the point of the phrase. Jesus in the New Testament isn't just any old mortal. He is *the* mortal.

One easy way to convey this in English would be settle on "mortal" or "human," and then capitalize the word when it refers to Jesus. So we'd have "humans" in general building the Tower of Babel. Ezekiel would be addressed as "human." And Jesus would be "the Human."

That would be a concise, accurate, and easy solution to translating the New Testament, but for one thing. Jesus is also called the "son of God," a phrase that matches "son of man," except that in place of the Greek word for "of man" (*anthropou*) we find "of God" (*theou*).

On one hand, the same objections we saw about "son" in the phrase "son of man" apply here as well. It's the same Greek word *huios*, and it means "member" or "child" or "son," not just "son." For instance, the infamous fallen angels, the "*nephilim*" of Genesis 6:4, are called literally the "sons of God," but the point is "divine beings." According to Romans 8:14, people who are led by God are the "sons of God," that is, "holy people," just as Galatians 3:26 asserts that people become more godly ("sons of God") through faith. So in one sense, "divine one" for the Greek would be just right, and would match "human one."

But on the other hand, according to the theology of the New Testament Jesus is actually God's son, born through Mary. In that regard, "son of God" is exactly right. So even though there is nothing to recommend the translation "son of man" for Jesus, "son of God" has some merit.

We end up with a dilemma. We could express the transition from human to divine with "the Human" and "the Divine," a pair of terms that reflects much of the original point. But it misses the father-son relationship inherent in "son of God." If, then, we use "son of God," we are all but locked in to using "son of man," the more accurate "son of humanity" not matching "son of God" in quite the same way. So to capture the ways in which Jesus is actually God's son, we have no choice but to use English phrases that, as we saw, hide the down-to-earth nature of the original along with its gender inclusivity.

More broadly, we learn that simply reading the words of the Bible is not enough to understand them.

29

KEEPING KOSHER

Does the Bible tell people to keep kosher? **No.**

Most of the past twenty chapters have focused on how direct statements in the Bible get distorted through mistranslation, misunderstanding, and misquotation, whether by accident or on purpose (or both). Below, we'll contrast these direct messages with the Bible's indirect messages. Before we get there, it will be helpful to expand the third category of things the Bible "says": things it doesn't say at all. We've already seen that the fruit in the Garden of Eden wasn't an apple, and the jubilee year wasn't a year of jubilation. But because there are no modern practices based on either one, the misguided popular conceptions and translations rarely translate into action. But there are also central religious practices that—again contrary to popular conception—are not in the Bible.

We start with the Jewish custom of "keeping kosher." Jewish practice divides food into two major categories: "kosher" and "nonkosher." The kosher foods are the ones that may be eaten, and, therefore, the nonkosher foods are the ones that may not. Pork, for instance, isn't kosher, so some Jews do not eat it. (By extension, the word "kosher" means anything that is religiously permissible, and by further extension, anything at all that is permissible, genuine, or appropriate.)

Perhaps the most widely known aspects of eating kosher are that mixing meat and milk at the same meal is forbidden, and, as we just saw, that pork products are prohibited. The details are much more complex, and extend beyond single foods and permissible combinations to the manner in which an animal is killed and the way in which the food is prepared. Meat from ruminants (animals like cows and deer, which chew their cud) that have a split hoof is potentially kosher, so long as they are slaughtered properly. Animals, like camels, that chew their cud but don't have a split hoof are forbidden, along with animals, like pigs, that do have a split hoof but don't chew their cud. Dairy products from kosher mammals are potentially kosher. (This categorization based on the shape of an animal's hoof is not unique to the details of kosher food. We saw in chapter 18 that Pliny the Elder, writing in the first century A.D., observed that—except for the unicorn—no toed or solid-hoofed animals have horns. In his same chapter 45 of book 11, he also notes that animals with split hooves have two horns, unless they have foreteeth in the upper jaw. He was responding to Aristotle, who, much earlier in his *On the Parts of Animals,* connected the multiplicity of stomachs in ruminants to their lack of foreteeth.)

Fruits and vegetables are in principle always kosher. Fish with fins and scales are kosher, while other fish are not. (There is debate about fish like swordfish, which have scales when young but not once they mature.) Shellfish are considered fish, and, not having scales and fins, aren't kosher. Some birds, like chickens, are kosher; others, birds of prey in particular, are not. Birds that naturally interbreed with kosher birds are kosher, as are birds whose eggs look like the eggs of kosher birds. Dairy products, though kosher, are not kosher in combination with meat products; for this purpose birds are considered meat but fish are not. This prohibition extends to serving meat and dairy at the same meal, or even mixing utensils for meat and dairy. In fact, a waiting period is required after eating meat before dairy becomes permissible again.

Most people assume that all of these fundamental religious dietary laws come from the Old Testament. They do not.

We do find some precursors to the system of keeping kosher, mostly in terms of which animals are kosher and which are not, in Leviticus 11 and Deuteronomy 14.

Leviticus 11:2 starts a list of land animals that are permissible: animals with true, split hooves that chew the cud. Then the text, just to be clear, explains that merely chewing the cud is insufficient to make an animal permissible, just as split hooves are not enough. That's why, according to Leviticus 11:4, the camel and the hare are forbidden; they chew their cud but don't have split hooves. (Unfortunately, hares don't actually chew their cud, so even though they appear in the text, they turn out not to be a great example.) According to 11:7, pigs are not permissible even though they have split hooves because they don't chew the cud.

Leviticus 11:9 explains that only fish with scales and fins are permissible. Then Leviticus 11:13 lists the impermissible birds—alas, using words whose precise meaning we no longer know. One translation starts, "eagles, vultures, black vultures, kites, falcons . . ." Another translation of the same text offers instead, "eagles, vultures, ospreys, buzzards, kites . . ." Then Leviticus 11:20 warns against winged swarming things (insects), with the exception of locusts and grasshoppers, which are permissible. And Leviticus 11:27 apparently rules out mice and various reptiles, though, again, there's some uncertainty about the meaning of the technical words. Later passages similarly exclude things that crawl on their belly (snakes) and things that have many legs (say, centipedes).

Other passages deal with the proper way to slaughter an animal.

So the Bible certainly divides animals into two categories—generally translated as "clean" and "unclean"—which correspond pretty closely with the kosher and nonkosher foods of today. We see that pork in the Bible isn't any better or worse than any other non-kosher meat, even though nowadays the pig is often considered the "most unkosher" animal, or a prominent symbol of nonkosher status. Like the camel, though, it was originally just an example of an animal that has one but not both of the qualities required for a mammal to be kosher.

More to the point, though, we have yet to see anything about one of the most important aspects of keeping kosher: the absolute division between milk products and meat products. And that's because the division isn't in the Bible.

Many modern Jews don't eat veal parmigiana or cheeseburgers, because those dishes mix meat with dairy. Many have two sets of utensils, one for meat, one for milk. Some even have two kitchens, so ingrained is the division to separate milk from meat. But the only biblical prod in that direction comes from a single, narrow instruction: "Do not boil a kid in its mother's milk." The word for "milk" in Hebrew may mean milk fat (and of course the word for "kid" refers to a young goat, not a human child).

The phrase appears three times in the Bible: in Exodus 23:19, Exodus 34:26, and Deuteronomy 14:21. Much of Deuteronomy is a repetition and consolidation of the previous three books, and it's not unusual to find Exodus repeated there, just as immediately above we saw repetitions of Leviticus in Deuteronomy. Both times the phrase appears in Exodus, it is in the context of regulations about holidays, and as the second half of a two-part commandment, the first part allocating the first fruits of the earth to God. So apparently this prohibition about the kid and its mother's milk has some connection to the holidays, and is related to allocating fruit to God. Even though we find it three times, this does not appear to be a particularly central theme of the Bible.

And at any rate, the commandment is only narrowly about cooking a baby goat in its own mother's milk. This seems like a law about preventing cruelty to animals, as though there is something particularly unkind about cooking a baby goat in the very milk that was supposed to sustain it and give it life. Other commandments in the Five Books of Moses point in the same direction, including the remarkably similar provision in Deuteronomy 22:6–7 that warns a traveler who sees a mother bird with her eggs not to take the mother with the eggs, but first to scare off the mother.

Yet this one line about baby goats and their mothers' milk is the basis for not eating any milk products with any meat products. The baby goat becomes not just any baby animal but any form of meat, just as the mother's milk becomes any dairy product. As we just saw, chickens are considered meat for these purposes, even though there is obviously no chance of boiling a chicken in its mother's milk. It's especially difficult to fathom how a provision about boiling a kid in its mother's milk might be understood, even by the strictest of interpretations, to be about a chicken.

So of the three aspects of keeping kosher—a division between permissible and impermissible animals, the proper way of killing animals, and keeping meat and milk apart—the Bible lists only two. It takes a massive expansion and interpretation of the text to put the third aspect back into the Bible.

Furthermore, even the Jews in the Bible don't seem to keep kosher. In Genesis 18:8, Abraham serves three guests a combination of "curds, milk, and calf" meat. Below we'll take a more methodical look at how to reconcile different parts of the Bible (particularly in chapter 39) and how to learn from examples (chapter 31), but for now we note that no less than the father of monotheism, the founder of the Jewish people, serves milk and meat together, while the only reason to think the Bible prohibits such an action is to assume that by "kid" the text meant "any form of meat," by "boil" it meant "cause to be together in any fashion," and by "its mother's milk" it meant "any dairy product."

Yet keeping kosher has been a defining practice of many Jews for millennia.

Our purpose in focusing so carefully on the gap here between current practice and the text of the Bible is not to ridicule. (There are, sadly, people who do mock religion for things like this. They have misunderstood religion.) Nor is this a condemnation of modern Jewish dietary practices. Rather, our goal is to highlight how religious tradition uses biblical texts and to compare that with what the Bible originally said. When we do, we see very clearly that we cannot use religious interpretation directly to deduce what's in the Bible. In this case, any reasonably objective look at the Bible shows precursors of only two out of three of the major elements of keeping kosher, even though Judaism attributes the entire obligation of keeping kosher to the Bible.

This kind of confusion between religious practice and what the Bible says is widespread. We see another example next, this time in the realm of Christianity.

30

THE RAPTURE

Is the rapture in the Bible? **No.**

According to a national survey of Americans conducted by the Pew Research Center in 2010, some 41 percent of Americans believe that Jesus Christ "definitely" or "probably" will return to earth by the year 2050. Only 10 percent are convinced that he will not. According to a similar survey in 2006, 80 percent of Christians believe in "the second coming of Jesus Christ."

This second coming of Jesus—which also goes by the name "second advent"—is part of a fundamental theology that holds that Jesus's work is not finished. Life on earth, according to this view, has three major stages. The first was before Jesus's appearance. Then Jesus came to earth and brought the world the second period, marked by the existence of Christianity. Someday Jesus will return to usher in an era of perfection, the third stage.

For instance, the fourth-century Nicene Creed, which defines much of most mainstream Christian traditions, teaches that Jesus Christ came down from heaven and became human before suffering crucifixion and returning to sit by the right hand of God. But Jesus "will come again, with glory, to judge" the earth, and then God's kingdom "will have no end."

In fact, the general concept of an eventual era of judgment is not unique to Christianity. We saw in chapter 20 that the prophet Isaiah (many centuries before Jesus) wrote about the day when God would "judge between the nations" and "arbitrate for many peoples," so that war will be replaced by peace. We find an eventual war between good and evil detailed in the War Scroll from Qumran, one of the Dead Sea Scrolls. And more generally, much of the writing in and around Jerusalem two thousand years ago dealt with this theme, in part because the period was so tumultuous.

Likewise, mainstream Judaism today—continuing a particularly old understanding—identifies three periods of history: before Israel received the Old Testament (or sometimes just the Five Books of Moses), the current period, and an eventual messianic era. In fact, much of the debate about Jesus two thousand years ago concerned the question of whether he was the Messiah whom the Jews awaited. The Jews who thought he was became the Christians.

Discussion of an eventual cataclysmic shift in the nature of the world is so widespread that it has its own technical term: eschatology. The Christian second coming is an eschatological belief, as is the Jewish belief in the eventual coming of the Messiah. In English we sometimes use "end of days" or "end of times"—both biblical in origin—to refer to the time when these eschatological events will take place.

Not surprisingly, different traditions have different details when it comes to eschatology and the end of days. In our case here, various Christians understand this third and final epoch on earth differently, with passages like Matthew 24:27 setting the stage: "For as the lightning comes from the east and flashes as far as the west, so will be the second coming of Jesus."

The Greek word we translate here as "second coming" (*parousia*) has a literal meaning closer to just "coming," but it was obviously a technical term in the New Testament, so we use the similar technical term "second coming" here to make the original text clear to English readers. We see an example of this word and its intent elsewhere, as well. In Matthew 24:3, Jesus's disciples ask him, "Tell us, when will this be, and what sign will there be of your second coming [*parousia*], and of the end of times?" Clearly, with Jesus sitting right there, they are not asking when he will arrive but rather when he will return. Similarly, James 5:7 urges patience until "the second coming [*parousia*] of the Lord." In fact, this Greek word is so theologically central that it has become part of English, and it is so closely tied to the second coming that the meaning of the English word "Parousia" is "second coming of Jesus."

In addition to being marked by final judgment, the second coming will involve the resurrection of the dead—again, a belief that extended well beyond ancient Christianity. Like Jesus's second coming, the belief in final resurrection is enshrined in the Nicene Creed, among other places. Its source was the general fascination with eschatology two thousand years ago. Everyone was talking about what would eventually happen to the earth, and various themes kept recurring: a final era of justice, punishment of the wicked, reward for the righteous, the resurrection of the dead, the coming of the Messiah, an end to strife, the destruction of the world as we know it, the rebuilding of the world, and more.

Various traditions combined these themes in different ways. For instance, the War Scroll from Qumran envisions the world finally perfected. Revelation, in the New Testament, also foresees the world's final perfection—the "New Jerusalem"—but only after the world is first destroyed.

Christianity's primary eschatological accounts come from the books of Daniel and Revelation.

For instance, Daniel 9:24 describes a vision of seventy weeks that will produce an end to transgression and sin, and bring everlasting righteousness. The next verse talks about seven weeks that separate the announcement of Jerusalem's rebuilding and the time of an anointed prince. These sevens and seventies, along with a final accounting, are typical eschatological themes, as are the trumpets and other military metaphors that we find here and elsewhere. (Daniel is in the Old Testament, so it's in the Jewish Bible, too, but Jews downplay the book, putting it with other mundane writings like Chronicles and attributing little prophetic value to the text. Christians put Daniel with major prophets like Isaiah and see it as closely connected to Revelation.)

Revelation, too—more fully, the Book of Revelation of Saint John the Divine—addresses the end of times. The language, which is unlike anything else in the New Testament, is at once vivid and vague. The first attribute has ensured the book's endurance in both religious and popular circles. The demonic nature of the number 666 traces its roots to Revelation. So do the four horsemen of the Apocalypse, the Whore of Babylon, and much more. Filled with sevens and other symbolic imagery, the book is ripe for interpretation. But alongside the vivid descriptions, the vagueness of the text has made it possible to interpret it in diverse ways.

In addition to Daniel and Revelation, the Gospels also have eschatological accounts. We already saw Matthew 24:27, which compares the second coming of Jesus to lightning. That verse is part of a longer passage dubbed "the Olivet Discourse" (because it takes place on the Mount of Olives) in which Jesus describes the end of times. Verses 29–30 predict that "immediately after the suffering of" the days in which Jesus comes back, "the sun will be darkened, and the moon will not give its light; the stars will fall from heaven, and the powers of heaven will be shaken. Then the sign of the Son of Man will appear in heaven." The Olivet Discourse appears in Mark and Luke as well.

The book of 1 Thessalonians, too, has eschatological content, such as chapter 4 verses 13–17, which start with the admonition "We do not want you to be uninformed about those who have died." Then the text explains, starting in verse 15, "we who are alive, who are left until the second coming of the Lord, will by no means precede those who have died. [16] For the Lord himself, with a cry of command, with the archangel's call and with the sound of God's trumpet, will descend from heaven, and the dead in Christ will rise first. [17] Then we who are alive, who are left, will be caught up in the clouds together with them to meet the Lord in the air; and so we will be with the Lord forever."

Taken literally, these various accounts of the end of days defy reconciliation, and there isn't even any widespread agreement about which texts need to be reconciled. Jews, as we just saw, discount Daniel, and, naturally, don't consider the books of the New Testament at all.

As part of an attempt to turn the text of the Bible into a unified theology, some Christians envision a two-staged return of Christ. The first stage matches 1 Thessalonians, the second, Matthew 24.

Because the King James Version uses the word "tribulation" in Matthew 24 where our translation has "suffering" (they mean roughly the same thing), the part of Jesus's second coming according to the Olivet Discourse in Matthew comes "after the tribulation." If so, there is a period of suffering or tribulation that comes before Jesus's second coming in Matthew 24. If, in addition, the events of 1 Thessalonians also take place before Jesus's second coming, then it makes sense to ask about the timing between the tribulation and the events of 1 Thessalonians. They both take place before the second coming, but does 1 Thessalonians describe what happens before the tribulation, during it, or after it?

At this point we should be clear that the text does not offer any direct or even indirect advice in this regard. Answering this question is similar to answering a question about what the Bible says about how long Jews should wait between eating meat and milk. It doesn't. As we saw in the last chapter, the Bible doesn't even say not to eat milk and meat together, so it certainly doesn't enumerate any details about how not to eat them together.

Similarly, the passages from Matthew 24 and 1 Thessalonians are only two samples of the broad-ranging eschatological themes woven into the New Testament. Still—again like Jews regarding kosher food—Christians have used these and other texts to build a religious tradition. And in this case, part of that tradition—for some—involves an answer to the timing of the end of days.

Specifically, we have the resurrection of the dead in 1 Thessalonians, the period of tribulation, and Jesus's second coming. (In addition, based on a reading of Revelation 20, there's a potential period of a thousand years before something called the final judgment. We don't care about that for our purposes now.)

One commonly accepted answer is that these three—the resurrection, tribulation, and second coming—are all the same, so they happen simultaneously.

Another answer is that the resurrection of the dead in 1 Thessalonians takes place before the period of tribulation.

The reason we care about the timing so much here has to do with details of a verb in 1 Thessalonians 4:17. Remember that "we who are alive . . . will be caught up in the clouds." The verb for "caught up" in Greek is *harpazo*, and, when translated into Latin, *rapio*. (Readers who look for these verbs in the text need to search for their conjugated forms: *harpagisometha* in Greek and *rapiemur* in Latin.)

As it happens, the Latin verb *rapio* produced a variety of words in English, including "rapture." That word's secular meaning now is "joy," which is why Gilbert and Sullivan were able to combine the two words in their famous song "Oh Joy, Oh Rapture Unforeseen," from their operetta *H.M.S. Pinafore*. Originally, the word had to do with seizing or carrying away. This is how Shakespeare used the word when he had Pericles say, "And, spite of all the rapture of the sea . . ." He meant "in spite of the piracy." Then, because one's mind can metaphorically be taken to a happier place, "rapture" came to mean a state of being especially happy, as well. And then its original meaning all but vanished. So today, "rapture" is extreme joy.

But because the original meaning of "rapture" had to do with being carried away, it matches the text of 1 Thessalonians 4:17 ("we will be caught up"). The Latin use of the verb *rapio* from which "rapture" is derived makes the connection even stronger. Accordingly, "the rapture" is connected to the second coming of Jesus through its original meaning of "carrying off." The idea is that believers will be carried up to heaven, that is to say, raptured.

We now return to the issue of timing, and rephrase it as a question about whether the rapture (in 1 Thessalonians 4) takes place before, during, or after the period of tribulation (referred to in Matthew 24). Traditionally, most people assumed that 1 Thessalonians 4 and Matthew 24 described the same second coming of Jesus, so they used "rapture" informally to mean "the second coming."

But then in the early 1800s another view arose, separating the rapture from the second coming, and, in particular, putting the time of tribulation between the rapture and the ensuing second coming. With this new theology, "rapture," for some people, ceased to be a colloquial synonym for "second coming" and came instead to mean a time when believers will be raptured (taken up) to heaven, thereby avoiding the period of tribulation.

And that is "the" rapture, the one that vividly entails ordinary people who believe in Christ suddenly rising from their earthly existence to meet Jesus while nonbelievers remain on earth. Because the matter is of some importance, it has earned its own nomenclature. People dub this rapture the "pre-tribulation" rapture (or "pre-trib," for short), and use "post-tribulation" for the more traditional view.

Unfortunately, the Pew study with which we started this chapter didn't ask specifically about the rapture, only more generally about Jesus's return, but strong anecdotal evidence suggests that belief in this pre-tribulation view from the 1800s is widespread, especially among fundamentalists. It is this pre-trib view that forms the basis of the popular books *Left Behind* and the movie of the same name, for instance.

What we see, though, is that the path from the Bible to the (pre-trib) rapture involves separating 1 Thessalonians 4 from Matthew 24, putting 1 Thessalonians 4 before the tribulations of Matthew 24, and taking the text in 1 Thessalonians 4 literally while ignoring other eschatological passages.

There is no rapture in the Bible.

Rather, there is a lot of discussion about the end of days, and the rapture is consistent with one way of interpreting the text. We should be clear that this is not a condemnation of those who believe in the rapture or a critique of that belief. Rather, it is a statement about the Bible, and the way that belief in the rapture belongs to the same category as a belief in strictly separating milk and meat products: Neither one is biblical, even though both are promulgated by religious groups that value the Bible.

31

SLAVERY

***Does the Bible encourage slavery?* No.**

Having looked at a few things that the Bible doesn't say at all, we now return to the theme of indirect statements and messages in the Bible getting turned into "what the Bible says." This category is particularly nuanced, so we start with a modern analogy.

A well-known story about George Washington relates that the founding father didn't lie when he was asked about cutting down his own father's cherry tree. The story is so famous, in fact, that the phrase "I cannot tell a lie"—which could be no more than a general saying—is almost universally associated specifically with Washington.

The anecdote comes from an 1800 publication by Parson Mason Locke Weems called *The Life of Washington*. In it, young George Washington's father asks his son, "Do you know who killed that beautiful little cherry tree yonder in the garden?" George responds, "I can't tell a lie, Pa; you know I can't tell a lie. I did cut it with my hatchet." In response, Weems writes, Mr. Washington (Sr.) tells his son how glad he is that he killed the tree, because "such an act of heroism in my son is more worth than a thousand trees, though blossomed with silver, and their fruits of pure gold."

The full title of the work gives us a sense of its nature: *The Life of George Washington; With Curious Anecdotes, Equally Honourable to Himself, and Exemplary to His Young Countrymen.* This is a book from which morals are supposed to be drawn.

We all "know" that the moral of this well-known account is to be honest, though the author suggests another value, namely, heroism. But there's a third moral that might be read directly from the text: Killing cherry trees is good. After all, none other than the great George Washington, a founding father of the United States of America, killed a cherry tree. Shouldn't we all strive to be a little more like George? Weems even writes in the title that his accounts are supposed to be "exemplary," that is, examples to learn from. Or, because we know from Weems's account that this particular tree was a favorite of George's father, maybe the moral is more general: We should all destroy things that our fathers like.

Obviously, these are absurd ways to read the story, which is about how George Washington deals with his mistake, not about the mistake itself. To mimic Washington, we should exhibit honesty and heroism.

What we learn from this brief encounter is how perilous it can be to take part of a story out of context and assume that the purpose of the story is that its readers should emulate that part. This holds, naturally, whether or not the story is historically accurate. In the case of young George and his hatchet, most people think that the account is fictitious, so we ask why Weems made it up. But even if Weems was reporting history, we would still ask why Weems included it.

The broader relevance here is that one of the most widespread ways of interpreting the Bible is to take a single account out of context and claim that the Bible tells us to emulate the people in the account. In other words, people interpret the Bible—frequently on their own, though sometimes in the context of more organized religion—by making the same kind of misguided mistake that turns a story promoting honesty into a call to kill trees.

For instance, some people simplistically note that the Israelites in the Old Testament exhibited a good deal of violence; the Old Testament, they say, must therefore approve of violence. We'll return to the general issue of violence in chapter 35, but for now we'll note the folly of the argument. Whether or not these accounts of violence in the Old Testament are historical—and, according to historians, there's violence in both the nonhistorical and the historical sections—the way to connect the accounts to a moral is to ask why the accounts were included.

The professional atheist Christopher Hitchens made just this error in a widely viewed online video that he prepared for *Vanity Fair*. In it, he contrasts the commandment "Thou shalt not kill" (which, as we'll see in chapter 38, is actually a mistranslation) with Moses's actions afterward, when, Hitchens says, Moses ordered all his supporters to draw their swords and kill their friends. His implication is that the Bible has no value because it is so massively inconsistent, first warning not to kill and then describing killing. But Hitchens—and more like him—have made a fundamental mistake, wrongly assuming that every part of the Bible is meant as a simplistic "do this" message. The same reasoning, as we just saw, would mean that the only way to learn from George Washington is to wantonly cut down trees.

In Hitchens's example, we might equally note that Moses ends up getting punished by God: Even though his life's goal was to lead his people into Israel, God doesn't let him enter the Promised Land. The text of Numbers 20:12 vaguely explains that the punishment is because Moses didn't believe in God. Because Numbers 20:11 explains that Moses hit a rock twice to get water from it, while in Numbers 20:8 God tells Moses to speak to the rock, tradition connects Moses's punishment to his hitting of the rock. And that's certainly a reasonable interpretation. But it is not the only one. Perhaps the hitting of the rock was just the final straw, the deal breaker, as it were, sealing Moses's fate after continued bouts of violence.

Obviously, this is only one alternative to Hitchens's facile understanding, and for our purposes now we don't care whether Moses was punished for his violence or not. All we really care about is the faulty reasoning: It's a mistake to pick one episode of the Bible and naively jump to the conclusion that the point of the episode is that we should behave the way the characters did.

With this important lesson in mind, we turn to the issue of slavery in the Bible. On one hand, there are slaves in both the Old Testament and the New Testament. And particularly in the Old Testament, the Israelites' journey from slavery to freedom is an ongoing, major theme. In the opening line of the Ten Commandments, God is "the one who brought you out of Egypt, out of the house of slavery," as if this quality were God's preeminent role. (To this day, freedom from Egypt is considered a defining element of Judaism.)

Exodus 20:10 extends the Sabbath to slaves: "The seventh day is a sabbath to the Lord your God; you shall not do any work—you, your son or your daughter, or your male or female slave." Similarly, the commandment against taking (usually wrongly translated as "coveting," as we saw in chapter 8) forbids taking someone else's wife, and also their "male or female slave" (Exodus 20:17). According to Exodus 21:2, "when you buy a male Hebrew slave, he shall serve six years, but in the seventh he shall go out a free person." Exodus 21:20 prescribes punishment for a slave owner who strikes and kills a male or female slave. Nehemiah (7:67) records that 7,337 slaves accompanied the 42,360 Israelites who returned to Jerusalem from Babylonia after the first exile in 586 B.C. The Old Testament acknowledges slavery and—at least by failing to condemn it—seems to permit it.

In the New Testament, Jesus acknowledges the subservient nature of slaves in Matthew 10:24: "A disciple is not above the teacher, nor a slave above the master." Slaves play a role in the parable of the weeds among the wheat, where (Matthew 13:27) the "slaves of the householder" bring a report of weeds. We already saw (in chapter 14) that the phrase "live by the sword" comes as a distortion of Matthew 26, where a supporter of Jesus cuts off the ear of one of the high priest's slaves. The New Testament, too, acknowledges and permits slavery, at least in the sense of not condemning it.

We do not know the exact nature of the slavery in the Bible. It seems unlikely to have been as draconian as many modern, recent forms of slavery, though scholarly opinions differ. Ancient slaves may have been paid, so they may have been more like indentured servants than slaves; in some cases, slaves had to be let go after seven years, so they may even have been closer to contracted workers. On the other hand, the Bible acknowledges sex slaves.

But whatever the case, almost all of these passages allow two reasonable but contradictory interpretations. The first is that slavery was a fact, unfortunate though it may be, and the goal of the passages was to mitigate the severity of that slavery. So, for instance, the rationale behind giving a slave a day off on the Sabbath and letting a slave go after seven years was to make sure that slaves were treated as humanely as possible. In the other interpretation, these passages suggest a tacit approval of slavery when they regulate or mention it but do not forbid it.

By analogy, we might imagine a Western man who travels to India, and rents an apartment that comes with a slave boy. (Eric Weiner wrote about this exact predicament in an essay that appeared in *The New York Times Magazine* on February 3, 2008.) Suppose our hypothetical man gives the boy a bit of money. Does that mean the man approves of slavery, because he has agreed to let a slave wait on him? Or does he reject it, because he treats his slave better than most? We don't know. Perhaps the man himself doesn't know.

Most of the passages that acknowledge and even address slavery in the Bible are similar. We don't know for sure what their stance on slavery is.

But a handful of passages from the New Testament jump out as seeming to support slavery. One is Ephesians 6:5: "Slaves, obey your earthly masters with fear and trembling, in singleness of heart, as you obey Christ." This verse follows a passage about children obeying their parents just as the Ten Commandments dictate. Ephesians 6 seems to be not just an observation about its day, but a divine and eternal pro-slavery commandment. Colossians 3 is similar in structure and content. And Titus 2:9 likewise relates, "Tell slaves to be submissive to their masters." The book of 1 Timothy 6 demands that "all who are under the yoke of slavery regard their masters as worthy of all honor."

These three passages (and a few others) were singled out by the Reverend Ebenezer W. Warren in his 1864 pro-slavery book, whose title includes the promise of "A Vindication of Southern Slavery from the Old and New Testaments." (The full title is *Nellie Norton: Or, Southern Slavery and the Bible. A Scriptural Refutation of the Principal Arguments upon Which the Abolitionists Rely. A Vindication of Southern Slavery from the Old and New Testaments*.) Reverend Warren's point is that the Bible encourages slavery, and to abolish slavery would be to go against the Bible.

But even these passages are equivocal. Ephesians 6:5 ("slaves, obey your masters") is matched in verse 9 with "And masters, do the same to them." Titus 2 ("tell slaves to be submissive to their masters") seems to be about overcoming unfortunate tendencies. The chapter starts by telling older men to be temperate and sound in faith, older women to be reverent and not to slander, young women to love their husbands and be self-controlled, and younger men to be self-controlled. Then comes the passage about slaves, which continues by warning them not to steal. And 1 Timothy 6 doesn't say that someone should be a slave, but rather how someone who already is a slave should behave.

By comparison, the New Testament also acknowledges the Roman Empire. For instance, in Acts 22, Paul protests an impending flogging by telling a tribunal that he is a Roman citizen, and Roman citizens cannot be treated too harshly. "I was born a citizen" of Rome, Paul explains in Acts 22:28. Even though Paul acknowledges Rome and even the benefits of being a Roman citizen, no one interprets this text as an endorsement of the Roman Empire (which was widely regarded as wicked by Jews and early Christians).

Similarly, even the passages that Reverend Warren (and others) cite are not endorsements of slavery. They are recognitions that slavery existed, but they take no position on whether it is a good thing.

We have worked through a lot of texts to come to a perhaps disappointing conclusion: The Bible neither condemns nor encourages slavery. Our strongest conclusion—though still weak—is that the Old Testament seems to recognize, at least in principle, that unchecked slavery is bad.

Most modern readers are appalled by slavery, so they are often quick to explain that the Bible was inspired for its day, or that the culture that created it treated slaves better than others, or that the provisions in the Old Testament were designed to make things as good as possible for slaves, or that the passages in the New Testament are metaphoric in nature. Maybe. But these and other attempts to make the Bible into an antislavery text are all interpretations. Some of them enjoy more solid founding than others. All of them ultimately distort the text.

Western culture has already come down firmly against slavery, and the issue is for the most part no longer a matter of serious debate. The detail in this chapter will be useful as we move forward to more controversial issues, when it will be particularly important not to confuse what the text advocates with what it acknowledges, and not to leap from example to moral.

32

MARRIAGE

Does the Bible support only a one-man-one-woman model of marriage? No.

In the last chapter, we saw how religious leaders can distort the text of the Bible to make it seem as though it supports their own personal view. In a sense, this is their job. Religious leaders are supposed to ground their religious teachings in scripture. And as we saw in chapter 23, the tradition of using scripture in new ways goes back at least two thousand years.

But there's also a sense in which people, particularly today with the advent of science, want to know when their religious leaders are reporting something that's already in the Bible, and when they are reading something new into it. And here we frequently find a surprising lack of transparency.

Perhaps the clearest example comes from the people who equate "biblical marriage" with "one woman and one man." In chapter 39, we'll address the issue of what the Bible says about homosexuality and same-sex marriage. And in chapter 37 we'll take a closer look at the power dynamics between married men and women as informed by the Bible. For now, we'll look at marriage more broadly, because many people are surprised to learn how popular polygamy was in the Bible. As early as Genesis 4:19, Lamech—one of Cain's grandsons—took two wives, Adah and Zillah. Abraham wasn't able to have children with his wife Sarah, so he gave it a shot with her maid, Hagar, demonstrating infidelity if not actual polygamy. And his grandson, Jacob, was clearly married to two wives who happened to be sisters: Rachel and Leah. We know not to use examples directly as morals (as we saw in detail in the last chapter), so these and other cases of men marrying more than one wife at a time may or may not be relevant. But we don't see any particular condemnation of polygamy where it occurs.

Clearly relevant, though, is Deuteronomy 25:5, which provides that the brother of a deceased man must marry his dead brother's wife, in what has become known as a Levirate marriage. (The word comes from the Latin *levir,* which means "brother-in-law.") The verses that follow in Deuteronomy underscore the importance of this obligation, and don't contain an exception if the surviving brother happens already to be married. So some Levirate marriages have the effect of not only permitting polygamy but actually requiring it. (Most Jews today do not follow this practice, but until the founding of the State of Israel in 1948, it was common among some Jews in Arab countries, as was polygamy more generally.)

This is the same Levirate-marriage tradition that Saint Augustine used (as we saw in chapter 6) to explain Jesus's different lineages as recorded in the Gospels of Matthew and Luke, so Saint Augustine obviously knew about the practice, and, apparently, either accepted it or even approved of it. For him, Levirate marriage was part of the line of Jesus. In the case of what Saint Augustine proposed, based on a suggestion he heard from Julius Africanus, we don't know if the first brother was already married when he took his dead brother's wife as his own, so we don't know if Jesus's lineage as understood by Saint Augustine involved polygamy, but it did involve a tradition that at least sometimes demanded polygamy.

Additionally, Exodus 21:10 addresses a married man's requirements if he marries a second wife. He has to continue to give the first wife her food, clothing, and marital rights. This passage is part of a longer discourse about slaves and, starting in verse 7, what happens when a man sells his daughter as a slave. So Exodus 21:10 may apply only to men who marry a slave girl, but either way it clearly allows polygamy.

So we have nonconclusive examples of biblical men who had multiple wives, descriptions of how to behave with additional wives, and at least one regulation requiring multiple wives. What about in the other direction? Is there any evidence that polygamy was forbidden or rejected?

The passages most commonly cited to support monogamy come from Genesis as quoted in Matthew 19. Genesis 2:24 reads, "Hence a man leaves his father and mother and clings to his wife, and they become one flesh." And Matthew quotes it, along with Genesis 1:27, in his discussion of marriage, but Matthew has a slightly different version of Genesis 2:24. His text, based on the Greek translation of Genesis 2:24, adds an extra word: "two." His text reads, "and the two of them become one flesh." These "two," say people who look for monogamy in the Bible, represent the only number of people allowed in a marriage.

We recognize this as a clear case of reading into the text. Certainly Matthew's statement is compatible with exclusive monogamy, but it's just as compatible with polygamy. A man could marry several women, becoming "one" with each of them simultaneously.

And at any rate, we know why Matthew brought up the example. It was to teach not about marriage but rather about divorce (in particular, to preach against it, a topic we return to in the next chapter). In verse 19:3, Matthew is asked whether it is lawful for a man to divorce his wife for any reason, and in verse 6, Matthew responds, having just cited Genesis, "so they are no longer two, but one flesh. Therefore what God has joined together, let no one separate." In verse 9 he adds, "whoever divorces his wife, except for unchastity, and marries another commits adultery." There's some uncertainty about the original Greek text here, so there are other English translations of this line, but they are all about divorce, not monogamy or polygamy.

Perhaps the most interesting lines are in 1 Timothy 3. Verses 1–7 deal with qualifications for holding high office in the Church. (This high office is commonly translated as "bishop," though there were no bishops back then as we now think of them.) One requirement (in verse 2) is that someone who "aspires to the office of bishop . . . be the husband of one wife." Verses 8–13 deal with the requirements for another office, commonly translated as deacon, including, again, that an aspirant be the husband of only one wife (verse 12). There are two reasonable ways of interpreting the phrase "husband of one wife." One is that he has never divorced and remarried; the other is that he is married to only one wife.

Either way, though, the obvious implication when this criterion is applied to those seeking high office is that it was not applied to everyone else. This understanding is reinforced by the only partial overlap between the qualities required for bishop and for deacon. And from qualities like "must be a good teacher" (to be a bishop) we see clearly that not everyone was expected to meet all of the standards listed in 1 Timothy.

So 1 Timothy seems to suggest, if not prove, that polygamy was accepted. It also suggests that monogamy was considered better than polygamy, because the other qualities in the lists all seem positive.

Some people also quote Deuteronomy 17:17 for similar effect, because it deals with how many wives a king can have. But the usual translation, according to which kings should not have "many wives" or "great many riches," correctly leaves unanswered the question of how many is too many. So Deuteronomy 17:17 might only suggest an ideal, of, say, not more than three wives. And like 1 Timothy, the clear implication is that this more stringent requirement is binding only on kings, not on the general population.

What we see, then, is that even though later mainstream Christian and Jewish traditions enforced monogamy, "biblical" marriage is not necessarily monogamous, and in some cases may even have to be polygamous.

We turn next to the flip side of marriage: divorce.

33

DIVORCE

***Does the Bible forbid divorce?* No.**

When the sixteenth-century king of England Henry VIII wanted a new
queen to replace the one to whom he was still married (Catherine of
Aragon), he appealed to Pope Clement VII, marriages being the prov-
enance of the Church.

As an apparently devout Catholic, Henry VIII knew that the
Church did not allow divorce. The only option for replacing a living
wife was something known as a decree of nullity, now commonly called
an "annulment." The Church would not sanction divorce, consider-
ing the dissolution of a marriage by anyone other than God to be inconsistent with the Bible (a claim we'll revisit below). But the Church
would, in certain circumstances, declare that a marriage was invalid
to start with, and this is what King Henry asked Pope Clement to do.
The pope refused.

So in 1533, over the objections of the pope, Henry left his wife
Catherine in order to marry Anne Boleyn (who, as has now become
famous, would be only the second of six wives). The pope responded

by excommunicating Henry VIII. Then Henry VIII declared himself the leader of the Church of England, replacing the pope's primacy in that regard. His new status was confirmed by Parliament in the 1534 Act of Supremacy, legislation that acknowledged Henry VIII as the "supreme head on earth of the Church of England." Because Henry VIII had already been dubbed "Defender of the Faith" by Pope Leo X in 1521 (for lashing out against Martin Luther and his new protestantism), it was easy at the time to pretend that Henry's new role was continuing an old position, not creating a new one. Still, this break between London and Rome over the king's marriages marked the creation of a whole new religious stream, the Church of England, which in turn led to the worldwide Anglican Church and to offshoots such as the Episcopal Church.

Marriage and remarriage are no less controversial now—and no less emotionally charged—than they were nearly five hundred years ago when they influenced global religion and politics. The Catholic Church still considers divorce inconsistent with the teachings of the Bible and does not recognize it; indeed, the Church puts adultery and divorce under the same umbrella of "Offenses Against the Dignity of Marriage" in the "Catechism of the Catholic Church," adding that "divorce is immoral." (As this book goes to press, Pope Francis has suggested a possible willingness to revisit this position.) A marriage only ends with the death of a spouse, though the Church still recognizes annulments, which publicly admit that a marriage previously thought to be valid in fact is not. (In 2002, the Church of England adopted a slightly more lenient position.)

What does the Bible say about divorce?

No one in the Bible divorces, at least not by modern standards. While we've already seen the perils of drawing conclusions based on examples, it's still interesting that this prevalent aspect of modern life isn't part of the biblical narrative. However, one reason we don't see divorce in the Bible is that a husband was able to take a second wife without leaving the first one, as we saw in the last chapter. Depending on how the husband and first wife behaved after he took a second wife, we might now recognize these marriages to a second wife either as essentially entailing divorce from the first or as polygamy.

But even though there are no actual divorces in the Bible, it recognizes divorce in principle and has provisions for divorcées. For instance, Leviticus 21:14 enumerates women whom a priest cannot marry, including widows, prostitutes, and divorcées; a priest can only marry a virgin. Numbers 30:10 declares that, in contrast to married women (as we'll see in chapter 37), widows and divorcées are responsible for their own oaths. There is clearly a category of "divorced woman" in the Old Testament, and there are laws that apply to her.

Marriage, divorce, and reconciliation also form persistent metaphors for God's relationship with Israel as expressed by the great prophets. With beautiful if complicated imagery, Hosea 2:16 looks forward to the day that the people of Israel no longer call God "my *ba'al*" but rather "my *ish*." The word *ish* means "husband," and represents reconciliation. The word *ba'al* has two meanings. One is "master"— for example, a slave owner who might own a sex slave, as opposed to being a husband. The word also means "false god," poetically connecting the marriage woes between Israel and God with Israel's mistaken idolatry. Israel's return to God's ways is compared to matrimonial reconciliation.

In addition, there seems to be something called a "bill of divorce" (*sefer kritut* in Hebrew). Deuteronomy mentions it in its laws concerning marriage and divorce. According to Deuteronomy 24:1, a man who finds fault with his wife can give her a "bill of divorce" and then send her away. If this woman remarries and her second husband gives her a similar bill of divorce, her first husband is not allowed to take her back. Every detail of this text points in the direction of divorce. And

Isaiah and Jeremiah both refer to this legal document metaphorically in connection with God's relationship to the people of Israel.

Jeremiah in verses 3:6–10 deals with "Israel and Judah," two parts of a divided Israelite nation. (It's potentially confusing that "Israel" represents both the entire nation and one division of it.) God is cross with "Rebellious Israel" and "Faithless Judah," a state of affairs the prophet expresses with the metaphor of marriage. Both of God's wives—Israel and Judah—have strayed. First Israel committed adultery, so God gave Israel a bill of divorce. But her sister Judah didn't learn, and she, too, strayed.

So far, we've seen that divorced women were common enough in the Old Testament that they had their own legal and moral category, and were familiar enough that the prophets could use them as metaphors. And while the priest wasn't allowed to marry a divorcée, he also wasn't allowed to marry a widow. The strike against the divorcée in Leviticus is that she's not a virgin. We don't find any particular condemnation of divorce in the Old Testament.

At first glance, Malachi 2:16 seems like it points in the other direction. The NRSV translation reads, "For I hate divorce, says the Lord." It seems pretty clear. But it's not. For one thing, the Hebrew there is so odd that it borders on ungrammatical. The word that gets translated as "divorce" here looks like a verb, not a noun, which is why the Septuagint translates it as, "if hating, you divorce [your wife]. . . ." Evidence from other translations, from the Dead Sea Scrolls, and from other sources agrees with the Greek. The oddness of the text, combined with the confusion over it, suggests that our version of it might be corrupted.

But even if we do have the right letters, and even if the NRSV and other modern translations of Malachi 2:16 are right, the line is still not about divorce in general. Like other prophets, Malachi was comparing God's relationship with Israel to a marriage. Two verses earlier,

Malachi says that "the Lord was a witness between you and the wife of your youth, to whom you have been faithless, though she is your companion and your wife by covenant." Malachi's point is that Israel (as represented by Judah) has abandoned God's path. In this context, "I hate divorce" makes the most sense as a statement about "the divorce we're talking about," not divorce in general.

So the Old Testament does not condemn divorce, though in singling out divorcées, it reflects the emotional impact of divorce.

We find a different picture in the New Testament.

According to Matthew 5:32, Jesus says that "anyone who divorces his wife, except on the ground of unchastity, causes her to commit adultery; and whoever marries a divorced woman commits adultery." That translation doesn't get it quite right, and the details of "committing adultery" and "causing someone to commit adultery" are complex. But the point is that divorce is tantamount to adultery, unless the divorce is on grounds of what the NRSV calls "unchastity."

The full text, which is part of a list of six modifications to the Old Testament, reads, "It was also said, 'Whoever divorces his wife, let him give her a certificate of divorce.' But I say to you that anyone who divorces his wife, except on the ground of unchastity, causes her to commit adultery; and whoever marries a divorced woman commits adultery."

The Greek word in the exception clause, *porneia*, generally refers to a variety of concepts related to sexual immorality, so "unchastity" isn't exactly correct here. The point is probably "unfaithfulness." (The Church's NABRE [New American Bible, Revised Edition] translation, reflecting Catholic doctrine, renders the Greek for "except for unfaithfulness" as the much less accurate "unless the marriage is unlawful." They use this passage to bolster nullification as the only way to end a marriage between two living spouses.) So Matthew 5:32 condemns a man who divorces his wife unless she is unfaithful. (There's no provision for a wife to divorce her husband.)

Matthew 19 agrees. There a group asks Jesus if a man may "divorce his wife for any reason." Jesus answers in verse 9: "And I say to you, whoever divorces his wife, except for unchastity, and marries another commits adultery." There's some textual confusion over the exact original language here. That, combined with the introduction "I say to you," suggests that this line is either a full or partial quotation of—or at least a reference to—the passage in Matthew 5 that we just saw. In the lines leading up to verse 9, Jesus explains some of the reasoning, including an often-cited suggestion in verse 6 that "what God has joined" in marriage, as in the marriage of Adam to Eve, "no human should separate."

In response, Jesus's disciples ask, "If this is the case of a man with his wife, wouldn't it be better not to marry at all?" The answer suggests that it would indeed be better not to marry, but "not everyone can accept this teaching." The text here thus presents a hierarchy according to which never marrying is best and staying married is second best.

The text in 1 Corinthians 7 agrees: "It is well for a man not to touch a woman." But because marriage is going to happen, and because (verse 9) it is better to marry than "to be aflame with passion," men and women should marry. Furthermore (verses 10–11), "the wife should not separate from her husband" and "the husband should not divorce his wife." The different verbs—a wife "separates" and a husband "divorces"—probably just reflect details of Greek grammar. The point is that neither spouse should leave the other. On the other hand (verse 15), if one of the spouses is a nonbeliever and that nonbelieving spouse leaves, it's okay.

So according to 1 Corinthians, one proper end for a marriage is if one nonbelieving spouse leaves. Some people correctly note that unlike 1 Corinthians, Matthew doesn't make an exception for nonbelieving spouses. In order to avoid any potential conflict in the text, they sometimes also note that 1 Corinthians doesn't specifically give the remaining spouse the right to remarry. Here, though, they are on shaky ground. After all, 1 Corinthians also doesn't mention any exception for unfaithfulness, yet this doesn't mean that 1 Corinthians is rejecting Matthew. (As it happens, we see the word *porneia* again here. In an example of the wide semantic range of the word, here the reason to have marriage at all is "because of *porneia*"—which the NRSV translates as "sexual immorality.")

Another passage, from Romans 7, is also frequently cited in connection to marriage. There, Paul starts off with a reminder that the "law" (in the Old Testament) "is binding on a person only during that person's lifetime." For instance, "a married woman is bound by the law to her husband as long as he lives; but if her husband dies, she is discharged from the law concerning the husband." That's why (verse 3) "she will be called an adulteress if she lives with another man while her husband is alive. But if her husband dies, she is free from that law."

Some people quote this in support of the notion that the only way to end a marriage is if one spouse dies. But that's not what the text says. The text only says that that death is one way to end a marriage, not that it's the only way. Paul only focuses on death because it sets the stage for his next point: "In the same way," he says in verse 4, "you have died to the law through the body of Christ, so that you may belong to another." In other words, people no longer have to follow the Old Testament, even though they were once bound to it, because death (on their behalf) has released them from their pledge, just as the death of one spouse releases the other from the pledge of marriage.

There are two contracts here: marriage and the covenant between God and the people of Israel. They are similar, Paul says, building on a theme we saw in the Prophets. And one way they are similar is that death releases the surviving party from the contract. Paul's point is about the Old Testament, not about marriage. He takes no position here on whether there might be other ways, such as divorce, to end a marriage; or on whether those other ways might be good or bad.

Still, even without connecting Paul's words in Romans to legal details about divorce, we see two clear trends in the New Testament that are absent from the Old Testament: First, marriage and the sex that goes with it are now only the lesser of two evils—it's better in some regards not to marry at all than to marry. And secondly, divorce is associated with harlotry, and, therefore, considered immoral except when the divorce is for reasons of sexual immorality. Alas, we don't have any clear idea of what that immorality might entail.

We also have to wonder whether it was divorce itself or its obvious implication that was the problem. Does Matthew 5:32 ("anyone who divorces his wife, except on the ground of unchastity, causes her to commit adultery") really refer only to divorce, or to the sex the divorcee will have after the divorce? Matthew 19:9 is clear that a man "commits adultery" only when he divorces a women and marries another one. It's not technically the divorce that's the problem. It's what comes next.

Jesus in Matthew 19:4–6, citing the precedent of Adam and Eve, goes a step further and says that no one should separate what God has joined. But those lines lead up to the conclusion in 19:9 (that a man commits adultery when he divorces and remarries), so the context suggests that the concern is about what follows divorce, not the divorce itself.

So the Old Testament doesn't forbid divorce, and only discourages it to the extent that a high priest cannot marry anyone who isn't a virgin, including divorcées.

The New Testament is more complicated. It speaks against divorce, primarily in the context of postdivorce sex, but in the same context speaks against marriage altogether. A strict reading of the text would prohibit marriage along with divorce. A slightly more lenient reading would allow marriage (in accord with the proviso in Matthew 19:11 that "not everyone can accept" the teaching of never marrying). More lenient yet is a condemnation of remarriage but an acceptance of divorce. And more lenient than that is a recognition that divorce is like other common sexual sins that are part of the human condition.

All of these positions find support in the New Testament, and none of them is exactly what the text says, because what the text really reflects is a variety of opinion on the matter of divorce.

In this regard, divorce in the Bible is a little like marriage: We saw in the last chapter that monogamy was considered better than polygamy, but both were accepted. Underlying the texts about divorce is a similar sentiment that divorce, like polygamy, is undesirable, along with marriage itself. But this judgment hadn't yet been codified in an absolute prohibition of divorce.

We turn next to another case of modern theological disagreement, but this time, only one side finds biblical support.

34

PROSPERITY

***Does the Bible say that God wants you to be rich?* No.**

It's hard to know for sure, but it seems that the most listened-to preacher in the English-speaking world in 2016 is Pastor Joel Osteen, with an estimated weekly audience for his TV ministry of seven million unique viewers, and a monthly total of perhaps triple that. Some twenty-five thousand people show up in person to attend his Lakewood congregation in Houston, Texas, each week. So when he wrote a letter in 2005 to tell his followers that "God wants us to prosper financially, to have plenty of money, to fulfill the destiny He has laid out for us," a lot of people were listening.

Pastor Osteen is not the only preacher to believe this. Pastor Kenneth Copeland has a similar message. Educated at Oral Roberts University and also from Texas, he was born in 1936 and began his Christian path in 1962, so he has been preaching prosperity for far longer than Pastor Osteen, who didn't begin speaking in public until the death of his televangelist father, John Osteen, in 1999.

Oral Roberts himself, founder of the institution that educated

Copeland and one of the pioneer televangelists, helped lay the foundation for this kind of thinking. Born in 1918, at age twenty-nine he left his church in Oklahoma after reading 3 John 1:2, "I wish above all things that thou mayest prosper and be in health, even as thy soul prospereth," according to a 2009 obituary in the *Guardian*. (Oral Roberts, naturally, was reading the King James Version. We might now prefer a slightly more modern translation: "I pray that you may prosper in all things and be in health, just as your soul prospers.")

This text led him to develop his "seed-faith" theology, according to which (as described, for instance, in his 1975 book, *A Daily Guide to Miracles and Successful Living Through Seed-Faith*) giving is like planting a seed. Both grow and return much more than the initial investment. Roberts applied this principle to both spiritual and material wealth: give a little love, get a lot; give a little money, get a lot. The path to riches, Roberts said, was giving money away. (In particular, Roberts urged people to give money away to his own ministry, in February of 1987 even telling his followers that if he couldn't raise eight million dollars from them by March, God would take him away from this earth.)

This seed-faith theology—which *USA Today* summarized on December 15, 2009, with the headline "Oral Roberts brought health-and-wealth Gospel mainstream"—influenced Copeland, Osteen, and many others, who developed and now preach what is often called the "prosperity Gospel": God's plan for believers includes material wealth.

Like most preachers, they claim to base their theology in the Bible. Does the Bible really support it?

We start with 3 John 1:2, the passage to which Oral Roberts attributes his epiphany. The book called 3 John, or, more fully, the Third Epistle of John, takes the form of a private letter to a man called Gaius. (Because of the letter's early obscurity, it took some time to be admitted into the Christian canon, but it is now part of the New Testament.)

The book opens, "The elder to the beloved Gaius, who I love in truth: Beloved, I pray that all may go well with you and that you may be in good health, just as it is well with your soul," according to the NRSV. The phrase "go well with you" corresponds to the older "prosper."

The original Greek word here, *eusdow,* ranges in meaning from general to financial success, but the nuances of that verb are hardly the point, because the context in which it is used is clearly a greeting to one particular person, Gaius. In perfectly common fashion, John opens his letter to Gaius with good wishes, the same as we might do now, with, perhaps, "Dear Gaius. I hope this letter finds you well." For the same reason, John ends his letter with "Peace to you" in the last verse, just as we might now sign off with "Take care." In other words, the "you" of 3 John 1:2 is Gaius, not the reader of the New Testament.

Oral Roberts took 3 John 1:2 completely out of context when he turned it into a statement about what God wants for us now. And others followed his lead. But 3 John 1:2 is not about prosperity. It's a social nicety.

Another particularly popular verse among prosperity-Gospel preachers is John 10:10: "The thief comes only to steal and kill and destroy. I [Jesus] come that they may have life, and have it abundantly." Jesus wants people to have not just life, but abundance, it seems.

John 10:10 comes at the end of a passage so confusing that the text itself says it's hard to understand. The chapter starts off with detailed imagery about sheep, pastures, and gates. Thieves and bandits enter surreptitiously, going around the gate; the sheep don't follow these trespassers, whose voices are unfamiliar. On the other hand, the sheep's shepherd enters through the gate, the gatekeeper opening the gate for him; the sheep follow him because they know his voice. Then the text adds, "Jesus used this figure of speech with" his listeners, "but they did not understand what he was saying to them."

So in John 10:7, Jesus elaborates, explaining that he is the actual gate for the sheep, while those who came before him were thieves and bandits. "Whoever enters by me will be saved," he says, "and will come in and go out and find pasture" (John 10:9).

Then in John 10:11, Jesus says, "I am the good shepherd," who takes care of the sheep, even laying down his life for them, as opposed to hired hands who leave the sheep and run away in the face of danger.

The extended metaphor—often called a parable, though John doesn't seem to use parables—is still hard to understand. Is Jesus the gate, as he says in John 10:9, or the shepherd, as he says in John 10:11? The image of Jesus as shepherd is widely attested (which is why it's a commonly depicted theme in Christian artwork), but it's not clear how Jesus could be the gate, too. Some people have suggested that we have two different metaphors here; others suggest that shepherds sometimes use their physical bodies as barriers, like gates.

John 10:10 bridges these two passages, contrasting the thieves with Jesus. The thieves come to kill and destroy. Jesus comes to help the sheep, so that they "have life." Then, using the Greek word *perossos,* the text adds "and have more." The exact nuance of this general word here isn't clear, but it does not seem to support a message of material prosperity, because it doesn't seem to mean "have life abundantly," in spite of some translations to that effect. Rather, it looks like it means "have abundant life" or even "have eternal life."

The last meaning suggests itself because, from reading the rest of John, we get a pretty good sense that "life" means the everlasting life after death that comes from believing in Jesus. For instance, John 3:36 teaches that "whoever believes in the Son has eternal life" while "whoever disobeys the son will not see life." The second time around, John uses "life" instead of the fuller "eternal life." In John 5:40, again, "life" means "eternal life" ("yet you refuse to come to me to have life"), as it does in John 6:53 ("unless you eat the flesh of the son of man and drink his blood, you have no life in you"). And the last line of the book explains its purpose: "These things are written so that you may come to believe that Jesus is the messiah . . . and that through believing, you may have life in his name." Finally, John's theme in chapter 10 is convincing the Jews to believe in Jesus to have eternal life.

All of this evidence indicates that John 10:10 is a theological statement about eternal life after death that has nothing to do with material wealth. The only connection between John 10:10 and prosperity is that they both involve having lots of something.

We'll look at one more "prosperity Gospel" verse, James 4:2: "You do not have because you do not ask." Taken in isolation, this line seems to suggest that all one has to do to get something is ask. And this is exactly how the televangelist Creflo Augustus Dollar, Jr., interprets the phrase. "When we pray," by speaking God's word, he writes on his website, "results are inevitable."

But again, this interpretation ignores the clear context of the verse, which offers a litany of things that go wrong when a person's motives are misplaced. Verse 4:2 starts with, "You want something and do not have it, so you commit murder." That's followed, in the same verse, by a parallel way of suggesting the same thing: "You desire something and cannot obtain it, so you engage in disputes and conflicts." Verse 3 has yet another unfortunate result: "You ask and do not receive, because you ask inappropriately, in order to spend what you get on your pleasures." Among these wrong ways to live life is the part of James 4 that Pastor Dollar and others stress: "You do not have because you do not ask."

James 4 is about the source of "conflicts and disputes," according to verse 4:1. They come from trying to acquire things for pleasure, instead of focusing on God. James is not about how to get things. It's about the perils of wanting them.

Indeed, the general thrust of the New Testament is a shift in attention from this world alone to varying combinations of this world and the next. Some parts focus on the world to come ("eternal life," for instance) and some on the connection with our life here and whatever comes next. Different authors express different views, but the point is always that our lives are bigger than the corporeal, physical, earthly existence that is most obvious. This approach necessarily has two parts, an emphasis on the world to come and a deemphasis of this world. As such, the prosperity Gospel is at odds with the thrust of the New Testament.

This is why so many people feel so strongly about it. Countering the prosperity-Gospel preachers are many other mainstream theologians and pastors, some of them with significant audiences of their own. Rick Warren, for example, whose weekly services attract some twenty thousand people, has rejected the notion that God wants everyone to have money.

Our purpose here, of course, is not to judge between these competing camps. Religious leaders have not only the right but the obligation to interpret scripture. Instead, our goal is to judge the degree to which the Bible, uninterpreted, promotes widespread prosperity. And we see that it does not.

Rather, the spirit and letter of the New Testament are better represented by passages like Matthew 19. In verse 19:21, Jesus tells a young man how to inherit eternal life. First, keep the commandments—do not murder; do not commit adultery; do not steal; etc.—then "sell what you own, and give to the poor." That way, Jesus says, the man "will have treasure in heaven." This passage is followed by the famous admonition that it is easier for a camel to pass through the eye of a needle than for someone who is rich to enter God's eternal kingdom.

The New Testament is more concerned with eliminating poverty than with creating wealth. (This is, apparently, a tricky balance, and modern economists continue to debate whether a rich upper class is good or bad for the poor. The Bible doesn't generally deal with economic theory, though it does have a few bits of specific advice, all but ignored today. Deuteronomy 24:14–15 demands that impoverished laborers be paid for their work before the sun sets; this would speak against withholding wages until weekly or monthly paychecks are distributed. Exodus 22:25 prohibits charging interest to the poor, and perhaps more broadly. And we've already seen that the misnamed jubilee year voided debts every half century. In a biblically based economy, people—at least the poor, and perhaps a wider segment of the population—would be paid immediately and would have access to interest-free loans. And every fifty years, debts would be erased.)

The message of 1 John 3:17 is representative of the New Testament's attention to combating poverty: "How does God's love abide in anyone who has the world's goods and sees someone in need and yet refuses help?"

In focusing on helping the poor, the New Testament is continuing a solid tradition that goes back to the earliest and most central parts of the Old Testament. Exodus 23:11 assigns whatever food happens to grow in the sabbatical year (which we discuss briefly in chapter 27) to the poor. Leviticus 19:1, part of the holiness code (which we explore in chapter 39), demands that people leave part of their harvest for the poor to gather, and, likewise, leave some grapes on their vines. Other parts of the Five Books of Moses repeat this requirement on land owners. Deuteronomy 15:11 reminds people that there will always be some people in need on the earth so they should give to the poor and the needy.

This strong tradition of helping the needy—not just the poor, but also the disadvantaged—at first applied just to the Israelite communities. Then the prophets demanded that it be extended more widely. Amos in verse 9:7 says that Israel is no better than nations like the Ethiopians. Isaiah (verse 42:2) highlights the importance of bringing justice to all of the nations. In verses 58:5–6, Isaiah rejects the idea of fasting simply as an empty ritual; rather, he says, fasting should be "to loose the bonds of injustice" and "to let the oppressed go free." Micah (6:8) says that God "has told you, O mortal, what is good, and what the Lord demands of you: to do justice, to love kindness, and to walk humbly with your God."

In fact, the theme of helping the needy is one of the most pervasive and consistent in the Bible. By contrast, personal wealth and prosperity is generally a minor matter, considered positive only when it helps the less fortunate, and otherwise deemed neutral or even detrimental.

35

VIOLENCE

***Does the Bible advocate violence?* No.**

One of the most common generalizations about the Bible is that the Old Testament is violent and the New Testament is peaceful. By extension, the God of the Old Testament is violent and the God of the New Testament is peaceful. By further extension, the God of the Old Testament wants violence and the God of the New Testament wants peace.

We have already seen (in chapter 31) the unfortunate pattern of misconstruing examples as morals, and, in particular, how an example of violence does not necessarily condone violence, so a more careful look at violence in the Bible is in order.

On one hand, there is no doubt that the Old Testament contains many violent passages.

Numbers 16 is a good example. There, three Israelites, Korah, Dathan, and Abiram, challenge Moses and Aaron's authority directly, and also indirectly by inciting some 250 leaders to rebel. Because Korah is a Levite, part of the priestly class, this is more than a popular uprising; it is a potential internal coup. God is left to choose either Moses and Aaron or Korah, Datan, and Abiram. After Moses and Aaron win, God tells those two leaders to stand back. Then (verse 16:32) the ground opens up and swallows the leaders of the potential coup, along with their entire households—"everyone who belonged to Korah and all their goods." And (verse 35) "fire came out from the Lord and consumed the two hundred fifty men" who had been convinced to follow Korah, Dathan, and Abiram.

Joshua 8 describes the battle to take a city called Ai, setting the stage in verse 1: "Then the Lord said to Joshua, 'Do not fear or be dismayed; take all the fighting men with you, and go up now to Ai. See, I have handed over to you the king of Ai with his people, his city, and his land." According to verse 3, Joshua "chose thirty thousand warriors and sent them out by night." By the end of the battle (in verse 25), Joshua and his men have killed everyone in Ai, twelve thousand people, both men and women. The text adds in the next verse, "For Joshua did not draw back his hand, with which he stretched out the sword, until he had utterly destroyed all the inhabitants of Ai."

In 1 Samuel 18, after David kills Goliath (a confrontation we explored in chapter 5), the women of all the towns of Israel came out singing (1 Samuel 18:7): "Saul has killed his thousands, and David his myriads." (A myriad is ten thousand.) Already this is a violent endorsement of Saul and David. Worse is Saul's despondent response in verse 8: "They have ascribed myriads to David, and to me only thousands." Saul is convinced that David will inherit the kingdom by virtue of his unmatched violence.

In 2 Samuel 8, David again wreaks havoc, killing (verse 5) "twenty-two thousand men of the Arameans" and (verse 13) "eighteen thousand Arameans." ("Arameans" here in verse 13 is probably a scribal error. The Greek text reads "Arameans" in verse 8 but "Edomites" in verse 13. In Hebrew, the difference between the two words is just one letter—a *d* or an *r*—and because of the shapes of those two letters, they are easy to mix up.)

We saw in chapter 4 that most of the Five Books of Moses was not meant to be historical, so the violence in Numbers 16 should not be attributed to history. And even though Joshua attempts to describe history, we know that the numbers are impossibly large. If Joshua really had an army of thirty thousand men we would expect to have some archaeological evidence of it, and we do not. Similarly, the "thousands" and "myriads" in 1 Samuel 18 are obviously not literal. (We are not surprised. Most of the numbers in the Bible are symbolic.) So none of the details here seem to have much historical plausibility.

On the other hand, the spirit of violence is unmistakable. And it's widespread. So certainly the text of the Old Testament contains violence.

So, too, does the text of the New Testament.

Jesus (in Matthew 10:34) warns, "Do not think that I have come to bring peace upon the earth. I have come to bring not peace but the sword." Luke 12:51 concurs. In Matthew 10:15, Jesus condemns cities who ignore his twelve apostles to a fate worse than Sodom and Gomorrah, whose inhabitants (Genesis 19:24–25) painfully burned to death when the Lord rained the infamous "fire and brimstone" down upon all of them. And 2 Thessalonians 1:8 lauds the "vengeance" that God will bring, causing people (verse 9) to "suffer the punishment of eternal destruction."

And lest there be any doubt, the book of Revelation seals the deal. Jesus (Revelation 14:14–16) will appear on a white cloud "with a golden crown on his head, and a sharp sickle in his hand." An angel will urge the crowned cloud dweller to use the sickle and reap, "for the hour to reap has come, because the harvest of the earth is fully ripe." So "the one who sat on the cloud swung his sickle over the earth, and the earth was reaped." Even more vivid is Revelation 1:16, where Jesus has seven stars in his right hand, "and from his mouth came a sharp, two-edged sword." (The text in these visions actually calls the figures each time "one like the Son of Man," leaving open two options. Either this is Jesus, or this is a person or angel that merely appears to be Jesus. Either way, the violence is detailed and massive.)

Revelation 6 describes a series of violent horsemen. The first horse (verse 2) is white and its rider comes out "conquering and to conquer," grasping a bow and wearing a crown. The second horse, bright red, carries a rider who "was permitted to take peace from the earth, so that people would slaughter one another." He has a great sword. In Revelation 19:17, an angel stands in the sun and commands the birds "to eat the flesh of kings, the flesh of captains, the flesh of the mighty, the flesh of horses and their riders." By verse 21, the birds are gorged with the human flesh they have eaten. According to Revelation 9:3–5, locusts from the earth are given the same power as scorpions, then "told not to damage the grass of the earth or any green growth or any tree, but" to torture people for five months. "Their torture was like the torture of a scorpion when it stings someone."

So like the Old Testament, the New Testament has its share of extreme violence.

Countering these are passages that praise peace. In Deuteronomy 20:10, the Israelites are commanded to offer a town peace before waging war against it. In Leviticus 26:6, God promises the Israelites "peace in the land" so that "nothing will scare them"—that is, neither people nor animals nor any other factor. That tranquil image is repeated in Micah 4:4, "they shall all sit under their own vines and under their own fig trees, and no one shall make them afraid." According to Exodus 18:23, if Moses heeds the advice of his father-in-law Jethro, then "people will go to their homes in peace." The priestly benediction in Numbers 6:26 calls God to "give you peace." The famous passage in Isaiah 9:6 refers to a child born to be a "prince of peace." Nahum (in verse 1:15) writes, "Look! On the mountains the feet of one who brings good news, who proclaims peace!" Psalm 34:15 offers the beautiful "turn from evil, and do good; seek peace, and pursue it."

In the New Testament, 1 Peter 3:11 quotes Psalm 34:15. Luke 2:14 contains the famous "Glory to God in the highest, and on earth peace, good will toward men" and the similar 19:38, "Peace in heaven and glory in the highest." (Those two verses form the basis of the well-known "Gloria in excelsis Deo.") Acts 10:36 refers to God's message of "peace" preached by Jesus. Most of the letters ("epistles") begin and end with wishes for peace, along the lines of the salutation in Romans 1:7, "Grace to you and peace from God our Father and the Lord Jesus Christ," or 1 Peter 1:2, "May grace and peace be yours in abundance." Clearly, the Old and New Testaments in the Bible contain vivid passages of both violence and of tranquillity.

We've already seen how easy it is to take a line or two out of context and misunderstand (or purposely distort) its meaning, and with so much material available to choose from, it is particularly easy to do so for the themes of war and peace. People who want to misrepresent the Bible as exhorting war and savagery will have no trouble, just as others will find it easy to make the Old Testament into a book of violence and the New Testament into one of peace.

But the real balance between the two is both more nuanced and more interesting. It's also tricky.

The biggest hidden stumbling block to understanding what the Bible says about peace is the word "peace" itself. At its core, peace is the opposite of war. But our modern, English word has other central connotations, most notably tolerance. Whether it's two people or two nations making peace, the point is to live side by side.

The ancient Hebrew word *shalom* and its Greek counterpart in the Bible *eirene* are, like our English "peace," the opposite of war. But rather than implying tolerance and coexistence, they imply the peace that comes between two parties when one of them is so thoroughly beaten that it can no longer fight back.

For instance, Psalm 29:11 was deemed so central by the Rabbis that it was incorporated into numerous sections of the traditional Jewish liturgy: "May the Lord give strength to his people! May the Lord bless his people with peace!" If there's going to be peace, what need is there of strength? The answer is that for the ancients, it was the strength that kept the peace because the strength was used to conquer the enemy. Likewise, Romans 16:20 warns that "the God of peace will shortly crush Satan." Crushing the enemy is no longer seen as peaceful.

Similar is the famous *pax romana* ("Roman peace"), which lasted for some two hundred years starting a couple of decades before Jesus. The longest period of "peace" the region had seen, it was still marked by the kind of viciousness that we no longer think of as peaceful. We need only look at the Roman ruler Herod and the way he was despised by the denizens of Jerusalem, who saw him as an oppressive ruler supported by the military might of an invading force. Jerusalem was occupied by Rome, we would now say, not at peace with it.

What's tricky here is that we have to disconnect the core meaning of the word from its implications. The core meaning of "peace" now and in antiquity was a lack of strife, and that hasn't changed. It's the implications that are different. But a word's implications, much more than its core meaning, are flexible. To see how, we need only reflect on the modern English word "peace." Though it usually means coexistence, we still use it to describe the *pax romana*. It was a peaceful time, just not the typical kind of peace that the word now implies in English. (There are still languages and cultures where "peace" is more closely aligned with victory than with tolerance; their "peace songs" are about warriors and bloodshed.)

Similarly, when we see the word "peace" in the Bible—whether *shalom* in Hebrew or *eirene* in Greek—we should not assume that it involves either the threat or the result of violence, but we should always be on the lookout for that strong possibility.

This ancient use of "peace" means that we have to evaluate "peace" in the Bible carefully. For instance, the passage from Deuteronomy 20:10 stipulates that "when you draw near to a town to fight against it, offer it terms of peace." That sounds peaceful. But the next line instructs, "if it accepts your terms of peace and surrenders to you, then all the people in it shall serve you at forced labor." We don't call that "peace" anymore. We call it "unconditional surrender." Yet at the same time it is also more in keeping with "peace" than unconditional war. It is both more peaceful than some alternatives, and—for reasons that we can appreciate only once we grasp the way in which the notion of "peace" has evolved—less peaceful than other alternatives.

Alongside such passages we find things like the famous passage from Ecclesiastes 3:8, which shows us that "peace" was the opposite of "war" just like "love" was the opposite of "hate": "a time to love and a time to hate, a time for war, and a time for peace." The great King Solomon is so named because "Solomon"—*shlomo* in Hebrew—sounds like *shalom*, "peace," and Solomon will give Israel "peace and quiet," according to 1 Chronicles 22:9. And the "peace" that we saw used in the salutations to letters in the New Testament has nothing to do with being conquered or with any other form of defeat.

Once we take all of this into account, we find a relatively clear pattern in the Bible. There's lots of violence and there's also lots of peace, but peace is always considered better than war. And the consistent hope for the future is that war will give way to peace.

Superficial appearances, then, are deceptive in this case. Most of the violence in the Old Testament is what happened, whether in a mythic or historical sense, while peace is what God generally commands for the future. In other words, we usually find accounts of past violence, and hopes for future peace. Furthermore, we know from chapter 5 not to read too much into examples of violence, because the examples are not necessarily behavior that should be emulated. So it doesn't really matter what David or even God did, no matter how violent. Perhaps the takeaway from those stories lies elsewhere.

The significant exceptions to this pattern of peace trumping violence are part of a system of justice, whether in the form of "an eye for an eye," capital punishment (which we explore in chapter 38), or eliminating forces that are themselves destructive.

A passage from Deuteronomy 25 is also often cited as an example of promoting violence—and, therefore, as a counterexample to the general theme that the Old Testament, while violent, doesn't usually condone violence. The text there deals with a people called the Amalekites, led by Amalek. Though they don't exist anymore, they were an archenemy of sorts to the Israelites. Deuteronomy 25:19 reads, "Therefore when the Lord your God has given you rest from all your enemies on every hand . . . you shall blot out any memory of Amalek from under the heaven; do not forget." This has been subsequently interpreted as biblical permission to attack, sometimes viciously. But we see that the text itself, in spite of its common interpretation, is not violent. (There's also a certain irony in being told not to forget to blot out a name. This very command to blot out the name has ensured the continuation of Amalek's name, to the extent that Amalek, though long gone, is far better remembered than most of ancient Israel's other enemies in the Bible.)

In the New Testament, too, the violence is what happened, while peace is what should happen, with, again, an exception for justice. We therefore find a hierarchy or sorts: Peace trumps violence, but justice in turn trumps peace.

Because this theme of justice is so important, we turn to it next.

36

JUSTICE

Does the New Testament replace the justice from the Old Testament with love? No.

As we saw in the last chapter, justice is a matter of great importance in the Old Testament. The famous "justice, justice shall you pursue" from Deuteronomy 16:20 illustrates with its double emphasis: We noted in chapter 1 that Hebrew sentences normally start with a verb, and one way of emphasizing something is to put it before the verb. The Hebrew here reads just like the English, with "justice" not only appearing twice, but also appearing before the verb. Because of the odd English that results from translating the line literally, some versions render it instead along the lines of "justice, and only justice shall you pursue," but that isn't really the point. This is a solid emphasis on justice, which we might represent in English with italics and boldface: "***Justice*** shall you pursue."

(The line has prompted a variety of interpretations, including a suggestion based on Sanhedrin 32 in the Talmud that the repetition of "justice" means that cases of law should always be brought before the most competent and learned judge possible. One "justice" is for the defense, the other "justice" for the prosecution, both of whom have an obligation to find an impartial judge, even as they advocate for their clients.)

The famous "eye for an eye and a tooth for a tooth" in the Old Testament seems to address justice, too. Then, because Matthew 5:38–48 in the New Testament rejects "an eye for an eye" in favor of "turn the other cheek," there's a perception that the New Testament more generally tries to replace the draconian justice of the Old Testament with forgiveness. But that simplistic view is inaccurate, and it misses the role that justice plays in the Old and New Testaments.

Justice is closely related with fairness. People who do bad things should be punished and people who do good things should be rewarded. One of the innovations of the Old Testament was to apply this principle evenly to every member of society, including the privileged class. Leviticus 19:15, part of the holiness code (as we explore in chapter 39), warns, "You shall not render an unjust judgment," adding, "you shall not be partial to the poor or defer to the great. You shall adjudicate with justice." Numbers 35:31–32 specifically prohibits rich killers from buying their way out of a death sentence or jail term.

Most people in Western democratic countries take this principle of judicial equity for granted and complain bitterly when the fairness breaks down. It is illegal for the rich as well as the poor to kill in these countries. But to this day, there are large swaths of the earth where the rich can act with impunity, their wealth serving to isolate them from legal consequences. The Old Testament would not approve.

More generally, we are all born with an innate demand for fairness. Children complain when they are punished for something they didn't do, but also when their friends get away unpunished after some illicit deed. The Old Testament reflects this fairness in two ways. The first, as we just saw, is to demand fair courts. People must treat each other fairly.

Beyond that, there's a broader fairness that humans are incapable of bringing about. Being a righteous person—giving to the poor, helping the underprivileged, donating generously, and in general following God's laws—ought to have inherent reward if life is to be fair. But those actions are largely unscrutinized by human systems of reward and punishment. Worse, the really important rewards and punishments are themselves beyond the reach of human actors: health versus sickness, prosperity from good crops versus ruin from natural disaster, peace versus strife in the home, and much more. No judge can make a sick person healthy, no matter how much merit there might be in doing so. For that matter, courts are imperfect and humans are not infallible. We can't even always promise the limited kind of justice with which we are tasked.

Therefore, the Old Testament promises two things. The first is that the imperfections of human justice will someday be replaced with God's universal and unflawed justice, as we saw in Isaiah's vision of a better future in our chapter 20.

The second is that in the meantime God will take up the slack, as it were. Deuteronomy 11 promises rewards for obedience to God, and, similarly, punishment for disobedience. "Keep this entire commandment . . . so that you may live long" (Deuteronomy 11:8–9) and people who keep all of God's commandments will be rewarded with "rain in its season" (verses 13–14). Contrarily, "the anger of the Lord will be kindled against" people who turn to other gods, "so that there will be no rain and the land will yield no fruit" (Deuteronomy 16–17); these worshippers of false gods "will quickly perish off the good land" (verse 17).

The problem is that life doesn't seem to work this way. We all know righteous people who suffer and evil people who thrive. And we deeply resent this cosmic injustice. This passionate response to a nearly universal condition explains the popularity of Woody Allen's film *Crimes and Misdemeanors,* which is about a gangster who literally gets away with murder and a kind rabbi who goes blind.

One purpose of justice—from pursuing "justice, justice" in principle to exacting "an eye for an eye" in practice, from the list of immoral behavior in the Ten Commandments to punitive damages as mandated by Exodus 21—is to promote good behavior by rewarding it and to discourage bad behavior by punishing it. But the system breaks down if both the really important behavior and the truly serious consequences are beyond the reach of human courts, and, in spite of the rhetoric, systematically unaddressed by God. This fundamental dilemma of the human condition is essentially unanswered in the Old Testament. Despite the great yearning for justice, there doesn't seem to be any.

This is where the New Testament comes in. There is justice in the world, according to the New Testament, and good people are always rewarded just as bad people are always punished. But sometimes the reward and punishment aren't doled out in this life. Life after death evens things out. Good people who were unrewarded in this lifetime will be rewarded in the world to come, just as unpunished bad people will eventually be punished. This is the system that gives us Heaven and Hell as ultimate, everlasting reward and punishment.

As it happens, the early Christians were not the only people to think of this, and the New Testament is not the only place where we find this religious doctrine. It's part of rabbinic Judaism, as recorded in the Talmud and Midrash. It's part of the Dead Sea Scrolls. And it's part of noncanonical religious writings from the same period, like the Apocalypse of Abraham and Enoch.

This message of eventual (and eternal) justice in the world to come was particularly attractive in a Jerusalem occupied by cruel Roman forces. The faithful may have been met with indifference or even contempt from the Roman leadership, but they would eventually earn eternal reward. And the evil Romans may have been beyond the reach of earthly justice, but they would eventually suffer.

In this context, the justice of this world came to be deemphasized. Compared with the perfect, final, and eternal justice of the world to come, the flawed and partial human justice of this world was practically insignificant. And this is the context that lets Matthew tell people to turn the other cheek. The minor indignity of unpunished aggression in this world is inconsequential compared with what awaits the aggressor in the world to come.

So justice is hugely important in both the Old Testament and the New Testament. The difference is that the Old Testament focuses more on what humans can do to bring it about, while the New Testament focuses more on what God will do. And because Judaism also incorporated a justice-giving life after death, today's Jews and Christians alike grapple with the amorphous connections among behavior, human punishment, and God. In fact, this may be why Woody Allen chose to end his *Crimes and Misdemeanors* with a subtle promissory note that things might even out. The gangster is never punished and the rabbi never regains his sight, but the closing song of the film is "I'll Be Seeing You."

With all of this in mind, we are in a position to finish our discussion of violence from the last chapter. There, we ended with a partially unsubstantiated statement that the New Testament, like the Old Testament, uses violence in connection with justice.

In the Old Testament, the connection was clear. Violence was called for to punish wrongdoers, as in the famous "eye for an eye." Fair was fair (though as we'll see in chapter 38, it didn't take long for everyone to agree that it wasn't fair after all). Violence was appropriate for killing murderers, for defense, and for attacking immoral enemies. The goal was always justice.

By contrast, the justice in the New Testament is primarily a matter for the world to come. Accordingly, so, too, is the violence. This is why alongside Matthew's "turn the other cheek," we find (as we saw in Romans 16:20 in the last chapter) "the God of peace will shortly crush Satan." This is why Jesus (Matthew 10:15, again from the last chapter) forecasts a fate worse than Sodom and Gomorrah for unbelievers. And this is why 2 Thessalonians 1:9 (yet again from the last chapter) calls for God's vengeance in the form of people "suffering the punishment of eternal destruction." This New Testament vengeance in the world-to-come takes the place of Old Testament vengeance in this world. Both are part of the same kind of justice system. They just differ in their timing.

So the superficial claim that the Old Testament calls for justice and the New Testament prefers love misses the deeper picture. Justice is an important theme throughout the Bible, and because the two prongs of justice in the larger sense are reward of the deserving and punishment of the undeserving, justice is closely connected to reward and punishment. And because punishment is often violent, violence and peace are inextricably intertwined with justice. Then, because the Old Testament focuses on justice in this world, it deals with reward and punishment, and with peace and violence, in this world. The New Testament, with its focus on justice in the world to come, similarly relegates the reward and punishment, along with peace and violence, to the world to come.

Interestingly, this is one case where the considerable difference in mentality between the Old and New Testaments has little practical impact among people who value scripture, because, as we saw, Jews and Christians alike came to roughly the same conclusions about justice and the afterlife. Christians recorded their revisions to the Old Testament in the New Testament, while Jews wrote theirs in their influential commentaries to the Bible.

In chapter 25 we saw that, according to the Talmud, some commandments are like contributions to an investment fund. People who follow the commandments enjoy interest on them in this life, but the real benefit is the growing fund itself, which is reserved for the world to come. This is another way of saying that good deeds in this life are rewarded in the next. And this Talmudic passage is so central that it made its way into the daily Jewish worship service. In the other direction, we'll see in chapter 38 that the same rabbinic tradition replaced "an eye for an eye" with a less violent alternative.

All of this reflects the Bible's insistence that peace is better than war, and tranquillity better than violence, even as the Bible recognizes that humankind has yet to achieve that ideal.

37

MEN AND WOMEN

***Are men and women equal in the Bible?* In some ways.**

Another common generalization about the Bible is that it values men over women. And particularly as Western democracies have reevaluated the role of women—in this regard, we note that 150 years ago not a single major democracy let women vote—the Bible's stance on men and women has been thrust into the spotlight.

For instance, the influential Council on Biblical Manhood and Womanhood (CBMW) was founded in 1987, the organization says, to combat the "widespread uncertainty and confusion in our culture regarding the complementary differences between masculinity and femininity." (By "complementary" they mean "different and reciprocal," not "flattering.") And they believe that the proper role of a woman in marriage is "willing submission" to her husband. Men and women are, and are supposed to be, different; and one difference is that the men lead and the women follow, in much the same way, they say, that Jesus led and his flock followed. Sin, they say, "inclines women to resist limitations on their roles."

The organization Christians for Biblical Equality (CBE) takes the opposite view, affirming that believers have "equal authority and equal responsibility in church, home and world" no matter their gender.

The phrase "church, home and world" in that statement accurately reflects the three areas of disagreement regarding how men and women should behave. One question is whether men and women should have equal access to positions of power in the church; the CBMW says no, the CBE says yes. A second question regards a man's and a woman's role in marriage. (The question assumes that a marriage will involve exactly one man and one woman. We saw in chapter 32 that this narrowing of marriage already represents a departure from the biblical view, and in chapter 39 we'll address what the Bible says about homosexual unions.) And the third question concerns men and women outside of the church and marriage.

Our goal here is not to evaluate the religious claims of these or any other group, but rather to focus on how the Bible itself presents men and women. But we get a flavor of the debate from passages quoted by these two organizations. For instance, the CBMW cites Ephesians 5:22: "Wives, be subject to your husbands . . . for the husband is the head of the wife just as Christ is the head of the church." The CBE prefers Galatians 3:25–28: "Now that faith has come . . . [28] there is no longer male and female; for all of you are one in Christ Jesus." Which is it? Are men and women equal, or are women subservient to men?

Further blurring a true appreciation of the Bible's message in this regard are widespread translation mistakes. We already saw in chapters 12 and 28 that the Greek word for "person" sometimes ends up as "man" in English translations, just as "member of" or "child of" becomes "son of." The same is often true for English renderings of the Old Testament. So people can read the same passage in different translations and draw different conclusions about it. In one translation, it's about "people," in another, about "men."

We take a step back before we turn to these issues, because many people instinctively feel that the Bible was written by men for men. But we don't know who wrote the Bible, so any claim that it was written "by men" is mere speculation. On the other hand, the principal heroes of the Bible all seem to be men. Jesus, certainly, in the New Testament, is unsurpassed in centrality and importance, and his human form was male. In the Old Testament, four candidates for supreme hero present themselves, and they are all men: Adam, Abraham, Moses, and David. The major prophets are men: Elijah, Isaiah, Jeremiah, et al. And sometimes the phrasing in the text for the "entire group of Israelites" is "you, your wives, and your children." There does seem to be a sense that this is a book about men directed toward men.

But it is not entirely about men. Ruth has a book unto herself; so does Esther. Many of the commandments specifically apply to both men and women. Exodus 21:28–29 deals with an ox that gores "a man or a woman." (Oxen are often used as what appears to be case law in the Bible. In this instance, there are two categories of oxen, those that have never gored anyone and those that have. Owners of the first group are not liable for a death caused by their animal, while owners of the second group are put to death as murderers. We have similar laws today, dealing, for instance, with attack dogs. The owners of previously violent animals have a higher burden of responsibility than other animal owners.) The Ten Commandments put mothers and fathers on equal footing. Both have to be honored. Similarly, Leviticus 19:3, in the holiness code, demands that people "revere" their "mother and father." Commentators are even quick to point out that "father" precedes "mother" in the Ten Commandments, but it's the other way around in the holiness code.

We start to sort things out by looking at Numbers 27. There, the "daughters of Zelophehad" come before Moses with a request. Zelophehad—a fifth-generation descendant of Menassah (according to Numbers and Joshua 17:3), so a seventh-generation of Jacob—has no sons, only five daughters. In Numbers 27:3–4 these women explain their situation to Moses: "Our father died in the wilderness . . . and he had no sons. [4] Why should the name of our father be taken away from his clan because he had no sons? Give to us a possession among our father's brothers."

The question is clear: Can women inherit property the same way that men can? And the precedent is equally clear: No. But in Numbers 27, Moses, citing no less an authority than God, reverses the precedent and gives the land to the women: "The daughters of Zelophehad are right" (Numbers 27:7). Furthermore, the text makes this a new precedent: "If a man dies, and has no son, then you shall pass his inheritance on to his daughter." This is clearly not complete equality between men and women; women are inheritors of last resort. But neither is it a complete exclusion of women. Daughters are second only to sons in the line of succession, ahead of (according to Numbers 27:9–11) a landowner's siblings, uncles and aunts, and "kin" generally.

This is exactly the kind of nuanced text that lends itself to co-option by people with an agenda. People who promote equal rights for men and women cite a woman's ability here to inherit. People who promote a higher status for men call attention to the woman's status as inheritor here of last resort. To that, people in the first camp respond that the text was progressive for its day; other cultures didn't let women inherit anything. (While we don't know if this is true—and the evidence from other cultures is both unclear and sometimes contradictory— we do know that the text of the Bible presents this as a step forward for women.) An objective look at this text sees it as a partial step toward equality of men and women.

A particularly revealing passage comes from Judges 13, which details how the mighty Samson came to be born. The story starts with a man from the tribe of Dan named Manoah, whose wife was barren.

Then an angel appears before the wife and predicts that she will bear a child, and he gives her instructions on how to raise him. The woman tells her husband what happened. He prays to God that he might get the information firsthand. So the angel returns, appearing to both of them and repeating the information.

The simple plot here masks a complex interplay between Manoah and his wife (whose name we don't know). When Manoah's wife tells her husband about the encounter, she calls the angel "a man" who looked like an angel (Judges 13:6). So Manoah prays for "the man" to return and repeat the information, apparently because he doesn't trust his wife to get it right. "Let the man return and teach us what we are to do concerning the boy who will be born," he pleads, even though his wife has just told him exactly what they are to do concerning the boy who will be born. Still, the angel returns, again appearing only before the wife, this time in a field. She runs to tell her husband. But when he hears the news, he doesn't run. He gets up and walks, as though just the act of standing required considerable effort, a characterization that seems to be reinforced by the literal meaning of *Manoah*: "sedentary," or perhaps even "lazy bum."

When they make it to the field, Manoah addresses the visitor as "the man" and asks for a repeat of the information about the child he will soon have. The angel answers that Manoah's wife will take care of things. Manoah—who still doesn't realize that he's talking to an angel—offers to cook a meal for "the man." The angel gives Manoah a clue about his true identity when he tells Manoah that he won't eat "your food," so Manoah should prepare a sacrifice to God. But Manoah still doesn't get it. It's not until "the man" ascends to heaven with the fire of the sacrifice that he figures things out. "We have seen God," he tells his wife (who has known this all along), "and we will certainly die." She counters that God wouldn't have done the things he did "if the Lord had meant to kill us."

Throughout the story, Manoah is a bumbling buffoon, the foil for his heroine wife. She sees things for what they are; he's clueless. She is entrusted with the upbringing of the future Samson; he is told to let his wife take care of things. She is enthusiastic and energetic; he needs all his energy just to stand up. Yet for all of this, he has a name and she doesn't.

What we learn from this—and the reason we have spent so long on this otherwise obscure passage—is that appearances can be massively deceiving. The simplistic way to look at the text is as one more case of a story about a man whose wife is so insignificant that she doesn't even have a name. But the more accurate way is to see it as a story about a wise, insightful woman who speaks with God, and her foolish husband who can't be counted on to do anything of importance. The namelessness of the woman seems to be only a matter of style, not a judgment about her merit.

If even the clear and obvious heroine of a story—a woman who speaks with God and who is entrusted to raise an important man—can remain nameless, we must ask about other nameless women. Have we, with our modern literary standards, misjudged their original importance, too? It's hard to know. One thing is clear, though: This story of Manoah and his wife is incompatible with a culture that always values men over women.

In addition, we see a particularly clear message from Song of Solomon, also called Song of Songs. This poetic book is about a sexual relationship between a man and a woman. (The man and woman are not married or engaged, or, it would seem, even dating. This, combined with the overt sexual imagery, made enough people sufficiently uncomfortable that they later recast the text as an allegory of God's relationship with Israel, for Jews, or, for Christians, Christ's relationship with the Church. For instance, the "breasts like towers" in Song of Solomon 8:10 are, according to the preeminent Jewish commentator Rashi, obviously synagogues and study halls, both of which nurture

Israel with words of Torah. It is those vital Jewish institutions that have strong walls.)

In the book itself, the woman calls the man *dodi* in Hebrew, "my lover." (Considerations of propriety among some translators inaccurately turn this into "my beloved.") And the man calls the woman *achoti kalah.* The second word in that phrase usually becomes "my beloved" or "my bride" or "my spouse" or "my wife"—though, again, "my lover" seems more accurate. And the first word literally means "my sister," which is why we have translations of Song of Solomon 4:9 along the lines, "You have ravished my heart, my sister, my bride." But that translation misses the point.

In ancient Hebrew (and in antiquity more generally), kinship terms were used to express family relationships, as they are now, but also power structure. So "father" and "mother" meant "more powerful than," just as "son" and "daughter" meant "less powerful than." "Brother" and "sister" meant "equal in power." The point of the text here is that the man repeatedly calls the woman "my equal." In other words, the Bible's only full-length examination of sexual relationships hits the reader over the head with the equality of the man and the woman.

When we looked at slavery, violence, and other matters, we were careful to distinguish between examples and lessons, and we want to be equally cautious here. Manoah's wife and the couple in Song of Solomon are examples, not necessarily lessons. But they are still relevant, because they show us something important about the culture that produced the Old Testament. In spite of common assumptions to the contrary, it was a culture that acknowledged the possibility of a woman who was smarter and more able than her husband, and it acknowledged the potential equality of power between men and women. This background complements the texts that we saw that give women the right to inherit land, and the many laws that apply equally to men and women.

Against these are passages like Leviticus 27, which deals with the valuation of human beings in the context of consecrating them to God. Men aged twenty to sixty are valued at 50 shekels, women only 30; men from ages five to twenty are worth 20 shekels, women 10. Boys younger than five but older than one month are valued at 5 shekels, girls 3. After age sixty, men are worth 15 shekels, women 10. Valuing females at only 50 to 66 percent of the value of males does not seem to accord with any vision of equality.

Similarly, Leviticus 12:1–5 explains that after childbirth a woman is ritually unclean for one week if she bears a boy, two weeks if she bears a girl. Then she undergoes a longer purification that lasts thirty-three days for a boy, sixty days for a girl. Again, this does not seem egalitarian in any sense.

The valuations offer the potential explanation that men were by and large generally able to do more remunerative work than women, so these shekel values may not represent the value of people but a measure of the financial contributions they could, on average, make. So people who were of an age that they could work—both men and women—were valued higher than men or women of any other age. And a person's "value" dropped after age sixty. (A twenty-to-sixty-year-old woman was valued at 30 shekels, double the 15 shekels of a sixty-one-year-old man.)

The lengths for ritual purification, being purely ritual, are more clearly sexist. Girls made a woman impure for longer than boys.

For that matter, Numbers 30 grants a husband the right to revoke any vow his wife makes.

In addition to these passages that truly deal with equality and inequality, modern readers are quick to read into other passages, most notably Genesis and the relationship between Adam and Eve. Because Adam and Eve were given different punishments for eating from the Tree of Knowledge, some people say, the Bible says that men are supposed to be different from women. Men have to work, women have to endure childbirth and suffer a love-hate relationship according to which they will long for their husbands who will rule over them. Women, therefore, shouldn't work, just as men shouldn't give birth. Men should rule over their wives.

But this passage in Genesis seems to describe the then-current state of affairs, not any particular ideal. While some people take these lines to mean that husbands should rule over wives, no one seriously suggests that the text prohibits anesthesia or meditation to mitigate a woman's pain in childbirth. (The modern Christian interpretation of these pivotal lines in Genesis is enormously complicated, because the exile from Eden that accompanied these punishments, generally called "the Fall," represents a state of sin. Accordingly, while men do work for a living, they wouldn't have to were it not for Original Sin. In an ideal world men wouldn't have to work.)

Similarly, some people suggest that men are better than women because (Genesis 2) man was created before woman and not the other way around. But in addition to competing passages in Genesis 1 that describe the creation of man and woman as simultaneous, jokes like "God made a rough draft before completing the final model" demonstrate the degree to which this sexist view is arbitrary. (On the other hand, 1 Corinthians 11:7–9 supports reading Genesis 2 in a way that assigns superiority to men.)

What we really find in the Old Testament, then, is a three-pronged pattern of grappling with the role of men and women. First, men tended to be stronger, a quality that lent itself directly to work, building, defense, shepherding, and many other crucial aspects of ancient life. Secondly, any particular man could fall anywhere on the bell curve, as could any particular woman. And thirdly, any inequality ran against the grain of the fledgling Israelite society.

Matching these three are passages that value men over women in general, passages that value a particular woman over a particular man (and vice versa, of course), and a running theme of equality as expressed not just in Song of Solomon but in the many places where men and women are addressed jointly.

So Genesis 3 observes that men work for a living and women painfully bear children, a dynamic according to which the love a woman has for a man gives him certain power over her. And Leviticus reflects the way men generally have a higher earning potential than women. Yet this doesn't mean that Manoah's wife can't rule over her husband, just as the couple in Song of Solomon can enjoy a relationship of equality.

Inequality between men and women in the Old Testament, then, seems to have been like warfare and like slavery: All three were established patterns that society would be better without.

The New Testament paints a different picture.

As we saw at this chapter's outset, Ephesians 5:22 tells wives to be subject to their husbands, because the husband is the head of the wife just as Christ is the head of the Church. According to 1 Corinthians 11, too, "Christ is the head of every man, and the husband is the head of his wife." (The word for "man" in Greek also means "husband," so the text flows better in Greek, but there's little doubt about the accuracy of the translations "man" and "husband" here.) And 1 Timothy 2: 12–13 permits "no woman to teach or to have authority over a man . . . [13] for Adam was formed first, then Eve." Though this last passage may refer more narrowly to wives not having authority over their husbands (because of the ambiguity of the Greek words), it joins the first two in assigning women subservient roles. And there are others.

Colossians 3:18 demands of wives that they be subject to their husbands. Interestingly, this is a passage that we mentioned briefly in chapter 31 in the context of slavery, because the text continues, "[19] Husbands, love your wives . . . [20] Children, obey your parents . . . [21] Fathers, do not provoke your children . . . [22] Slaves, obey your human masters." (The word "human" here, commonly translated "earthly," is probably intended to make it clear that the Greek word for "master," *kurios,* which also means "lord," doesn't refer to "the Lord" in this case.)

At least here in Colossians, gender inequality is closely connected to slavery. When we discussed slavery in chapter 31, we noted two possible interpretations. Either slavery is good; or, so long as slavery exists, there's a right way to do it, but slavery itself is bad. These same two interpretations potentially present themselves regarding gender relations in Colossians 3:18.

For that matter, Ephesians 5:22 ("wives, be subject to your husbands") is preceded by "be subject to one another," potentially making the deference of a woman to a man just one example of human deference more generally.

But these are technical, limited objections that ignore the broader picture. The real parallel between slavery and gender roles in marriage, according to Colossians, is that wives should be subservient to their husbands so long as there is marriage, just as slaves should serve their masters so long as there is slavery. And even though Ephesians starts with everyone being subject to each other, it falls in line with other passages from the New Testament when it presents the husband as being in charge of the wife.

The New Testament vision of marriage is one in which the man is in charge of the woman. And, depending on whether 1 Timothy 2 is about wives teaching husbands or women teaching men, the New Testament vision of teaching and religious leadership may extend primarily to men, too. This is not to say—as many are quick to point out—that men and women are not equally children of God in the New Testament. But they have different roles. The complementarians are right about the New Testament, at least when it comes to marriage. There's a role for the husband and a (subservient) role for the wife.

In a sense, we are not surprised. Other doctrines, including the rabbinic tradition that would eventually become mainstream Judaism, also subjugated women to men, while insisting that men and women alike were children of God. The Talmud, for instance, sometimes refers to "women, slaves, and children" as a single category. And Roman culture insisted that women were feebleminded (*imfirmitas consilii,* as the influential Roman philosopher and statesman Marcus Tullius Cicero wrote in the century leading up to Jesus's birth). Roman law recognized two categories of married women, those who belonged to their husbands (*in manu,* literally, "in the hand" of their husband, using a technical definition of "hand" associated with property), and those who remained under the control of their father's family. Even women in this second group, who enjoyed considerably more freedom than those in the first, were legally obligated to have a male guardian (*tutela*)—though those requirements were gradually lifted in some cases.

The only New Testament foundation for the countervailing view— that husbands and wives according to the Bible should be equal in all regards—is to assume that marriage is no longer what it used to be. In that case, wives would be subservient to husbands only in the Roman-style marriage, not in modern marriages. This isn't a completely crazy position to take. After all, biblical marriage allowed polygamy, while modern marriage does not. But it certainly pushes the boundaries of "what the Bible says" beyond what most people are comfortable with. If marriage is different only because of social norms, what else might be different? And how would we know?

For now, focusing on the clear intent of the New Testament passages in Ephesians, Colossians, and Corinthians, we note that the New Testament sees the husband as the head of the family, with the wife subservient to him. The Old Testament—with its emphasis on equality in Song of Solomon and its apparent struggle with inequality elsewhere—suggests a potentially more equal role.

38

KILLING

Do the Ten Commandments forbid killing? **No.**

In chapter 35 we looked at the issue of violence in general. Now we turn to killing specifically.

Four different kinds of passages in the Bible address killing, and in spite of common perception, they point in a reasonably unified direction.

First, and most obvious, are direct statements about killing. And of these, the most famous is "Thou shalt not kill," from the Ten Commandments (Exodus 20:13 and Deuteronomy 5:17).

At first glance, this seems to be a clear statement against killing of any sort. But that famous English phrase, which comes from the KJV, is a mistranslation. The Hebrew verb in the commandment doesn't mean "kill" but rather "kill illegally." This is why some more modern translations like the NRSV render the text instead as "You shall not murder." But that isn't quite right, either, because there are lots of kinds of killing that are illegal but still short of murder.

Here lawyers and laypeople often use English words differently, and legal terminology in English differs from jurisdiction to jurisdiction. For instance, many people think of "homicide" as the same as "murder," but technically "homicide" is any killing of another human, even when it's legal: self-defense, for instance, and at the hands of the state in capital cases. Similarly, manslaughter is always illegal, but it's not murder.

To make matters more confusing, the NRSV adds a footnote to its translation, "or kill." But the editors don't elaborate, as though the difference between legal killing and illegal killing isn't worth addressing.

As we expect, people pounce on these two translation options— "kill" and "murder"—and frequently choose the one they like more, rather than look for the point of the original text.

The Catholic NABRE, also a modern translation, still follows the four-hundred-year-old King James Version, and reads, "You shall not kill," in keeping with the Catholic stance on the sanctity of life. (They also have a footnote, longer than in the NRSV, explaining that "kill" is sometimes understood as "murder.") And pacifists more generally quote "Thou shalt not kill" as a biblical injunction against war, the death penalty, and more.

But the original Hebrew is clear, in spite of considerable confusion among translations: It only refers to illegal killing, and it refers to every kind of illegal killing.

In addition to naturally strong feelings about death and killing, another direct statement about killing sometimes prods people to reinterpret the commandment. Exodus 21:24 (among others) offers the famous *lex talionis* that we met in chapter 35: "an eye for an eye and a tooth for a tooth," as well as "a life for a life." This seems pretty clearly to support the death penalty as part of a larger pattern of matching a punishment to the crime.

And again, people often choose what they want the text to mean. One common tactic is to reverse the thrust of these Old Testament passages. Rather than requiring an eye for an eye, which would be cruel, people say that the point was to limit the punishment to not more than an eye for eye, which was a beneficent innovation compared with previous codes. In other words, it's not that the Bible demanded an eye for an eye, but, rather, that it prohibited anything more than an eye for eye.

But there is little evidence to support this common claim. The Old Testament passages here do seem to demand retaliation. And because the Ten Commandments only address illegal killing, they have no bearing on the legally sanctioned "life for a life." So the Ten Commandments and *lex talionis* are not in conflict.

In this context, a third direct passage about killing is relevant. Jesus in Matthew 5:38–48 rejects "an eye for an eye" in favor of the equally famous "turn the other cheek." His point is that victims of aggression shouldn't take vengeance but, in fact, should welcome more aggression. If someone hits you on one cheek, don't hit the person back, but, just the opposite, offer your other cheek as a target as well. (As we saw in chapter 36, the reasoning here is that the temporary injustice in this world pales in comparison to the final accounting in the world to come, but the effect is still to reverse *lex talionis*.)

Christianity is not alone in its discomfort with *lex talionis*. Judaism, too, went on to reject "an eye for eye." Discussion in the Talmud in the middle of the first millennium A.D. (Baba Kamma 83b–84a, for instance) notes that everyone's eye is different, so "an eye for an eye" cannot ever be fulfilled. If a blind man pokes out the eye of an artist, does the artist really inflict similar damage by poking out the useless eye of the blind man? The Rabbis argue that the best we can do in our imperfect human world is adjudicate monetary damages. (American law, too, rejects the *lex talionis* of the Bible in favor of financial compensation. But an interesting difference may set apart the American system and the Jewish one. In America, an aggressor who pays a victim has made things equal. The victim no longer has any claim against the aggressor. By contrast, the Rabbis' system suggests that the financial payment does not make up for bodily harm; it's just the closest we can come.)

In the other direction, some people cite *lex talionis* not as calling for moderation but as demanding the death penalty. While they correctly interpret "an eye for eye," they have missed the broader message about the death penalty—and, more generally, about killing—in the Bible. *Lex talionis* is just an abbreviation for a much more nuanced and detailed approach to retribution, which we turn to next.

The most elaborate discussion of killing is found in Numbers 35, where killers are divided into two broad categories, in English frequently called "manslayers" and the more serious "murderers." Murderers are to be put to death, while manslayers are to be confined to a biblical sort of jail. (The details of these jails are intriguing. They were cities—called "cities of refuge"—in which it was illegal to take vengeance upon a killer. In the rest of the land, an aggrieved party could kill a manslayer with impunity, but not in a city of refuge. Accordingly, manslayers would not leave the cities of refuge. Like jails, they punished killers by limiting their freedom and keeping them away from the general population. Unlike jails, they did not require guards. Also unlike in our modern system, killers were freed from cities of refuge when the high priest died, an ordinance that, apparently, did not unduly jeopardize the life of the high priest.)

Intentional killing comes under the category of murder, and is punishable by death, according to Numbers. At the other end of the spectrum, entirely inadvertent killing where death could not reasonably have been foreseen is not murder but manslaughter. So if someone sets out to kill another person and succeeds, that is murder. If someone, say, is throwing wood onto a fire, and the wood slips, hitting and killing another person, that is manslaughter.

This differs from modern, Western society, though, because entirely accidental homicide isn't a crime nowadays, and the killers in these modern cases are, therefore, not punished. For example, if a child runs into the street and gets hit by a driver who's driving carefully and legally, the driver now is deemed not guilty, while Numbers would insist on punishment in the form of sending the driver—deemed guilty of manslaughter—to a city of refuge.

The middle cases in Numbers are the most interesting and most mirror today's legal debates. For instance, remarkably parallel to modern hate-crime legislation, it's merely manslaughter to hit someone who ends up unforeseeably dying. But it is considered murder to do so in hatred. That is, the same act of accidentally killing someone is judged differently depending on whether the attacker hated the victim. Similarly, Numbers differentiates between potentially dangerous instruments like metal and other objects, assigning a higher level of responsibility to people wielding things that are apt to cause death.

These are the real details about killing in the Bible, and the sparse language of the Bible often hides the depth of the text.

Purposely killing another human is illegal (in accord with modernity), but so is accidentally killing another (in contrast to most modern law). The death penalty is legal. Blood vengeance—the practice of a family member of the victim executing the death penalty—is required. In these senses, the biblical laws are harsher than many modern ones.

In other ways, the biblical laws are more lenient. A person can be put to death for murder only if two people witness the murder. And the rich cannot buy their way out of a death sentence or out of the imprisonment required for a killer. (While most English readers take it for granted that murder is illegal among the rich as well as the poor, in most places across the world today, the rich can kill whomever they want with impunity.)

Most interesting, perhaps, is the conclusion: Blood pollutes the land, and the only way to make up for shedding blood on the land is in turn to shed the blood of the one who first shed blood. The second half of this claim is simply *lex talionis*. The first half, in accord with the Ten Commandments, notes the absolute horror of killing innocent people.

So far we've seen that illegal killing is a moral matter, not just a legal one. And in terms of that legality, purposely killing is permitted in certain cases of retribution.

What about self-defense?

The detailed legal code in Numbers doesn't address that issue, but other passages in the Bible do, most notably Exodus 22:2–3, according to which a homeowner is allowed to kill a thief who breaks in at night, but not during the day. The only thing clear about this passage is that it is sometimes okay for homeowners to use lethal force to protect their homes, and sometimes it's not.

Some people ignore the second half and cite this as justification of any lethal force in defense of a home. Others cite only the second half. In the middle, some people think that the difference between day and night is that at night, but not during the day, homeowners might reasonably fear for their lives. If so, homeowners would be allowed to use lethal force to defend their homes only if their personal safety is in jeopardy, not merely to protect their property.

While this middle-ground conclusion strikes many people as reasonable, and, equally, seems like a reasonable interpretation of Exodus, it is not the only reasonable interpretation. Perhaps the point was that lethal force was only appropriate if there was no convenient source of light (in which case it would never be okay in modern, electrified civilizations). Or perhaps the key difference is sleep-time versus waking hours. Or maybe the passage alludes to some other quality that separates the day from the night.

So the most we can say with confidence and without inserting our own biases is that lethal force, according to Exodus, is sometimes okay, and—apparently—only at night.

Some people also cite Luke 11:21 in support of self-defense: "When a strong man, fully armed, guards his castle, his property is safe." While this seems to support guarding one's residence by force, the passage in Luke actually has nothing to do with self-defense, and everything to do with might being overpowered by even more might, a lesson Luke applies to demon exorcists who are powerful, but not as powerful as God's kingdom. Luke 11:21 is not about self-defense.

So far, everything we've seen applies to what we might now call peacetime, in contrast to the laws of war.

Deuteronomy 20 addresses warfare. A preamble demands that a priest charge and encourage the troops, promising God's help in achieving victory. Then the text exempts certain people from serving in war: men who have built a home but not yet lived in it, men who have planted a vineyard but not yet gathered its grapes, and men who have proposed to a woman but not yet married her. Underlying this touching passage is the assumption that many soldiers, even with God's help, will not return.

As we saw in chapter 35, the Israelites were required to give a city the chance to surrender before it was attacked. (We also saw that the text uses the word *shalom*—"peace"—to make the point.)

Then the text divides cities into two categories: those that are far away, that is, outside the land of Israel; and those in Israel. In the latter case, the rules of engagement, as we might now dub them, call for killing every inhabitant of the city, because otherwise, those people might spread their ungodly practices. In the case of cities outside of Israel, the Israelites were to kill all of the men, but take the women and children.

In no case were the Israelites permitted to chop down fruit trees around a city, though they could eat the fruit. The reasoning is that the trees are not the enemy. (Trees were connected to warfare because they could be chopped down and fashioned into instruments of war.)

What unites these various laws of war is the observation that life is a compromise. Peace is better than war, but what if peace isn't possible? Life is better than death, just as God's moral ways are better than ungodly immoral ways; but what if the only way to stop people from promoting immoral behavior is to kill them? Most people prefer to live their life rather than risk it by serving as a soldier, but what if soldiers are necessary for people to live life? What if war comes at a particularly inopportune time for some people?

Because of the nuanced way the Bible recognizes war as a compromise, we have two different ways of incorporating the ancient advice today. One is to focus on the details, purposely killing every male enemy during war, for instance. The other is to focus on the balance, maybe noting that today we can (perhaps) win a war without the unfortunate killing.

Similarly and more narrowly, we might exempt certain vintners from military service, or more widely let farmers stay home until they have reaped their crops, or even more widely yet, let the chief of a start-up stay home from war until the company has brought its product to market. All of these are biblical approaches to war.

In summary, then, illegal killing is, obviously, always forbidden. And it comes in two degrees of severity (as detailed in Numbers). Illegal killing is also immoral (according to the Ten Commandments). It has to be punished, possibly by death. Lethal force may be an acceptable response to a home invasion. And killing during wartime was a necessary evil, to be used only as a last resort.

All of the details are essentially elaborations of two points: Killing is a matter of morality, and the blood of the slain pollutes the earth.

39

HOMOSEXUALITY

***Does the Bible say homosexuality is a sin?* No.**

We turn now to two of the most hotly debated social issues of the twenty-first century, homosexuality and abortion (next chapter). More than any other topics, these two divide both religious and secular communities.

In light of the modern social importance of the issue, many readers are surprised to learn that the Bible is largely silent on homosexuality. In fact, there are only three brief passages that address it directly, in contrast to the much more expansive texts on social themes like poverty, peace, justice, love, and equity.

One passage, which actually mentions homosexuality twice, comes from the Old Testament, in Leviticus. The other two passages are from the New Testament, in Romans and 1 Corinthians.

In addition to these direct statements, there are some passages that may allude indirectly to homosexuality.

We start with Leviticus because it is by far the most commonly quoted biblical passage about homosexuality, and also one of the most misrepresented.

Leviticus 18:22 warns a man not to "lie with a man as with a woman," because doing so is what most translations call "an abomination." Leviticus 20:13 uses similar language, and adds that the penalty is death. These two passages clearly denounce male homosexual sex.

Some people, though, read more into the passage than is there. They interpret it as applying to men and women alike, even though it only mentions men. Or they interpret it as referring to homosexuality in general, though it does not.

Some people even go a step further, claiming that Leviticus denounces homosexuality as a sin. But while it condemns certain behavior, it doesn't call it a "sin." That difference may seem vacuous or even absurd to modern readers—what does it matter if Leviticus calls something a "sin" or uses some other word to decry it?—but for many people, there's a huge theological difference between "sin" and undesirable behavior in general.

By analogy, we can look at the law. Lots of things are undesirable, and lots of things (including many of the undesirable things) are illegal. But in a court of law, the question of desirable or undesirable is almost irrelevant. All that matters is whether something is legal or illegal. We don't put people in jail if they haven't broken the law.

"Sin" is the religious parallel to "illegal," and arbitrarily deciding that something is a "sin" because you don't like it is like arbitrarily deciding that something is illegal just because you don't like it. So saying that Leviticus calls homosexuality a sin is a double misrepresentation.

In the other direction, some people try to diminish the impact of Leviticus. Perhaps "lie with a man as with a woman" doesn't mean homosexual sex at all, they say, because sex with a man is different from sex with a woman. But the biblical expression is clear, even if its literal translation allows for fudging. These verses in Leviticus are about male homosexual sex.

Still in the direction of limiting the force of Leviticus, some people suggest that maybe the Hebrew doesn't actually mean "abomination." Here they are right about the details but still wrong about the conclusion.

The Hebrew word that becomes "abomination" (*to'evah*) may actually mean "taboo," which is to say, it may denote a violation of a potentially fluid social norm and not an absolute wrong. But these lines in Leviticus come as part of a series of undesirable sexual behaviors, each one with a noun attached. For example, the very next verse (Leviticus 18:23) calls bestiality a "perversion." The point of the text is not to match up specific behaviors with specific descriptions, but rather to denounce all of the behaviors. So the exact nuance of "abomination" is all but irrelevant.

And at any rate, the severity of the offense is driven home by the punishment: death.

Most interesting, though, is the context in which these two lines appear, because failure to take the context into account is the most common way of distorting the intent of Leviticus.

These lines are part of a detailed passage about right and wrong, commonly called the "holiness code." The passage is loosely divided into sections, and these lines come in sections about sexual behavior. So alongside the prohibition of male homosexual sex, we find prohibitions against bestiality (as we just saw), incest (among siblings and other close family members), adultery, and more.

Other sections of the holiness code deal with other matters, including expiration dates for eating sacrifices (three days from the day of sacrifice), leaving food and drink for the poor (specifically, not reaping an entire field or harvesting an entire vineyard), theft, deceit, fraud, timely payment of laborers, witchcraft, foreigners, deferential treatment of the elderly, and inappropriate mixtures.

This last item seems to have been a matter of some importance in antiquity, though modern readers often find it odd. Leviticus 19:19 warns against letting different kinds of animals interbreed, against sowing a field with two kinds of seed, and against something called *sha'atnez:* garments made from wool and linen. (Though most people ignore this last one today, there are still Jews who follow it, which is why in some parts of the country stores offer blazers and other articles of clothing that are certified "*sha'atnez* free.")

So from this context we see that, according to Leviticus, male homosexual sex is like adultery but also like insolence toward the elderly; it is like bestiality but also like mixing wool and linen. (The similarity comes from the inclusion in a common list. The punishments are not identical.)

The problem for modern readers is that this is now a ridiculous category. We don't have anything today that is like bestiality and also like mixing wool and linen. One is a revolting crime to which most people have a strong, visceral reaction, the other, for most people, at most a mild curiosity.

This vast range makes it easy for people to distort the importance of what Leviticus says about male homosexual sex. Some people claim that they are locked into an antihomosexuality position by Leviticus. We've already seen that Leviticus doesn't address homosexuality in general, but even if it did, these people would be bound to follow it only in the same sense that they are locked into an anti-*sha'atnez* position. To claim no choice about denouncing male homosexual sex is to claim no choice about denouncing clothing that mixes wool and linen.

Other people deny that Leviticus takes a strong position on homosexuality because, they say, it includes it along with trivial things like *sha'atnez.* But this isn't quite right, either. *Sha'atnez* probably wasn't trivial. And even it was, the triviality of part of the code doesn't necessarily extend to the entire code. This situation is similar to a set of laws that makes it illegal to steal and to jaywalk. The illegality of something trivial like jaywalking doesn't mean that stealing is any better than it would be if jaywalking were legal. Equally, jaywalkers don't have the luxury of saying that the only reason they don't steal is that it's illegal. Rather, they are interpreting the law for themselves.

So Leviticus addresses the very limited question of whether male homosexual sex is okay, and answers with a clear "no." But Leviticus doesn't make it clear how important an issue it was.

Next we turn to Romans 1, in the New Testament. The text of Romans takes the form of a letter from the apostle Paul to the Romans, which is why its full name is "Epistle to the Romans." In it, the hugely influential Paul explains the nature of salvation through Jesus.

Verses 26–27 in chapter 1, as translated by the NRSV, seem pretty clear: "For this reason God gave them up to degrading passions. Their women exchanged natural intercourse for unnatural, and in the same way also the men, giving up natural intercourse with women, were consumed with passion for one another. Men committed shameless acts with men."

Paul was a gifted writer. Unfortunately, the Greek he used to compose his works is difficult for us to understand with precision today, because at times he wrote in his own unique dialect. He invented some words, and used other, familiar words in novel ways.

So the details of verses 26–27 are not as clear as they seem. We know they are about sex. And we know they are about the distinction between natural and nonnatural. But beyond that, we have to guess at what exactly the words mean. One reasonable interpretation is that the passage refers to female and male homosexual sex, which (according to the text) is unnatural. Another reasonable interpretation is that the passage refers only to unnatural female and male homosexual sex, potentially contrasting it with natural male and female homosexual sex.

The lack of a clear understanding of the text once again opens the door to people with an agenda. Some people cite Romans 1:26–27 as proof that homosexual sex is unnatural, others as proof that homosexual sex, like heterosexual sex, comes in two varieties: natural and unnatural.

More importantly, verses 26–27 are actually a punishment for exchanging God's truth for a lie, as Paul describes in verse 25. That is, Paul isn't telling people not to engage in unnatural sex. Rather, he's telling people to follow God, because if they don't, they will be punished with unnatural sex. As with "sinful" acts versus "undesirable" acts in connection with Leviticus, the distinction here may seem trivial. But for many people there is a big difference between a choice we have as humans (to follow God or not, according to Paul) and behavior that God ordains.

So stripped of biased interpretation, Romans 1:26–27 makes a statement about the naturalness of homosexual sex, but we unfortunately have no way to know for sure what that statement is.

Thirdly, we have another passage by Paul, this time in 1 Corinthians, another letter he wrote. Here Paul provides a long list of people who will not inherit God's kingdom: "Fornicators, idolaters, adulterers, male prostitutes, sodomites, thieves, the greedy, drunkards, revilers, [and] robbers" (chapter 6, verses 9–10, as translated in the NRSV).

So far, this doesn't seem to be about homosexuality, but rather about improper sex in general, by fornicators or idolaters, for example. The evangelical NIV (New International Version) translation, though, reads "men who have sex with men" instead of "male prostitutes, sodomites." Unfortunately, this is one of the cases where Paul actually invented one of the words, and we don't know whether the NRSV or the NIV is a more accurate description of what Paul meant when he wrote *arsenokoites* in Greek.

Paul is clearly adamant that sex can be immoral. But, just as in Romans, we don't know if he meant that all homosexual sex is immoral or if, like heterosexual sex, it comes in two varieties: natural and unnatural.

Unlike in Romans, Paul is clear here that people will be punished for whatever kind of behavior he is describing. So while he doesn't actually use the word "sin," this is pretty close—certainly closer than Leviticus or Romans. Yet even here, the text doesn't say that homosexuality itself is a sin (though many people report it that way). It says either that some homosexual sex is a sin, or that all of it is.

In short, these three passages combine to create only one clear message: Leviticus frowns on male homosexual sex. The rest—the degree to which it is undesirable, homosexuality more generally, its connection to sin, etc.—is all a matter of interpretation.

In terms of that interpretation, a couple of passages seem to provide examples of homosexual relations, a couple of passages have been interpreted as denouncing homosexuality, and one passage has been used both to support and to decry homosexuality.

Though we know not to leap from example to precedent, it's still worth looking at the examples, if for no other reason than that people quote them so frequently.

The book of Samuel in the Old Testament describes King David and his potential rival, King Saul's son Jonathan. But instead of acting as rivals, David and Jonathan apparently loved each other. And though their love has traditionally been interpreted as platonic, the language is particularly intimate and vivid: "The soul of Jonathan was bound to the soul of David, and Jonathan loved him as his own soul" (1 Samuel 18:1). And because the word now translated as "soul" (*nefesh* in Hebrew) may have actually meant "body," as we saw in chapter 17, this line is open to a variety of interpretations.

After Jonathan dies, David composes a lamentation: "I grieve for you, my brother Jonathan; you were dear to me. Your love for me was more wonderful than the love of women" (2 Samuel 1:26). So this might be an example of homosexual love in the Bible.

The second potential example comes from the book of Ruth, which tells the story of a woman from Bethlehem named Naomi and her daughter-in-law Ruth. In verse 1:14, the text tells us that "Ruth clung to" Naomi, which, though pretty clearly platonic, is reminiscent of how Adam "clung" to Eve in Genesis 2:24. Both texts use the same word. Some people note, therefore, that Ruth loved Naomi the same way that Adam loved Eve. This may be true, but basing the conclusion on one similar word is an unwarranted leap. In English we use "love" for spousal emotions and for parental emotions, but that doesn't mean that the emotions are the same. Similarly, the "clinging" in Ruth and in Genesis might be different.

More intriguing is the poetry that follows. In verse 1:16, Ruth declares to Naomi: "Where you go, I will go, and where you stay I will stay. Your people will be my people, and your God will be my God." This beautiful expression of love is so powerful that it has made its way into traditional marriage ceremonies. Particularly in light of this common usage, some people claim that Ruth and Naomi's love must have been the same as the love between a husband and a wife. But, again, it's an unwarranted leap. It is common to repurpose poetry.

We turn next to the story of Sodom and Gomorrah in Genesis. It begins in Genesis 19:1 when Lot (Abraham's nephew) sees two "angels" arrive in his city of Sodom. Lot invites them to stay in his house. But the Sodomites, who apparently have heard that "men" have arrived in town, demand that Lot produce them for the purpose of sex. In response, Lot tries to pimp out his daughters: "I have two daughters who have never known a man. Let me bring them to you, and you may do to them whatever you want" (Genesis 19:8). His goal is to protect the angels/men.

The reader already knows from Genesis 18 that God is going to destroy Sodom along with its sister city Gomorrah, and, indeed, the city is eventually destroyed by what has traditionally been translated "fire and brimstone."

Early traditions attributed the destruction of Sodom to its inhabitants' greed, nastiness, and lack of hospitality. But by the first century A.D., homosexual tendencies had been added to the list of the Sodomites' sins. In fact, this is where the English verb "sodomize" comes from.

But even among modern readers who ardently look for antihomosexual messages in the Bible, it's hard to maintain that the Sodomites' behavior is worse than Lot's offer of his own daughters as prostitutes. In spite of the etymology of the word "sodomize," and in spite of popular perception, the story of Sodom and Gomorrah does not seem to have originally been about homosexuality.

Finally we have the creation narrative in Genesis, in some ways the most important text, because Adam and Eve are supposed to represent all of humanity. Adam's name means "human," and Eve's name is connected to the word for "life." Adam and Eve represent what it is to live life as a human. This is why Adam's punishment for eating from the Tree of Knowledge (he is destined to "work by the sweat of his brow," for example) is usually interpreted as applying to all men, just as Eve's punishment (including pain in childbirth) is attributed to all women.

Obviously, Adam and Eve were engaged in a heterosexual union. So some people argue that the only legitimate pattern for humans is to follow Adam and Eve is this regard; they take Genesis as prohibiting homosexual unions because Adam and Eve were heterosexual. But there is nothing in the text to suggest that people who mimic Adam and Eve are supposed to mimic their sexuality.

Moving on, Eve is created as specific kind of helper for Adam according to Genesis 2:18. Literally, she is "opposite" him. So in a similar vein, some people argue that a person's spouse must be of the opposite sex. But here the reasoning is particularly faulty, because even though the Hebrew description literally means "opposite," it probably actually means "like."

How could "opposite" and "like" be confused in this way? One easy way to understand the situation is by envisioning a two-columned table such that each item in the first column is lined up with a similar item in the second. On any given line, the items in the two columns are both opposite each other and like each other. In this sense, "opposite" and "like" are closely related.

So "complementary" is a reasonable interpretation of Genesis 2:18, perhaps in the way that men complement women. But it is not the only reasonable interpretation. Just as plausible is "complementary" more generally, in the way that any partner complements another.

Equally, the first part of Genesis 2:18 explains why Eve had to be created in the first place: "Because Adam shouldn't be alone" or "Because the human shouldn't be alone" or "Because people shouldn't be alone." If people shouldn't be alone, and if some people can only find companionship with same-sex partners, this may be the strongest support of homosexuality in the Bible.

Interestingly, then, the exact same passage has two reasonable interpretations: The first is that people should behave like Adam and Eve, a man marrying a woman and a woman marrying a man; the second is that people should behave like Adam and Eve, finding a partner—whether a man or a woman—so they are not alone.

And here a nuance is relevant: If it turns out that some people can only find companionship with the same sex, and if it further turns out that they didn't know about this aspect of human sexuality in the days of the Bible, then the same text that used to demand heterosexual partnering might now demand, with equal urgency, the acceptance of homosexual partnering.

At any rate, we've seen one clear limited statement in Leviticus, two potentially ambiguous passages from Paul in the New Testament, two unconvincing cases of homosexual love, one clear case of reinterpretation, and finally, here, the paradigm for life as a human that offers no clear guidance about homosexuality.

So in the end, the only truly biblical stance on homosexuality is limited to rejecting male homosexual sex with the same vehemence as, for example, clothing made from wool and linen mixtures; and to remaining open-minded about everything else. Any more specific position is an interpretation.

40

ABORTION

***Is abortion the same as murder in the Bible?* No.**

We just saw that the Bible offers very little direct advice about homosexuality. It offers even less about abortion.

However, unlike homosexuality, the underlying issue behind abortion—the sanctity of life—is a central theme throughout the Bible. People are created in the image of God (Genesis 1:27), as we discussed briefly in chapter 2. Taking a human life, as we saw in chapter 38, is not just a legal matter but a moral one, too. The penalty for murder is death, and the rich cannot buy their way out of this most severe of sentences.

In a broader sense, the whole of the Bible is about how humans relate to each other, to God, and to what God has placed on earth. For instance, the Bible doesn't tell us what animals have to do to earn eternal life in the world to come, or how animals should interact. There's even less information about plants, and almost nothing about rocks and soil, except to the extent that people come from the soil and return to it. The Bible is about people. So it's crucial that we know what counts as a person.

In particular, if we want to understand what the Bible says about abortion, we need to know if a fetus is a person. Unfortunately, the Bible doesn't say.

In fact, there's only one direct mention of a fetus in the Bible, and that's in Exodus 21:22, which addresses the damages people have to pay if they accidentally hit a pregnant woman. We get a sense of the details from the NRSV translation: "When people who are fighting injure a pregnant woman so that there is a miscarriage, and yet no further harm follows, the one responsible shall be fined what the woman's husband demands, paying as much as the judges determine." That is, someone who causes a woman to miscarry has to pay a fine.

From this statute it follows that the fetus couldn't possibly be a human being, because we know—from Numbers, as we discussed in chapter 38—that there are only two acceptable penalties for wrongly killing a human: death or life imprisonment (technically, imprisonment until the death of the high priest). We even know, from the same passage, that it is illegal to buy one's way out of either sentence. So not only is there no provision for monetary damages for a killer, we are specifically warned against monetary damages when it comes to killing a human. The damages demanded in Exodus 21:22 are inconsistent with a fetus being a human.

However, the original text is unclear in some regards. The NIV, in fact, doesn't think this is about miscarriages at all. According to that translation, the fine is for causing a woman to "give birth prematurely." That's because the original Hebrew refers to a woman "whose offspring leaves her" after she is hit. We don't know if the offspring leaves her dead (in which case this would be a miscarriage) or alive (a premature birth).

Furthermore, the text specifically refers to the offspring leaving the woman "without harm." The next verse then explains what happens "with harm": *lex talionis* applies and the punishment is "a life for a life, an eye for an eye" and so on. Based on that, it's reasonable to assume that the "harm" is to the woman. If all she does is lose the fetus, the attacker pays a fine. If, in addition, he injures her, he is punished more severely. But the ancient Greek translation in the Septuagint seems to think that the harm applies to the child, and that the text refers to a woman who, after being hit, gives birth either to a not-fully formed child or to a fully formed one. Curiously, though, the fine applies in the case of a child who is not fully formed, while the "eye for an eye" clause only applies to the fully formed child, so the Greek text doesn't make much sense without emendation.

If the "harm" clause applies to the woman, as seems most likely, then it's hard to see how this text might be about a woman who is induced to give premature birth. After all, why would there be any fine at all if both mother and child are fine? More likely, this is an extension to the eye-for-an-eye reasoning, essentially asking what happens if a person without a fetus damages someone's fetus. Obviously, the punishment cannot be "a fetus for a fetus." Exodus 21:22 tells us what it is instead.

So based on the preponderance of evidence, and in accord with most accepted translations, we conclude that Exodus 21:22 is about inadvertently causing someone's miscarriage. And we learn that a fetus is not treated like a human.

People who want to allow abortions use this conclusion to report that the Bible allows abortions. But this is an unwarranted leap. Exodus 21:22 is about inadvertently causing someone else's miscarriage, not purposely performing an abortion. And it is not about what a woman does to or for herself.

In the other direction, people who want the Bible to militate against abortions take one of two tacks. The weaker one, following the probably inaccurate translation in the NIV, argues that this isn't about miscarriage. But if so, the Bible certainly has no position on abortion. The stronger one is to focus on the word here for the fetus that comes out of the woman: *yeled*. Elsewhere, this Hebrew word means "child" (generally in contrast to "adult," not to "parent," like the English "youngster"). Therefore, they argue, a fetus must be the same as a child.

We find "child" or "children" used elsewhere as well for what we would now call a fetus. For instance, in Genesis 25:22, the newly pregnant Rebecca is concerned because her twin "children struggled within her." Here we find the Hebrew word *ben*. Unlike *yeled,* which refers to "child" in the sense of "young person," *ben* means "child" in the sense of "son" or "daughter." But the implication—say some people—is the same. If the fetuses are already Rebecca's children, they must be people.

But this reasoning, too, is flawed, because we commonly use words in more than one way, as the very next verse shows us. In Genesis 25:23, God explains to Rebecca that "two nations" are in her womb. Certainly, we don't conclude from this that a fetus is a nation. Or to look at a modern example, someone's "long-deceased father" is, obviously, dead, but that doesn't mean that all fathers are dead, or that the dead father is still alive. Or parents might recall their honeymoon, when their child was just a hope; but killing that hope isn't the same as killing a child. Or a photo of a young George Washington might be captioned "The Founding Father as a Child," even though, as a child, he wasn't yet a founding father.

Similar reasoning is similarly flawed. For instance, in Numbers 12, Moses and Aaron worry about their sister Miriam, who has become leprous. Aaron, apparently asking his brother Moses to intercede with God, asks his brother to make sure that Miriam will not be "like someone who is dead coming out of his mother's womb." If the woman carrying the stillborn in the simile is already a "mother," some people like to argue, certainly the fetus must count as a human child. Likewise, Mary visits John's mother Elizabeth in Luke 1. In verse 41, Elizabeth's "infant leaped in her womb." Some people think that this demonstrates that a fetus is an infant. But it does not.

The basic linguistic pattern at play here is that words can generally be separated from the time at which they apply. This is why "the founding father as a child" means "the person who will be the founding father." It's why we can talk of "two-year-old Mark Twain" even though when he was only two, he was still called Samuel Clemens, not yet having assumed his pen name. It's why a teacher might meet a former student and exclaim, "Look at my student, all grown-up now." It's why a woman, even before she's pregnant, might say she's already thinking about her children. And it's why the words "mother" and "child" in connection to a woman carrying a fetus are (perhaps) a linguistic curiosity, but they do not tell us what the Bible says about the nature of that fetus.

So far, our only clue about the biblical status of a fetus is that destroying one by accident is punished, but not in the same way that killing a human by accident is, so our only solid conclusion is that a fetus is valuable, but not the same as a human in the Bible. And we have only one verse to back that up.

Another approach is to turn things around. Rather than probing the status of a fetus, we might ask if we have any evidence about when life begins.

Here some people point to the close biblical connection between breath and life. According to Genesis 2:7, the first man became a living being only after God breathed the breath of life into him. In Ezekiel's wonderful vision of the dry bones, the prophet sees dry bones in the desert. God will dress the bones with sinews and flesh, and then put breath (using a different Hebrew word than we saw in Genesis) into them and they will live. Adam wasn't alive until God breathed breath into him, and, more generally, people live when they have breath and die when their breath leaves them. So, some people argue, life begins when people can breathe on their own.

If so, accordingly to some, a fetus, which doesn't breathe on its own, wouldn't be alive at all. We recognize this as a leap from the text; it is not what the text says. The connection between breathing and life is not a definition of life. Worse, similar reasoning leads us to conclude that a person on a respirator would also not be alive, yet no one seems to think that that's the right result. The Bible links breath and life, but probably because of the obvious observation that when people die their breath leaves them. The connection doesn't help us when it comes to abortion.

Yet another approach is to look at Exodus 23:26: "No one shall miscarry or be barren in your land." Though the translation "miscarry" is uncertain—the Hebrew word may be a synonym for "be barren"—this only tells us that bearing children was generally considered good and not being able to bear children was generally considered bad. It doesn't mean that any particular pregnancy must be good or bad. (If it did, Exodus 23:26 might put abortion in the same category as choosing not to get pregnant.)

In the end, the Bible gives us no direct information about abortion and very little indirect information. All we know is that a fetus, though valuable, is not the same as a person, and it looks like a fetus is similar to a body part.

If, in fact, the fetus is the same as a body part, then some biblical passages suggest that purely elective abortions are frowned upon: Leviticus 19:28 and Deuteronomy 14:1 warn people not to make cuts on their bodies, just as 1 Corinthians 6:19–20 declares that people's bodies belong to God, not to themselves. Abortions might then be like other surgery—permitted only for a good reason, with, unfortunately, no biblical insight into what that reason might be. But even this falls in the category of guesswork. And if we're wrong that the fetus is a body part—if it's more like property—then even this bit of speculation doesn't apply.

This lack of guidance is particularly vexing in light of the huge value the Bible places on human life. The Bible emphasizes the supreme importance of the question of when life begins, but nonetheless doesn't give any sort of answer.

In this sense, the issue of abortion highlights the way the Bible focuses our attention on what matters.

For instance, how we treat trees is more important than how we treat rocks, which is why the Bible doesn't even address minerals. Animals are more important than plants, which is why the laws of keeping kosher deal only with animals. And people rise above animals, plants, and minerals.

These conclusions sometimes seem too obvious even to bother committing to paper or mentioning out loud. For instance, modern legal codes almost universally prohibit the senseless murder of people, while animals can be killed—in many places, even just for fun—but not tortured. And our modern laws generally take no position on chopping up a plant or a rock. Most people can't even imagine an approach that puts more value on rocks than on, say, pets.

But if we take this hierarchy for granted, it is precisely because the mission of the Bible has succeeded, not only offering suggestions about what matters, but so thoroughly influencing human thought and behavior that most of us find it abhorrent to stray too far from its basic message.

Or to look at things differently, the reason most people care so much about abortion is that the Bible tells them to, just as it mandates careful attention to matters of human life and death, quality of life, justice, equity, the limited role of violence, and, more generally, the human condition.

As with most matters of importance, an ongoing tendency has focused our collective attention on areas of disagreement—whether over slavery in the nineteenth century or women's rights and abortion today. But, perhaps surprisingly, both sides on these divisive matters are united in agreeing that they are important, a lesson we learned from the Bible.

Naturally, there are exceptions. We saw in the last chapter that the Bible doesn't care very much about homosexuality; politics seems to be the driving force behind that issue's modern centrality, with the Bible coming into play only as a tool. But in general, we are still debating the issues that the Bible insists are important.

CONCLUSION

We began with five ways the ancient text of the Bible is commonly misunderstand today: through mistranslations, ignorance, accident, misrepresentation, and culture gaps. And running through those five, we identified two common elements: mixing up tradition with the original text, and taking the text out of context.

Now, forty chapters later, we've seen how those themes combine to distort the Bible.

Mistranslation played a role right off the bat, in chapter 1, when we noted that the first words of the Bible are generally mistranslated as "In the beginning." That phrasing wrongly stresses the unasked question "What did God do?" instead of the correct original question as reflected in the Hebrew: "When?" And because a book's opening words flavor everything in the book, this translation mistake has the effect of distorting everything that follows.

Other isolated translation mistakes include "Do not covet" for what should be "Do not take" in the Ten Commandments, "God so loved the world" for what should be "This is how God loved the world," various important wordplays that translations fail to convey (from the connection between the truth and freedom in chapter 11 to God's very name in chapter 13), and perhaps Moses's horns (as we saw in chapter 25). Even the double-faceted nature of being human—the tangible and the intangible—gets hidden by mistranslation, as we saw in chapter 17.

Chapter 1 also showed us how tradition gets confused with the original text. Rashi's alternative take on the Bible's first words—"When God began to create"—worked its way into some translations, which thus inadvertently moved the reader even further from the intent of the main text.

The same (understandable) tendency to impose tradition on the words of the Bible masks the original intent of Isaiah's poetry (as we saw, for example, in chapter 20) as well as such central matters of morality as the Ten Commandments, which, as we saw in chapter 38, do not say "Thou shalt not kill." Courthouses and houses of worship widely display a traditional mistranslation.

Ignorance and historical accident further warp the message of the Bible. There's no apple in the Garden of Eden (as we saw in chapter 26), even though we are not the first generation to picture the original fruit in that way. There's no rapture in the Bible, as we saw in chapter 30, and of the three aspects of keeping kosher, only two are even mentioned in the Bible, as we saw in chapter 29. And there's some confusion over the length of the Great Flood, Jesus's lineage, Goliath's killer, and even Jesus's killer, among other accounts in the Bible. But historical trends have pushed the ambiguities to the side in favor of a single if simplistic portrayal.

In addition to ignorance, more devious motives sometimes prompt people to misrepresent the Bible: they have an agenda they want to promote, so they superimpose their ideas onto the Bible. This is how pro-slavery advocates sometimes supported their position, as we saw in chapter 31. And it's how modern preachers justify their stances on homosexuality and abortion, even though the Bible barely addresses the first issue and does not address the second.

Frequently in these cases of misrepresentation, the strategy is to lop off the relevant context. This was precisely how a greeting from one person to another was turned into a biblical message that God wants humanity to be rich, as we saw in chapter 34.

Finally, and perhaps most centrally, we find a huge culture gap separating our modern, Western society and the Jerusalem of old that created the Bible. On a limited scale, this is how Psalm 23, originally about a mighty warrior, came to be misread as focusing on a placid and peaceful guide, as we saw in chapter 16. It's why modern readers tend to find modern notions of royalty in the "kings" of the Bible (as we saw in chapter 19), and to focus on the nonexistence of the unicorns and dragons (of our chapter 18) in the Bible, instead of on what they were meant to convey.

One sweeping gap we saw was the disconnect between our scientifically driven society and the pre-science days of the Bible. We as modern readers are like children enchanted with a shiny new toy. Our toy is science, and we can't stop playing with it, shoving it in where it doesn't belong, particularly into the prescientific Bible. In this sense, dividing the Bible into "scientific" and "unscientific" makes as little sense as doing so for art.

For instance, in chapter 2 we saw that the reason not to read the Bible literally isn't the way it contradicts science, but rather the way the Bible contradicts itself. The value of Genesis is hidden from many readers who analyze only its scientific accuracy, just as the two lineages of Jesus (in chapter 6) stand side by side, in spite of their contradictions, to offer a unified message.

Not surprisingly, even the approach to text in the Bible was prescientific. This is why, as we saw in chapters 21 through 23 and elsewhere, people now misunderstand how the New Testament quotes the Old Testament. (Then a translation mistake that wrongly renders *plirow* as "fulfill" instead of "matches" makes things worse in some cases.)

All of this brings us back to the opening line of the introduction. There are no miracles in the Bible.

That's because miracles are by definition extra-scientific. The only way to have miracles is to divide the world into two categories: things that science allows, and things that science does not. A miracle has to fall into the second category. Because they didn't even have those categories in the Bible, they certainly didn't have miracles.

What they had instead were wonders. Some things were so amazing, so breathtaking, so incredible, or so magnificent that ancient communities were compelled to preserve them even in an era when mass communication was exceedingly difficult: freedom from slavery, a life of dignity, families, beauty, a sense of purpose, a sense of the divine.

In exploring these themes, we have stripped away the accidental and purposeful grime that discolors the Bible's original message. In so doing, we now see, we are forced to give up miracles.

But what we gain is a renewed sense of wonder.

BIBLE CITATION INDEX

GENERAL INDEX